FOCUS

Memoirs of a life in photography

FOCUS

Memoirs of a life
in photography

Beaumont Newhall

A Bulfinch Press Book
Little, Brown and Company
Boston • Toronto • London

First Edition

Newhall, Beaumont, 1908–1993
                    Focus : memoirs of a life in photography—1st ed.
                        p.   cm.
                    "A Bulfinch Press book."
                    Include bibliographical references and index.
                    ISBN 0-8212-1904-9
                    1. Newhall, Beaumont—1908–1993   2. Photographic historians—United States—Biography. 3. International Museum of Photography at George Eastman House. I. Title.
TR140.N48A3   1993
770'.92—dc20
[B]   92-37376

Frontispiece: Beaumont Newhall, c. 1957. Photograph by Nancy Newhall. (Courtesy of Scheinbaum & Russek Ltd., Santa Fe, New Mexico)

Bulfinch Press is an imprint and trademark of Little, Brown and Company (Inc.)
Published simultaneously in Canada by Little, Brown & Company (Canada) Limited

Designed by Sametz Blackstone Associates
Imagesetting in Perpetua and Gill Sans by Graphics Express

PRINTED IN THE UNITED STATES OF AMERICA

To Christi and Theo

CONTENTS

I

BEGINNINGS

In Deerfield, Massachusetts, 1918. Photograph by Mathilda Weil, a member of the Photo-Secession.

I WAS BORN IN 1908, IN LYNN, MASSACHUSETTS, A SEACOAST CITY TWELVE miles north of Boston. My mother was Alice Lillia Davis (1865–1940), daughter of Joseph Davis (1836–1887), a prosperous manufacturer of boots and shoes in Lynn. My father was Herbert William Newhall (1858–1933), a physician.

My parents met quite by chance in Europe in 1885. Mother was on a grand tour with her father, mother, three sisters, and a nursemaid for the youngest, who was five years old. Father, having graduated from Harvard Medical School in 1884, was completing his training as a physician in the universities of Würzburg, Vienna, and Strasbourg. After a semester in Würzburg, Father took a vacation trip through southern Germany and Switzerland. In Lucerne he made the acquaintance of Joseph Davis, who, they were both surprised to learn, lived just around the block in Lynn. Mr. Davis invited him to call upon the family at their hotel. Father noted in his journal his disappointment that the Davises were planning to spend the winter in Dresden, so there would be little chance of seeing them again in Europe. However, they changed their travel plans and in January 1886 came to Vienna, where Father was then enrolled in the university. He wrote his sister:

> They have come to Vienna to spend a week or so. They were so kind as to hunt up my address through the police, such is the wonderful system here that it took them only a couple of minutes to do so. Having found my address they sent me a card, and I of course embraced the opportunity of calling upon them. It was the first glimpse of home life that I have seen in Europe, and their little girl [Mother's sister Ruth] fairly captivated me with her blue eyes and golden hair, her prattling talk and a good night kiss. They all united in sending their regards to father.

At dinner a few days later, Mr. Davis proposed an excursion to Budapest and invited Father to join him, along with "Miss Lillie," as mother was called, and a friend from Lynn, Miss Child.

Mother wrote in her journal on February 8, 1886: "At 4:30 the gay little party, comfortably situated in a second class car, left for Hungary. We passed the last hours playing whist, the Dr. and I receiving the most points. At 11 o'clock we reached the capital, ¾ hour delayed on account of snow." Next day the "gay little party" went on a sleigh ride through the city of Budapest. "We secured an antiquated sleigh," Mother wrote, "which just seated the four Lynnites and by an elastic stretch of imagination fancied the frozen and not over-clean horse blankets rich and costly Russian furs which kept out the cold. Dr. and I sat on the bare edge of nothing opposite Papa and Miss Child."

Left: Herbert William Newhall. Photographer unknown.

Right: Alice Lillia Davis Newhall, April 23, 1894. Photographer unknown.

Although they stayed in Budapest only two days, their sight-seeing was thorough. On the first morning they admired "the rich buildings that line the wide avenues." They spent an hour and a half looking at the paintings of the now-forgotten Russian realist Vasili Vasilievich Vereshchagin, who specialized in oriental genre and sensational anti-war scenes, based on his experience as a correspondent in the Russo-Turkish War. They then looked at a collection of old masters. Mother liked especially Murillo's *Madonna* and *Flight into Egypt*. After a two-thirty dinner the party crossed the Danube, "not blue as song and poetry represents, but of a grey, dirty color," to visit the Royal Palace on the summit of a steep hill reached by an inclined railroad. They got back to the hotel just in time to "brush up" before attending the opera *Il Trovatore*, which they found "more than enjoyable." They walked back to the hotel for a late supper.

On the second day of their visit, the "little party" went to the parliament building and saw the National Picture Gallery, consisting mostly of paintings of Hungarian history. After dinner, taken again at two-thirty, they went with a guide to the largest dance hall in Budapest—not to dance, but to view the rich, gilded decoration that rivaled that of the Opera. In the evening they attended a light opera. At five-thirty the next morning they were on their way back to Vienna. Mother noted in her journal: "We voted our excursion to Pesth a great success and shall keep the memory of it green and bright."

Father wrote his mother from Strasbourg, on May 16, 1886: "It must have been a source of great glee to the Lynn gossips that I had met the Davises. Indeed I wonder that they waited for that news. No. I am not engaged. I am not struck or smitten. Miss D. is a nice girl, and I am no fortune hunter. That's the whole story."

I find it remarkable that my forebears showed such intense appreciation of art and knowledge of its history. My grandfather Davis, on his first visit to Europe, in 1876, had visited the Alte Pinakothek in Munich. In his privately printed *Random Notes on a Trip to Europe* he wrote:

We were told that the oldest and best art gallery, the Pinakothek, was to be closed today, and not opened again for two weeks; therefore, if we desired to see the fine paintings there, we must go before twelve o'clock. Accordingly we took an early breakfast, and spent the forenoon in this celebrated gallery; and how richly we were paid, for here we saw some of the most magnificent pictures extant, pictures that seemed to speak to us like living realities.

I cannot tell you much of these paintings, except that they are all by the "old masters" and are considered wonders of art. The most famous, perhaps, are those by Rubens, such as the "Last Judgment," "Triumph of Religion over Vice," "Massacre of the Innocents," "Fall of the Condemned," and numerous others by the same artist, all contained in one room. There are said to be (I did not count them) more than fourteen hundred pictures in this gallery, none of them painted later than the first part of the eighteenth century, and some as far back as the thirteenth. Now I do not pretend to have much appreciation for art in its highest sense, though I confess to a love of things beautiful, in art as well as in nature; neither my early nor my later life has fitted me for playing the role of a connoisseur, but I tell you, friends, that I have been wonderfully impressed with some of the grand old paintings and statues I have seen in the art galleries of this old world. There is, probably, a hidden power within us to see and understand these things that we do not dream of until some occasion puts us to the test; at any rate, I know that many of these beautiful creations of art will long linger in my memory, and that never more shall I criticize those Americans whom we often hear dilating in such extravagant terms upon the wonderful pictures they have seen in Europe.

It was not twelve o'clock, we were not half satisfied with our view, but the doors of the gallery were to be closed, and we were reluctantly obliged to leave. We spent the afternoon quietly at our hotel.

My father, too, was greatly moved by the great masterpieces he saw in Europe. From Paris he wrote in 1886: "I never tire of the Louvre. I go there now nearly every morning. There is one magnificent hall which I think is worth all the rest. I know nearly all the pictures in it by heart. I like to go there now; for it seems like meeting old friends. This hall is called the 'Salon Carré.' The great masterpieces are all here." He enumerated the artists whose work he admired most: Murillo, Veronese, Raphael, Titian, Correggio, and Leonardo da Vinci. "There are a lot of statues here, but a poor picture is to me more pleasant than a moderately good statue." However, he had nothing but praise for the *Venus de Milo*: "At first you see only the deformities, the broken arm, and the imperfections of the marble where it has eroded. But all these faults and flaws vanish in a few minutes, after you get the right distance, and the right light. You can form no idea of its wonderful beauty. The gracefulness of the position, the pose of the head, the perfect regularity of the features, the divine expression! No one can see the beauty at first glance."

One day my father met Oliver Wendell Holmes, the famous jurist, author, photographer, and physician—and his former Harvard Medical School professor—in the Louvre. Father wrote:

> He inquired his way from me, when I surprised him by announcing myself to him as the son of one of his old pupils, and as a former pupil myself. I don't think he remembered my face or name, but he was very gracious, and readily accepted my guidance to find the pictures he had admired 25 years ago. He is here quite "incognito." He recognized one old painting after another. It was marvelous how well he remembered the names of the less famous masters. He seemed a great lover of what I had called old fashioned pictures, and showed me many points of excellence which I had overlooked. I was with him for over two hours, and I think I found every picture he inquired for. Finally I got a *fiacre* for him, and we parted, he thanking me very much, and I assuring him that it would always be a pleasant reminiscence for me. Now that was quite an adventure, was it not?

As my parents' trip took place before the invention in 1888 of the first amateur camera, the Kodak, it was common for tourists to collect "views" of the places they visited. So while neither Father nor Mother took any photographs in Europe, they avidly collected hundreds of commercial photographs of the cities, landscapes, sculptures, and paintings they had seen and admired during their Continental tour. They carefully pasted these sepia-toned photographs, printed on the thinnest of paper, in their albums. It amazes me that their albums are so similar in the choice of the photographs. Surprisingly, after more than a century, the majority of the photographs are in pristine condition. They form a vivid accompaniment to their journals.

Father opened his office for the practice of medicine on his return to Lynn in the fall of 1886. On January 15, 1891, he and Miss Lillie were married.

From the day I was born, June 22, 1908, until I went to boarding school in 1925, I lived in Lynn with my parents. The city was then known as the shoe center of the world; it was estimated in 1904 that between 20 and 25 million pairs of boots and shoes were produced in Lynn annually. Immigrant shoemakers made up a large part of the population. They lived in West Lynn, near the numerous redbrick factory buildings. We lived on Broad Street, the main thoroughfare of the residential area of East Lynn, at its junction with Nahant Street, which led to the ocean beach.

Around the corner from our house, adjacent to our backyard, was the New Universalist Church, or "Meeting House," as it was originally named, where, I was told, I was baptized. This was our family church. Built in 1872–73, it was an imposing structure of stone, cruciform in plan, with an unusually steep slate roof over the nave and transept and a square tower at the crossing. Grandfather Davis was very proud of the church, and rightly so, for he and two friends contributed thirty thousand dollars each toward its construction. In his *Random Notes on a Trip to Europe*, he wrote in 1877:

Although I have seen nearly all the great churches of Europe, there is not so hallowed and none which causes so much fondness in my heart as our own little church, so beautifully situated in our dear city of Lynn. As I write today, our church in its simplicity and quiet architecture seems like a gem, and I hope before many months have passed to sit again with my family and friends within its sacred walls in humble worship of that good providence who has vouchsafed to us such health and happiness during our journeys in this distant land.

In 1905 Grandfather Newhall made a present of the three-story house next door to his residence and medical office.[1] A large and handsome house, it had been built in the half-timbered style so popular in England in the sixteenth century. It seemed out of place among the simple frame houses and three-story apartment buildings that lined Broad Street. In those days, doctors often had their offices in their homes, and our house was both residence and dispensary. Father's medical office was on the first floor, with its entrance directly on the street. Also on the first floor were an ample kitchen, two pantries, and a dining room. The main residential entrance was from a side porch that opened on a front hall. On the

1. Edward Newhall (1822–1905) graduated from Harvard Medical School in 1848. He studied medicine in Europe for two years, mainly in Paris.

Stereotype of the New Universalist Meeting House, Lynn, Massachusetts. Photographer unknown.

Newhall residence, Lynn, Massachusetts, c. 1900. Photographer unknown.

second floor there were three bedrooms, a sewing room, and a spacious living room that ran from one end of the house to the other. This was our family room, with a fireplace at one end and a book-lined library at the other, where in the evenings we read or listened to recordings of classical music or, later, the radio.

My parents frequently hosted meetings of friends: the Shakespeare Club, whose members read the plays aloud; Le Cercle Français, where only French was spoken; and a book review group. Every month or so Father invited fellow physicians to discuss clinical reports issued by the Massachusetts General Hospital in Boston, where he had been a house doctor. These meetings were closed to Mother, my aunt Annie—Father's sister, who lived with us—and myself. I well remember the refreshments: peanuts, ice water, and cigars. It was my responsibility to get a bag of peanuts at the near-by drugstore along with a box of cigars. Next day I would return the box to the druggist and pay for the cigars the doctors had smoked.

On the third floor, directly above the living room and of the same size, was the most unusual room in the house: a spacious, fully equipped professional photographic studio. Here Mother made portraits of family and friends and, on a semi-professional basis, anybody else. Exactly when Mother became an ardent photographer I do not know. Her early interest in photographs is shown by the hundreds of pictures she avidly collected on her European travels with her family. As a young woman she delighted in directing her friends to assume humorous poses for tintypes. These were inexpensive photographs on metal that were taken and processed "while you wait" in local studios and by itinerant photographers. They were the souvenirs of good times: a portrait of friends in a carriage bound for the tennis court, or such gag shots as that of Mother wearing, with two other girls, a fat boy's belt. In 1901, at the very time that her studio was built, Mother won national recognition with the

Opposite left: "The Tennis Party" (tintype). Alice Lillia Davis is seated in the rear seat. Photographer unknown.

Opposite right: Ruth Davis. Photograph by Alice Lillia Davis Newhall.

Left: Alice Lillia Davis (*left*) and friends wearing "Waldo's Belt," 1887 (tintype). Photographer unknown.

Right: A camera similar to the one used by Mother. Photograph by Barbara Puorro Galasso. (Courtesy of International Museum of Photography at George Eastman House)

reproduction in the photographic periodical *Photo-Era* of her charming portrait of her sister Ruth Davis. In the same issue were prints by Alfred Stieglitz, Gertrude Käsebier, and other members of the prominent group of master photographers known as the Photo-Secession. Her photographs were also reproduced in *Photo-Miniature*.

Mother's photographic studio was spacious, occupying one half of the top floor. In the center of the room, set into the sloping roof, was a huge skylight that I remember as about six by eight feet. It faced north, considered at the time to provide the ideal natural light exposure for portraiture. Mother used no artificial light at all, but relied entirely on daylight. The studio was bare except for a mobile burlap-covered screen that served as a background for her sitters' portraits, an iron stove at one end of the studio, and a few chairs. On the wall hung a large painting, commissioned while they were in Italy, of Grandfather and Grandmother Davis with their four daughters: Lillia, Florence, Ruth, and Edith. It was very large, so large that there was no other place in the house to hang it except the studio. I often wondered if Mother recalled the family's 1885 trip to Europe whenever she looked at the painting.

Mother's camera was of the bellows type, for 6 x 8-inch glass plates. Her lens was a Bausch and Lomb Rapid Rectilinear, with a shutter that was opened and closed by squeezing a bulb attached to a long rubber tube. The camera was firmly mounted on a sturdy camera stand with casters so she could easily move it around the studio to get the best light for her subject. Her darkroom was adjacent.

She did all of her own processing. One of my earliest recollections is standing beside my mother in her darkroom while she developed glass plates by the red glow of the safelight. I was fascinated to watch the image appear, as if by magic, in the glass tray. One day, wondering what the magic fluid tasted like, I dipped a finger in the tray of hypo and put it on my tongue. Mother was horrified. She yanked me out of the darkroom, spoiling her plate as she opened the door, dragged me to the nearby bathroom, and washed my mouth out with soap.

Unlike so many of the "Pictorial" photographers of her generation, Mother had no use for "soft focus." Her images are solid and convincing. Her posing of the sitter is direct, with a strong feeling of presence. She printed on platinum paper, which gave soft, luminous highlights and open shadows. These prints she mounted on gray or brown cardboard. She also used Autochrome color plates when they came on the market in 1907. These could be exposed in any standard plate camera, and processed in any darkroom. The result was a brilliant color transparency. I was my mother's favorite model. I seem to remember often posing for her in costume: as the *Blue Boy* in Gainsborough's famous painting, or as the Indian changeling in Shakespeare's *A Midsummer Night's Dream*.

In 1914 Mother completely lost interest in photography and stopped using the camera. I never understood why she gave up photography so suddenly. She said it was because when World War I broke out she found it difficult to obtain photographic chemicals, most of which were imported from Germany. She showed no interest in photography whatever for the rest of her life, and the studio became a playroom. Later, when I was about fifteen years old, I taught myself photographic processing in Mother's abandoned darkroom.

The few photographs taken by Mother that I possess are portraits of the family. I treasure in particular several of my sister, Ruth, who died of typhoid fever in 1912 at the age of

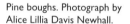
Pine boughs. Photograph by Alice Lillia Davis Newhall.

seventeen. As I was only three when that tragedy occurred, I have no recollection of her except that conferred by these photographs. On the death of Ruth, e. e. cummings, her closest friend, who was also seventeen at the time, sent my parents the following lines, which they treasured more than any other tribute.

Reverently we think of her,
A soul that dwelt in happy eyes
Within a house of pain.
The suffering that crucifies
One little body, by God's grace,
When all the world is glad and vain,
Could never draw one small demur
From those hot lips; across that face
One faintest shadow of surprise.

The Angel of the Golden Key
Opens the doorway of your youth,
And you are free at last.
Nay, falter not, 'tis really truth,
Really the rose-leaf for the thorn;
Swing back the portals of the past;
Fear not to cross the threshold,—we
Fear not, who have not even borne
Your trials, only loved you, Ruth.

e. e. cummings
January 1912

EARLY TIMES

My schooling was somewhat erratic. At kindergarten, held at a neighbor's house, I learned to read and write English in the mornings. The teacher became irate when I refused to capitalize the initial letters of my name, and soundly boxed my ears. I have a more pleasant recollection of afternoon hours with a governess I knew only as "Mam'selle," who taught me to speak and write French.

At about age eight or nine I went to a very small private school on one of the upper floors of the Lynn Women's Club, which was next door to our house. There were only a dozen or so pupils. Mr. Parker, the sole teacher, was a pleasant and very energetic young man. In the mornings we had traditional book learning. In the afternoons we sometimes walked to the ocean, which was not far away, to play games on the sandy beach that stretched for two miles to the peninsula of Nahant. I always enjoyed skipping along the edge of the sea as the waves broke on the sand. On Wednesdays we went to the local moving-picture theater. We laughed at the antics of the screen comedians, particularly one I remember as Mr. Penny, a name I cannot find in any standard book on film. It may have been on one of these Wednesdays that I saw *The Birth of a Nation*; however, it was more likely my mother who took me to that classic, which made a great impression on me, and which I saw many times thereafter.

Mr. Parker was something of an artist as well as a schoolteacher. From him I learned to draw with charcoal. Curiously, what I remember most vividly was his collection of Tom Swift novels. This series of proto-science-fiction adventure stories included *Tom Swift and His Sky Racer, or, The Quickest Flight on Record; Tom Swift and His Submarine Boat, or, Under the Ocean for Sunken Treasure; Tom Swift and His Photo Telephone, or, The Picture That Saved a Fortune*, and so forth.

When America entered World War I in 1917, Mr. Parker enlisted in the armed services. He closed his school, and I never again met him. I was sent to a public school, the Brickett School, within walking distance. There I became a chum of Edward Poole Hollis, whose father was a most remarkable parent. He was in the real estate and insurance business, but seemed to have plenty of free time, for he would meet Edward and me almost every day after school in his Hudson touring car and take us either to a Salem amusement park, or to the beach, or to hike across the peninsula to Nahant.

We were particularly interested in Mr. Hollis's miniature railway. Behind their substantial two-family colonial-style house was a two-story garage. The top floor was Mr. Hollis's metalworking shop, which housed an elegant model railroad. It was very cleverly put together. The two-inch-gauge tracks ran on waist-high shelves around the entire circumference of the room. To enter the room one had to lift the drawbridge that crossed the doorway. This broke the electric current and stopped all traffic until the bridge was lowered, and the trains merrily proceeded around the room once again. The miniature locomotives and rolling stock were imported from the English firm of Basset-Lowke. These were not toys, but beautiful examples of the model-maker's craft, perfect in every detail.

I soon became fascinated by sailing ships and model-making. Mr. Hollis had a complete set of *The Model Engineer*, an English magazine I always read from cover to cover. I did not realize at the time that I would become a contributor to that British periodical. I learned to use wood-working tools in the manual training course at junior high school, and began to make ship models in my workshop at home. In those days there were no kits of ready-made model parts that needed only to be assembled. My models were built entirely by hand. From the Science Museum in London I obtained blueprints of a model in its collection, the *Santa María*, the ship on which Christopher Columbus sailed to America. I used these drawings to make a detailed model, complete with sails made by my mother, an expert needleworker.

Next I restored to its original condition a model made in the nineteenth century of the ship *Caroline Augusta* for the descendants of her onetime captain, Andrew M. Putnam. The model was in a sad state: the spars were broken, the masts and rigging gnarled up. I removed every

Santa Mari

piece of rigging, made new masts and spars, cleaned up the decks and sides of the ship, and rerigged it completely. I described this in *The Model Engineer* for November 26, 1925. "An Interesting Ship Model Repair" was my first published writing, for which I received payment of two guineas.

The more I became fascinated with model-making, the deeper my research into the subject. I recall vividly my hours of study in the Peabody Museum in Salem, Massachusetts. Founded in 1799 as the East India Marine Hall, this museum has specialized ever since in maritime history. Its large collection of models of all types of sailing craft delighted me and was a source of inspiration. It also had, tucked away in the back of the building, a fine library of books on, and photographs of, ships. As a boy I would ride my bicycle to the museum and wheel it right into the entrance corridor, where it was safe under the watchful eye of the friendly constable, as the museum's principal guard and receptionist was called. Then I would greet the jovial marine curator, Lawrence Jenkins, if he was free. He was wonderfully kind to me when I was an eager youth, and would show me book after book that he thought might interest me. I pored over them.

For the descendants of the original owner, I made two identical models of the clipper ship *Aurora*, built in 1853 for the China trade. I went back to original sources. I carved the hull from measured drawings and profiles I had made from the original builder's half-model in the Peabody Museum.[2] I was paid one hundred dollars for each, which I used toward my tuition at Harvard. In retrospect, I realize that my models were

2. The rigging, which was fitted to only five other vessels, I found clearly described by the inventor, Ralph Bennett Forbes, in his pamphlet *A New Rig for Ships and Other Vessels, Combining Safety, Economy, and Convenience* (Boston: Weir and White, 1849). The classical square-rigger of its time was a sailing ship with three masts, each of which carried four rectangular sails. The topsails, which were the second abovedeck, were the largest and the most difficult and dangerous for the crew to handle. Captain Forbes divided these enormous sails in two. The "double topsail rig" was later modified by Captain Frederic Howe and became universal.

historical research reports. Indeed, I delivered with each model of the *Aurora* a two-page description of the very unusual rig, which was subsequently published in the April 1938 issue of *The Mariner*, a periodical devoted to maritime history.

I did my first teaching in my workshop, where I showed half a dozen or so eager boys, mostly children of my parents' friends, the principles of woodworking and the handling of tools. I remember that one mother was concerned that some of the tools we used were very sharp; she feared that her son might hurt himself. I pointed out that dull tools are the most dangerous, for they can easily slip out of control. By being paid fifty cents a lesson, I collected enough to buy a handsome chuck for my Goodell-Pratt foot-operated lathe. I am amazed at the generosity, tolerance, and understanding of my parents. They had no interest at all in ships and maritime history, and must have been bewildered by my passion for building things, but they never complained.

Years before my model-making, when I was still a child, they played along with me. There was "the Elevator." Mother used to take me with her on shopping trips in Boston. I always liked the elevator at Stearns, one of the most elegant and fashionable stores in the city. It was operated by a man in uniform. As we approached each floor he would recite the goods sold there. When he stopped the car he would throw open the door and say, in French, *"Place aux dames!"* How

A portrait made in 1925, at the time of my high school graduation. Photographer unknown.

many understand this as "Ladies first!" I do not know. Our living room at home was on the second floor. When the downstairs maid announced that supper was ready by tinkling the bell on the dining table, I would assemble the family at the head of the stairs, loop a strong string from one newel post to the other, and then, after a few seconds of buzzing, announce "First floor! Dining Room! *Place aux dames!*" and throw back the string. Sometimes the folks would find a circular toy railroad track on the dining table ready to bring on a flatcar the salt or pepper shaker, the sugar bowl, or the cream pitcher to anyone who needed it.

As I grew older Mother gave me the use of what she called the "sewing room" for my workshop. It was right beside the living room. In it I had a workbench as well as a jigsaw and a lathe. Both were foot-powered and fairly quiet, but there was always a lot of commotion, plenty of shavings and sawdust, and the smell of paint and varnish. The family liked having me near and watching me work.

During my high school days I had few companions. When making models I worked entirely alone. If I was not in my shop in the afternoon, I was quite likely exploring Lynn and its surroundings. Although I had a bicycle, I preferred to walk a mile or so directly across the city to Lynn Classical High School. After school I would take a circuitous route home. I enjoyed window-shopping. Often I would visit a cabinetmaker's shop to watch the craftsmen at work or to pick scraps of wood to take home to my shop. The men were very friendly, and I learned a lot from them.

Every week or so I would treat myself to a trip to Boston. I liked particularly to go on the Boston, Revere Beach, and Lynn Railroad, a narrow-gauge line that stopped at many seaside towns before it finally arrived in East Boston. There you boarded a ferry that crossed the harbor to Atlantic Avenue. I liked to wander around the piers and look at the ships. Once in a great while a square-rigged ship would be tied up to a wharf, and sometimes I would be invited to come aboard.

It was but a short walk from the wharf to the Old State House on Washington Street. One room of that historic building was devoted to ship models. I was so impressed by a large model of the U.S. frigate *Constitution* that I wrote an article about it for *The Model Engineer*. Unlike most models (including my own) this was a miniature working ship that could be sailed in the ocean. Right around the corner from the Old State House was Wilkinson's hardware store, which was the model-maker's delight, where you could buy screws and nuts and bolts by the piece, sheet metal by the square inch, and brass rods by the foot.

Along the coast north of Lynn many boats were being built, ranging from the rowboats, locally called dories, to impressive racing yachts. I particularly enjoyed bicycling to Marblehead, which was a great yacht-racing center in the summer. Strangely, despite my great interest in boat-building of all kinds, I had no desire at all to sail on them.

Our family was Europe-oriented. Both Father and Mother had traveled extensively in Europe, and although they never again crossed the Atlantic, they kept in touch through French and German periodicals, and hired either French or German governesses for me. When I was a freshman at Harvard, my uncle, Johnson O'Connor, a psychologist, invited me to a dinner party in his

Boston home. The other guests were psychoanalysts. Although Prohibition was then in force, wine was served. I was not used to liquor of any kind. When the party broke up and I was about to leave for Cambridge, my uncle quietly said, "I think you had better spend the night here. You've had quite a bit of wine."

At breakfast next day Uncle Johnson asked me, "When did you learn German?" I answered, "Why, I'm just beginning at Harvard."

"Well, last night you were speaking fluent German! One of the analysts said you must have had a German nursemaid."

When I next saw Mother I asked her—without telling her why—if I had had a German nursemaid when I was a baby. She immediately answered, "Yes, indeed. You probably heard more German than English in the first two or three years of your life!"

My father was a highly respected and popular physician. He was a general practitioner of the old school: every morning he made his rounds from house to house, at first in a horse and buggy and later in a chauffeur-driven automobile. In the afternoons, and often in the evenings as well, he was in his office on the ground floor of our house. He had no receptionist, no nurse, no medical assistant. He kept his own books. In his minuscule chemical laboratory he conducted routine clinical tests. I used to marvel at the beautiful, highly polished brass microscope that he kept under a large glass bell. Although he was on the medical staff of the Lynn Hospital for forty-three years, from 1889 to 1932, he never talked to us about his work and never mentioned his patients.

Not until I had left college did I fully realize the extent and the wisdom of my parents' laissez-faire policy toward me. I had no idea that Father, successful as he was in the practice of medicine, very much disliked being a physician. During my first steady employment, in the Pennsylvania Museum of Art in Philadelphia, I wrote him my thanks for having made it possible for me to have entered the museum profession. He answered, "I think it was because I had taken up my father's profession, as it seemed the easiest thing to do rather than from any real desire to become a doctor, that I determined that you should be free to follow your own course."

Father's greatest interest was botany and gardening. He loved to collect all kinds of wild plants, roots and all, from the woods and fields. These he would carefully plant in the backyard. At one time he had specimens of all the ferns that grow in Massachusetts. In 1918 he bought two acres of country land in West Peabody, Massachusetts, and built a small house on it. It was an easy seven-mile drive from Lynn, so Father was able to commute to his office and continue his medical practice. We lived there every summer for twelve years. He named our summer home, an idyllic place, "Eskerdell," a word he coined from two geological terms. He defined them in a poem:

What is the esker?
A glacial ridge, which like a snake
Crawling in sinuous folds across my land
Has stopped to rest, abasking in the sun.

What is the dell?

A little vale bedecked with mosses green

And lichens gray

With asters and with juniper.

In it lies a pool of pond-lilies.

Stately, dainty irises grow on the brink.

Towering over all

Above the esker and its cedar tall

There rises from the dell a giant ash

Whose mighty trunk two men with

Outstretched arms cannot encircle.

We had a large vegetable garden at Eskerdell; so much was grown on it that we took produce to the city market. What we could not sell we gave to friends and neighbors. I was given a somewhat smaller plot of my own. I am sure that Father was disappointed that I showed little interest in gardening, but he never questioned my dislike and supported me in my passion for marine research and the building of ship models, which must have seemed very curious to him.

In the last years of his life, when he had all but retired from the practice of medicine, Father wrote poems for his own satisfaction and for distribution to his family and friends. It was a sad day in 1931 when it became necessary, for financial reasons, to sell the country house and land. In what is to me the most poignant of his poems he memorialized the one place in the world he loved the most, Eskerdell.

The Sale

So many thousand feet of land,

Bounded so and so,

The house that stands upon it

And a right of way,

So runs the deed.

No mention of the ridge,

From which the cedar rears

A towering spire to the sky;

No mention of the dell

Where stands the giant Ash

Upon whose top-most bough

The scarlet tanager lights;

Or of the mossy slope

Where hare-bells blue

Nod beneath the trees;
Or of the banks of ferns whose fronds
Brush the cheeks of passers-by;
Or of the Norway spruces
Broad and tall, the stalwart sentinels
That guard the little road.
All these we sell,
But not the memories of summer days
When lying near the pool
We watched the clouds sail by.
Of glorious sunsets,
When golden islands floated
In seas of softest green;
Of evening when the wood-thrush sang
And his call was echoed by his mate
Again and again.
Or of the inky blackness of the night,
When fireflies danced and flashed their lamps,
Or of the peaceful mornings
When across the fields
Came ringing sweet and clear
The full and mellow notes
Of the Sabbath bell.
These memories we keep.
For those who follow us at Eskerdell
We have the kindest wishes,
And hope that they will find
All the joys we left behind,
And more besides.

CAMP MERRYWEATHER   In the summers of 1921 to 1924 I went to Camp Merryweather on Belgrade Lake in Maine. This unusual boys' camp was conceived and managed by Henry Richards and his wife, Laura, the daughter of Julia Ward Howe, author of "Battle Hymn of the Republic."

As I recollect, forty or fifty boys, aged between twelve and seventeen, were there each summer. "Skipper," as we called Mr. Richards, was aided by his son, "Captain John," and a half-dozen or so counselors who were college students or masters in private schools.

The main building was a sprawling, one-story structure on the edge of the lake with a large room where we dined, a room for reading and writing, and a kitchen. There was neither plumbing nor electricity. We bathed and brushed our teeth in the lake. The rooms were lighted with oil lamps.

Mornings began right after breakfast, when we were assigned various tasks, such as sweeping the floors, picking up trash, and cleaning the oil lamps. At eleven o'clock sharp we raced to the boathouse, put on our bathing suits, and went swimming, rowing, and canoeing. Watermanship was a specialty at Camp Merryweather, which owned a fleet of canoes, rowboats, kayaks, and racing shells. We campers were not allowed to take boats beyond the cove where the camp was situated, unless accompanied by a counselor. After lunch we reclined beneath the trees in an area called Pine Parlor and listened to Mrs. Richards reading classics by Charles Dickens, Robert Louis Stevenson, and other authors. We then played games.

If, at breakfast, the day promised to be fair, Skipper might say but one word: "Scouting!" We would shout with joy. This was a make-believe war game. Campers were divided into two sides: the Iroquois and the Algonquins. Our "battlefield" was a stretch of an acre or two of scrubby forest. Wearing special caps of khaki, we lined up on opposing sides of the field, out of sight of one another. On the shouted command of Skipper, who stationed himself in the middle of the field, we began to crawl and creep stealthily through the underbrush, hoping to reach the other end of the field without being seen by the enemy. If an opponent recognized you he called out your name. You were honor bound to stand up, turn your cap, which had a white lining, inside out, and walk to Skipper's headquarters, which was called the Boneyard. Opposite your name on the roster Skipper drew crossed bones, signifying that you had been killed in action. When Skipper blew the whistle to mark the end of the game, the side having more campers who crossed enemy territory won.

Another time Skipper might declare an All-Day Excursion. We would help to launch rowboats and canoes and line them up in formation. The oversize war canoe, paddled by ten campers, was the flagship. Skipper himself steered it with a huge paddle. To port and starboard were two rowboats. Beside them were two canoes, and on either end of the line were one-man kayaks. On the command of the Skipper, shouted through a huge megaphone, we started across the lake nonstop. Lagging craft were urged forward by Skipper, those rushing beyond the line were ordered to slacken their speed. Once ashore, we built fires on the beach and cooked our lunch. Then we returned to camp in a style equally rigorous.

The Tinkletrap   When I graduated from high school, my aunt Annie gave me a Ford Model T, which, because it was a demonstration car, was marked down to $225 cash—a bargain even in 1925. Nobody knew how far it had been driven because, like all Model Ts, it had neither speedometer nor odometer. However, the tires looked new—or, as the dealer said, "The rubber's good."

As part of the deal, the salesman taught me to drive. It didn't take me long to master the gearshift. There were three foot pedals. You pressed down the left-hand pedal and were in low. When you took your foot off, you were in high. On pressing the middle pedal, you were in reverse. If you pressed any two pedals down at the same time, you stalled with a snarl of clashing gears.

You sat in a seat on top of the gasoline tank. There was no gauge, but your neighborhood filling station gladly gave you a stick marked in gallons. To "fill her up" you took out the cushion of the front seat, stuck the measuring stick down into the tank, and told the man at the pumps how many gallons you needed. Then he sold you as many quarts of oil as gallons of gasoline, which he also poured into the tank. Like most Model T owners, I bought such accessories as a speedometer, a rearview mirror, a windshield wiper, a thermometer, and a radiator cap.

After the second or third lesson, I found that I was doing all the driving to Lynn Woods every afternoon. It took me a little while to figure out that the salesman liked demonstrating a lot more than selling cars. Only with reluctance did he finally agree that I was ready to take the road test for a driver's license.

I loved that Model T. My best girl, a student at Wellesley College, called it "The Tinkletrap." When I drove it, I knew that I was behind an engine. I often wondered what would have happened if the muffler hadn't parted company with the manifold and the floor boards had not caught on fire, back in 1926, just after I had the car painted Wellesley blue.

❖

EDUCATION

To my family, "Harvard" and "college" were synonymous. After all, two generations of Newhalls and one generation of Davises had gone to Harvard, and both Father and Mother hoped that I would follow what had become a family tradition. But my high school scholastic record was so poor that the principal told Father that admission to Harvard was practically impossible. My parents thought otherwise, and decided to send me for a year to Phillips Academy in Andover, Massachusetts, in the hope that my academic record there would meet the standards of the Harvard faculty.

I disliked Andover. The classes were rigorous and demanding. We learned largely by rote. In the French language class, for instance, we were told in the fall that we would learn one hundred idioms and in the spring we would be examined on them. If we missed one our grade was 90, two and it was 80, and so on. If we missed five out of the hundred, we had flunked the examination.

In Latin class the teacher opened the lessons by reading the roll from a little black book, then asked a question of each of us as we stood at attention. He quickly noted in his book how many questions each of us had failed. One morning, after going around the room, he delighted in announcing "Every one of you has failed. This is a record." Of course, an after-class session was prescribed.

I disliked attending church eight times a week, and I detested sports. I worked out my antipathy for athletics by signing up for "hurling the javelin." Nobody else was interested in this sport, so every afternoon I would go out to the field and hurl this javelin, run after it, pick it up, hurl it again, run after it, hurl it, for half an hour. I passed the requirements.

I understand that today Andover is a much more liberal institution than it was in 1925. Although I was able to present a report card that satisfied the dean of admissions at

Harvard, I think it was not my grades that impressed him as much as the article my father showed him on ship-model repair that had been published in *The Model Engineer*. It was the first of more than 650 articles that I have written over the years.

FILM AND PHOTOGRAPHY In 1926, when I was eighteen, the chance viewing of a motion picture determined my future. That summer marked the end of one age and the beginning of another—a halcyon three-month interval between graduating from Andover and entering Harvard. One night, while visiting an Andover classmate in Salem, Massachusetts, and wanting to see a movie, we wandered into *Variety* (1925), an experimental German film starring Emil Jannings, directed by Ewald André Dupont, and photographed by Karl Freund. This film was different from anything I had seen on the screen before. *Variety* told its story with images created through the use of extreme camera angles. It was a circus tale of two jealous trapeze artists in love with the same girl. One was going to let the other fall by failing to grasp his partner's hands while he was swinging in midair. The camera followed the action, climbed with the acrobats to dizzying heights above the audience in a Berlin theater, swung on the trapeze the hero was grasping. It seemed to penetrate everywhere. There was also multiple exposure; the rumors that were circulating were shown metaphorically using multiple ears. The film was, to my eyes, a triumph—not of Jannings's acting, not of Dupont's direction, but of Freund's imaginative camerawork. I chased *Variety* from theater to theater. It went the rounds of the Boston suburbs, and a ten-cent trolley ride brought me to each neighborhood playhouse. I'd see a late-afternoon show, have dinner at a local cafeteria, then see the show over again.

During my college days, as other motion pictures came to theaters in the area, I would follow them, night after night. I would bike around all the small towns, following the circuit, writing extensive reviews of those that interested me. These remarks were not intended for publication but simply as notes. As I wrote in a review of *Serenade*, a whimsical, lighthearted musical starring Adolphe Menjou: "I go to the cinema usually to see the direction of a picture—to absorb the technical tricks of the trade. Why, I don't know, but it is the most fascinating part of a movie to me. But here is one that I enjoyed for its jollity, for its carefree, natural, happy-go-lucky character." Although these notes seem somewhat juvenile and naive today, they were of great importance to me back in the days before there were art houses or film libraries or any way to study the medium seriously. Just about this time Iris Barry was founding the London Film Society. Her arrival in this country and her attaining the position of curator of the Museum of Modern Art's newly established Department of Film later created a new opportunity to see films.

There was an exception. A small group formed the Shady Hill Film Society, which brought many film classics to Brattle Hall in Cambridge. I served as an usher and so saw many memorable films, making extensive notes on those that most interested me. Among these was a French film made by Henri Chomette, the brother of René Clair (who had dropped the family name), titled *De quoi revient les jeunes films?* (What Are the Young Films Dreaming About?), which appears now to be lost. After seeing this film in 1927 I wrote the following notes:

Along with the remarkable *The Cabinet of Dr. Caligari* was a laboratory experiment by Henri Chomette. I cannot begin to give all the effects that were thrown upon the screen, so I shall only give a very few. Here we see the true possibilities of that most versatile machine, the motion picture camera. Crystals. Kaleidoscopes. Soap bubbles. Dynamos. Shells. Lights everywhere. And best of all a trip through Paris. First we went at breakneck speed through the subway. Lights looked like white lines, in fact that is all that there was on the screen for several feet. Then a square light in the distance. Just the merest speck. Nearer, and nearer, until it looked like a newspaper. Bigger and bigger, until at last we realized that it was the entrance to the tunnel. Railroad tracks shooting by and merging one into the other, or rather melting. A double exposure of two tracks, the one going, so I heard, at two-four time, the other at two-three time. Subway cars rushing at you, upside down, or pointing to the sky. Under bridges on the Seine, until you thought that you had been under all the bridges in the world. The negatives of foliage, queer white branches against a black background. A profile, repeated across the screen to make a pretty pattern. A series of studies in dissolves. Distorted mirror pictures, and again crystals, and bubbles and wheels, all, not symbolic of anything as the audience would have us believe, but simply as pretty and interesting things, revealing, as it were, the remarkable possibilities of the camera as something more than a mere machine for reproduction. American photographers might sit up and take notice. Most interesting for one interested in the future of the movies and the possibilities of the motion picture camera, most boring for one seeking sentiment and a story. So these experiments fail in America.

At about the same time I first saw *Variety*, I found on the shelf of new books in Harvard's Widener Library a volume of the most startling still photographs I had ever seen. It was a collection of photographs of American skyscrapers and such industrial buildings as grain elevators and factories taken by the German architect Erich Mendelsohn and published in 1926, *Amerika: Bilderbuch eines Architekten* (America: Picture Book of an Architect).[3] I knew nothing of this architect's stature: his observatory in Potsdam, the so-called "Einstein Tower," was as unknown to me at the time as the buildings of Le Corbusier and Mies van der Rohe. But the layout of the book was fantastic to me: on one whole page there was nothing but a tiny photograph of the New York skyline. This was followed by full-page pictures of skyscrapers seen in distorted views—for, possibly by accident, probably by design, Mendelsohn did not always hold his camera level. He did not use a wide-angle lens, nor did he use the front and swinging back of the conventional view camera to eliminate what is called "perspective distortion." When he looked up and craned his neck he tilted the camera too. To me these were extraordinary photographs because of the camera angle as well as the choice of subject: photographers didn't choose skyscrapers and grain elevators as their subjects then—they photographed the pretty and the picturesque. I found Mendelsohn's images as gripping as Freund's in

3. Erich Mendelsohn, *Amerika: Bilderbuch eines Architekten* (Berlin: Rudolf Mosse Buchverlag, 1926). Only recently have I read the enthusiastic review of this book by the Russian Constructivist artist El Lissitzky, reprinted in his *Proun und Wolkenbugel, Briefe, Dokumente* (Dresden, 1977), pp. 64–69.

The Salmon Tower, at the northeast corner of Madison Avenue and Fortieth Street, taken from a window in the Murray Hill Hotel, April 22, 1927—my first New York City photograph. (Courtesy of Scheinbaum & Russek Ltd., Santa Fe, New Mexico)

Variety, and was inspired to try to find industrial subjects of equal excitement in Cambridge and New York for my folding camera.

I wanted to go to Hollywood and be a film director, but my parents wanted me to go to Harvard, which I did in order not to disappoint them. When the time came for me to choose a field of concentration for my college studies, my parents suggested I consult their friend Alfred Tozzer, a professor of anthropology at Harvard. I was disappointed that no courses were given in motion pictures or photography. Professor Tozzer said, "Why don't you try art history? After all, paintings are pictures too." So I enrolled in an elementary art appreciation course. I liked it so much that during my undergraduate years I took every course in Western art that Harvard offered.

At that time, Harvard's approach to art history was basically what I term "archeological." The aesthetic, the spirit, of painting and sculpture were never discussed. Instead we were shown slides and had to memorize hundreds of images in order to pass the exams. We certainly did build up a terrific pictorial vocabulary. There were, however, several visiting European art historians who made a deep impression. I remember in particular Adolph Goldschmidt, a retired German professor. Although his specialty was medieval ivory sculpture, he lectured on seventeenth-century Dutch and Flemish painting. He opened our eyes to a new approach, different from the factual, with its emphasis on dates and rote memorization. Instead of the usual slide examination, he showed us just *one* slide: he gave us title and artist, *The Lace Maker* by Vermeer, date, provenance, and technique, thereby exhausting everything we knew about the work. "Gentlemen, describe the painting," he said. Another innovation was his use of two slide projectors, so paintings could be seen side by side for comparative study—a technique that is by now quite universal, but that was unknown at Harvard in the 1920s.

During the summer of 1928 I worked in the library of the Harvard art department cataloging lantern slides of works of art. In their lectures the art professors used hundreds of black-and-white glass slides of the now obsolete 3¼ x 4-inch format, printed by contact from copy negatives of the same size. Paper prints were also made from each slide negative, and these were mounted on index cards. It was the task of the cataloger to furnish data for each slide: name and life dates of the artist, title of the work, medium, date of production, and the present owner (museum, private collector, or dealer). We catalogers had to provide, along with this data, exact bibliographical references of our sources for this information. Since the slide collection included works of art of virtually every period and every country, we became familiar with a great number of paintings, drawings, sculptures, etchings, engravings, lithographs, and other graphic arts. In addition we became familiar with a large number of architectural monuments of all ages and countries. Furthermore, we came to know the literature of art history and had opportunity to make use of the foreign languages we had learned as a matter of course—in my case, French and German. It was a privilege to have unlimited access to the extremely large library of art books and the collection of photographs of art and architecture.

Left: La Porte Guillaume, Chartres, 1929. Photograph by Beaumont Newhall. (Courtesy of Scheinbaum & Russek Ltd., Santa Fe, New Mexico)

Right: House designed by Robert Mallet-Stevens, Paris, 1929. Photograph by Beaumont Newhall. (Courtesy of Scheinbaum & Russek Ltd., Santa Fe, New Mexico)

To celebrate my twenty-first birthday in the summer of 1929, my parents very generously gave me a trip to Europe. It was a perfect time for me to go abroad, for I already knew a good deal about art, but my knowledge was for the most part secondhand, through black-and-white photographs rather than from originals. I spent most of my time in London and Paris, with excursions in England, France, Germany, and Holland. I kept a careful journal.

Like my father, I enjoyed the Louvre. I wrote home in July 1929: "What a colossal place it is! I gave up all hope of making a survey tour, and went to see several of the masterpieces: the *Venus de Milo*, the *Winged Victory*, and *Mona Lisa* being the outstanding. I took away the fondest memories of the *Winged Victory*—veritably a thing of life and beauty. *Mona Lisa* was a disappointment, but Vermeer's *Lace Maker* was more than I had expected." However, as I pore over these voluminous and often monotonous letters and journals, a clear pattern emerges: after viewing the standard masterpieces, I sought out the little-known, ancient piece of architecture. Chartres Cathedral was of course magnificent, but I preferred discovering the forgotten city gate:

> July 10, 1929. Arrived at Chartres and immediately went to the Hôtel du Grand Monarque. After leaving my luggage I went to see the cathedral. What a building! I have now seen many marvelous cathedrals; this really is the finest yet. There is no over-decoration—all is dignified and full of meaning, yet so different than I had anticipated....A walk about town was the next thing I did. There is an old city gate, the Porte Guillaume, that few travelers see. Of course it is overpowered by the cathedral, but as a specimen of fourteenth-century French military architecture it is worthwhile. I photographed it.

In planning this European trip it was my intention to photograph the monuments and buildings that I knew from my studies. For this purpose I bought in Boston a German Voigtländer "Avus" camera for glass plates, sheet film, or film pack, 9 x 12 centimeters (3¼ x 4½ inches) in size. It was a beautifully made bellows camera with a ground glass for exact focusing and a 150 cm focal length Skopar ƒ/4.5 lens. The incredible price of thirty-nine dollars included a half-dozen plate holders and also a leather case. With each purchase came a sample photograph taken with the camera and a certificate stating the exact focal length of the lens. The Avus could be used either hand-held or fastened to a tripod. I made a lot of landscapes and pictures of buildings that interested me. Soon I gave up photographing the cathedral of Nôtre Dame in Paris, the Eiffel Tower, or the Palace of Versailles. I could buy postcards of them for less than the price of film.

What astonishes me, looking back now more than half a century, was that I also had a keen interest in the architecture that at the time was considered "revolutionary"—the "International Style." On this 1929 trip I photographed a group of houses in Paris designed by the architect Robert Mallet-Stevens. I noted in my journal: "These buildings are the best expression I have seen of the new spirit in architecture. Utterly simple, depending on mass and color for decoration, the houses seem to me most practical and livable. Orange awnings against buff cement walls form a pleasing color scheme; many terraces on roofs, many huge windows give the impression that the dwellers really enjoy their houses."

Of special interest to me was the city of Nancy, for I was writing my Harvard honors thesis on the charming eighteenth-century inner city, or *troisième ville*, a gem of city planning. It was in Nancy that I first became aware of *art nouveau*.

> It is an architecture inspired by growing things. The attempt was to build houses with the same logical means that God creates flora. Hence one sees many stems and stalks supporting lintels, balconies, window frames. In spite of the fact that to my eyes it seems illogical to build a house like a tree, there is a certain grace and beauty of form to the structures. The simplification, the stylization of natural forms, seems to me the real precursor of our modern style. Also the fact that the whole ensemble is in the same style—furniture, decoration, and even paintings.

I was greatly impressed by the amount of modern architecture in Holland, particularly in Amsterdam. On a visit to the marine museum to see the ship models there, I passed through the area known as Vondelpark and was greatly surprised that, as I noted in my journal, "all the buildings, and there are dozens of them, are constructed in the modern style. The result is superb. One feels that the contemporary style is more than a fad, but as vital as the Renaissance."

I visited Europe again in 1930, after receiving the degree of Bachelor of Arts cum laude from Harvard. This time I spent several weeks in Munich, where I boarded with a German family. No English was spoken, and I had hoped to perfect my knowledge of the German language, which I had found indispensable in my art-history studies. But the highlight of the trip took place in Paris, where I viewed the great exhibition at the Louvre of the lifework of the painter Eugène Delacroix. "No less than 900 paintings, drawings, and prints have been assembled," I wrote Mother. "Rarely does one have the opportunity of studying so well one of the great masters. One could, for example, see certain paintings, such as *The Death of Sardanapalus*, in all stages, from the embryonic first sketches to the huge (8 x 9 feet) finished work. The fact that I saw about all the Delacroix paintings in America in Chicago last April makes me most fortunate in the study of his work. It is as close an approach to the complete study of an artist as can be made."

PAUL SACHS   In the spring of 1930 I was delighted to receive a letter from the dean of the Graduate School of Arts and Sciences of Harvard University stating that I had been appointed to a university scholarship. Beyond the honor was the stipend that covered the cost of tuition for the academic year. This enabled me not only to obtain an M.A. degree, but it determined my future profession: art-museum curator and, eventually, director.

I enrolled in the graduate course "Museum Work and Museum Problems" given by Paul Joseph Sachs, associate director of Harvard's Fogg Art Museum. This was the first course in the management of art museums given anywhere. A most remarkable man, Professor Sachs came to Harvard in 1915 from New York City, after retiring as a partner in his father's banking firm Goldman, Sachs. He became associate director of the Fogg Museum. In this extraordinary course he shared with us his vast experience as a collector, an art historian, and a museum executive. He gave two informal seminars a week, one a lecture at the Fogg and the other held at Shady Hill, his home in Cambridge.

This old building (which no longer exists) had at one time been the home of Charles Eliot Norton. The founder of art history in the American university systems, Norton began teaching art history at Harvard in 1873. In the 1920s and early thirties, Bernard Berenson was a model for the type of training students received in identifying and classifying works of art, enabling them to become excellent museum curators. Sachs, who was a collector, knew Berenson.

Sachs ran these seminars as if they were business conferences. We students kept no notes, for his secretary recorded the minutes of each meeting, typed them up, mimeographed them, and distributed them to us each week. In addition to the informal seminars, we had weekly lectures by specialists in all aspects of museum work, from the conservation of paintings to museum security to the preparation of an operating budget. Visiting scholars were also a regular feature.

"P. J.," as we affectionately called him, taught by involving us in real-life problems rather than hypothetical exercises. For example, at one meeting he brought an armful of correspondence that had come to his desk in the previous two days. He read and discussed with us all thirty-three letters, handing one to each of us and asking how we would answer it. We would then draft answers for him to use. He explained that he did this to give an idea of the diversity of problems that are presented to a museum administrator, and to build up an understanding and "feeling" for museum work.

He insisted that we share with him the responsibilities for the security of the priceless works of art placed in a museum director's custody. We were required to memorize the location of each art object in all the galleries of the Fogg Museum and were expected to check the galleries every day. At any moment, in the middle of a lecture, P. J. might ask, "Newhall, name the paintings in Gallery Six in the order of their hanging, left to right." He also talked to us about his experiences, confided what dealers to be wary of, and gave us his address book and letters of introduction when we traveled abroad.

Most surprising of all was P. J.'s trust in us and his belief in our capabilities, despite our youth. One day P. J. announced to the class that a city of 350,000 residents was seeking a director for an art museum. He said he did not know which one of us to nominate for the job, which paid the then generous salary of seventy-five hundred per year, so he asked us to vote for one of our fellow students. Gordon Washburn won the informal election and became director of the Buffalo museum now known as the Albright-Knox Art Gallery, one of America's most prestigious small museums.

I was less successful. The city of Springfield, Massachusetts, had received an unexpected bequest of $2.6 million for the construction and operation of a new art museum. The City Library Association had been charged with handling the building funds and sought the advice of Paul Sachs. Since the terms of the bequest called for an architectural competition, complete specifications were required. P. J. called for volunteers to go to Springfield, make a survey of the needs of the new museum, and prepare a detailed report for the trustees. I volunteered and so did a fellow student, Stuart C. Henry. Our report satisfied the Springfield trustees, and P. J. was so pleased with it he printed it in the "Museum Course Notes." When the trustees asked him to choose a director, he simply named Stuart Henry and myself. But the trustees of the new museum felt that we were too young, and did not accept the nominations.

Since 1923, Sachs had been training a new generation of museum curators. When the Museum of Modern Art was founded in 1929, Sachs was asked by the trustees to nominate a director. He chose Alfred H. Barr, Jr., aged twenty-six, as director and Jere Abbott, aged twenty-nine, as associate director. Both were completely inexperienced as museum executives, but Barr became one of the best museum directors of the century.

That was a great era of building new museums, and it was also a time of major collecting. We all got jobs. The list of museums directed, at one time or other, by P. J.'s students is extensive. It includes such major museums as the Museum of Modern Art, New York; the Metropolitan Museum of Art, New York; the Museum of Fine Arts, Boston; the Art Institute of Chicago; the National Gallery of Art, Washington; the Philadelphia Museum of Art; the Cleveland Museum of Art; and the M. H. de Young Memorial Museum, San Francisco, among very many others.

On the death of Paul Sachs in 1965, I wrote my fellow student Agnes Mongan, who had been appointed his successor as associate director of the Fogg Art Museum: "It is sad to think that our dear Paul Sachs is no longer with us. He certainly changed my whole life, and that of so many of our colleagues, not only by his generosity towards us, his advice, his counsel and his support, but by creating a climate in American museums which has made it possible for us to put to use and develop all that he taught us."

❖

At Harvard commencement in 1931, when I received my master's degree, Father wrote a very special poem, which I have cherished over the years.

To Beaumont

How gently flows the brook

Between its mossy banks,

The overhanging trees shut out the sky.

It does not hurry at the sight

Of meadows bright with sunshine.

I wonder if it hesitates,

Loath to leave the pleasant shade.

There may be shoals,

There may be rocks ahead.

There may be dams,

It may be forced to flow

Through mighty turbines

Ere the sea is reached

And its life is lost

In the ocean whence it sprang.

So now with you,

About to leave the quiet walls of Harvard,

Where you have spent so many hours

Living in the past,

Seeking the secret of the masters,

How they made their works divine,

What message they are sending us,

How we can keep the torch they lit

Still burning bright

To make the lives of men

More rich with joy and beauty.

You now go forth

To mingle with your fellows

In the world where many interests compete.

Your mission is to foster

The love of art and beauty.

You first must find the spark

That glows, however faint it be

In every human soul.

Show sympathy. Be tolerant

Of different points of view.

Walk boldly forth
And teach the truth that you have learned.

And as you say
Farewell to Harvard
And hail the outside world,
We stand by and wave our hands
And shout God-speed.

H.W.N.
June 5, 1931

❖

1931—1935: YEARS OF HOPE

Although P.J. did not find a museum directorship for me, he did succeed in placing me as lecturer in the vast museum in Philadelphia then known as the Pennsylvania Museum of Art. My duties were to lecture on Tuesdays and Sundays at three o'clock, and to give gallery talks on Wednesdays—or at any other time when requested. To quote from the printed program: "Anyone desiring to see the collection under expert guidance may secure the services of Mr. Newhall to the extent that his engagements permit."

The subjects of my talks ranged over the entire history of art. The most difficult part was being a docent. There would be a sign in the front hall announcing, "Mr. Newhall will lecture on Rembrandt at 3 o'clock in Gallery 7." So I would go to Gallery 7, prepared to speak on the subject. I stood alone, with people wandering around. As I began to talk they would walk over, listen, then one by one they'd leave the room. I stood alone again, with no one to talk to, and very upset. As I crept back to my office, Rossiter Howard, the head of the department of education, was comforting, but he'd say, "Look, you've got to learn how to interest them." So I worked away in the library, collecting humanistic stories. Rossiter offered me a few tips about lecturing: speak to all of the people, then pick out someone on the right to address, then someone on the left. "You are setting up a relation to the audience that way," he said. He reminded me that as a lecturer I was giving a theatrical presentation as well as telling the museumgoers about the paintings. His advice, more than anything else, enabled me to give lectures.

My pleasant job as an informal teacher ended quite abruptly. On New Year's Day 1932 I learned that due to the Depression the budget of the museum had been so severely cut by the city of Philadelphia that there were no funds with which to pay my salary. The director of the museum, Fiske Kimball, wrote me: "I need scarcely emphasize that this action is taken only under duress, quite irrespective of your services, with which we are entirely satisfied."

I at once reported to Paul Sachs the unhappy news of being laid off by the museum. Within a few days he telephoned me that the Metropolitan Museum of Art in New York needed an assistant in its Department of Decorative Arts and that he had recommended me. I immediately went to the museum and was interviewed by James Rorimer, a fellow alumnus of Paul Sachs's museum course, and now associate curator in that department. He explained that a staff member was needed to look after the small branch museum known as The Cloisters. We drove to Washington Heights at the northern tip of Manhattan and stopped in front of a churchlike building beside the columns and arches of a medieval cloister. Rorimer said that these were part of the long-abandoned monastery of Saint Michel de Cuxa in southern France. They had been acquired by the American sculptor George Grey Barnard, who imported them stone by stone and re-erected them in his garden near his studio. The adjacent building contained his collection of medieval sculpture and architectural fragments. John D. Rockefeller, Jr., purchased both the collection and building for a million dollars in 1925 and gave them to the Metropolitan Museum. The Cloisters opened to the public in the following year.

The prospect of overseeing this charming, unique, and almost unknown museum appealed to me greatly. I saw the position as an opportunity to offer gallery talks and guided tours and possibly to organize small special exhibitions of medieval artifacts from the vast collections in the main museum. I told Rorimer that I was much interested in the job and would accept it if it was offered to me. On January 14, 1932, Joseph Breck, then acting director of the Metropolitan, appointed me assistant in the Department of Decorative Arts. I reported to work February 1. To my surprise I was told that The Cloisters had been permanently closed! Thus the job to which I had been officially appointed only a fortnight earlier had been abolished.

It was only many years later that Rorimer explained to me that this sudden change of plans was the result of the gift by John D. Rockefeller, Jr., of $2.5 million to build a new and much larger museum of medieval art that would not only replace Barnard's original structure and house his collection, but would also serve as the home of many other medieval works of art. This new building would carry the same name as Barnard's original museum: The Cloisters.

As a result, I became Rorimer's assistant. I installed temporary exhibitions of new acquisitions, supervised the cleaning and restoration of medieval sculptures, and performed other tasks usually delegated to museum interns. In December, just as I was settling into an apartment I had rented on East Seventy-ninth Street, Joseph Breck dismissed me. He felt that I should leave the museum in order to continue my studies in art history, and asked me to submit my resignation at once. When I pointed out that I had just leased an apartment and was obliged to pay rent for several months, he extended the date of my separation to April 1, 1933. I was perplexed at this dismissal, particularly since no reason at all was given for it. I now realize that with the closing of the original Cloisters, the job for which I was hired no longer existed.

In April I returned to my parents' home in Lynn. I tried, without success, to find employment locally. Quite unexpectedly I was awarded a Carnegie Art Scholarship to attend the summer session of the Institute of Art and Archeology at the University of Paris.

Returning to Paris after an absence of three years seemed like coming home. This time I was not a tourist. Nothing seemed strange to me, and I knew my way around pretty well, including the often confusing maze of subway lines of the Métro. I had my favorite cafés and restaurants, and I found a very nice and quite inexpensive place to stay: the Hôtel d'Alsace on the rue des Beaux-Arts on the Left Bank. It was only a short walk from the hotel through the Luxembourg Gardens to the institute. During the five weeks of the summer session of the institute, four courses in the history of French art were offered; each student was limited to two of them. I chose "Art of the Middle Ages in Southwest France" and "Antiquity and Exoticism in French Art Since the Sixteenth Century." The latter proved to be the most interesting, particularly because of the discussions of the paintings of the Romantic period around 1830. The professors lectured in French in the mornings, and in the afternoons we visited museums or studied in the splendid library of art books given to the University of Paris by the wealthy collector Jacques Doucet.

While I was in Paris I received the sad news that Father had died on June 18, 1933. In the cable Mother stated with great fortitude that I should not come home at once, but should complete my studies at the university. "Father would want it that way," she wrote, and of course she was right.

When I did return home Mother quite simply and calmly told me how Father had passed on. Shortly after I left for Paris he was seized with a heart attack. Two weeks later he was apparently convalescing, and was sitting up in bed enjoying a cigarette while Mother left him to prepare his luncheon. When she brought up the tray she noticed he was motionless. The cigarette had fallen from his lips.

As I look back on the years we had together I find it difficult to express how much I owe to my father. Whatever I have been able to contribute is the only way I know to honor his memory. He backed me in all I did, however unconventional it may have seemed to him. The following obituary expresses the community's gratitude for his concern for their welfare.

DR. HERBERT NEWHALL. Descended from the first settlers in Lynn, Dr. Herbert Newhall, taken by death yesterday at the age of 75, was known to thousands of his fellow citizens and hundreds have reason to revere his memory.

One of the old school of physicians, his presence brought comfort to many a distressed household and his skill saved scores and scores of lives. Younger medics found his advice sound and he guided many an aspiring younger doctor to success in puzzling cases.

As an associate medical examiner for 14 years, Dr. Newhall had a part in many mystifying tragedies and as a member of the school committee of Lynn he aided in formulating the school programs over a long period of years. He was the chief physician at Lynn Hospital and during the world war was a member of the medical advisory board of this district.

His work in both the Massachusetts General and Boston Lying-in hospitals won him renown far beyond the borders of his native city.

Though ill two weeks the end was unexpected and Dr. Newhall succumbed to a heart attack. His wife, son, brothers and sisters have received condolences from a wide circle of friends.

I reentered Harvard Graduate School in the fall of 1933, intending to study for a Ph.D. in art history. It seemed to me simple: I only needed to pass four courses with grades of A or B, take an oral examination, and write a dissertation. I already had in mind researching and writing about some aspect of nineteenth-century French painting, possibly its relation to photography.

My first writing on the history of photography appeared in the August 1932 edition of the *American Magazine of Art*. It was a review of the book *Aus der Frühzeit der Photographie, 1840–1870* (The Early Years of Photography) by Helmuth Th. Bossert and Heinrich Guttmann.[4] Basically a picture book, it reproduced two hundred photographs. I didn't realize it then, but it was a scissors-and-paste job, cribbed from other books. The text is superficial, a journalistic compilation that is of no value whatsoever to a scholar. But, at that time, I was greatly impressed, and wrote: "The high level of the work of the many photographers represented, among them Nadar, Fox Talbot, David Octavius Hill, Charles Victor Hugo, and [Carl Ferdinand] Stelzner, will be a surprise and a revelation to many, particularly because of the astounding modernity of feeling." I went on to explain that these pioneers used the camera in a straightforward way, with no attempt to simulate painting in the "pictorial" manner so popular at the time of my review.

4. Dr. Helmuth Th. Bossert and Heinrich Guttmann, *Aus der Frühzeit der Photographie, 1840–1870* (Frankfurt am Main: Societäts-Verlag, 1930). The review appeared in the *American Magazine of Art*, vol. 25 (August 1932), pp. 130–31.

"Pure" photography was the only type possible. Today those working with the camera are, for the most part, realizing that this is their only legitimate aesthetic: that the ability of the camera to capture the utmost possible detail of the natural world is its chief characteristic, and should be fully realized.

For the student of painting the collection furnishes material for an illuminating study of the influence photography has had on both the artist and the lay public. It seems very strange to this reviewer that such an inquiry has never been thoroughly made.

The opportunity of undertaking such an inquiry came to me quite unexpectedly two years later. It was then the custom at Harvard for the chairman of the art department to choose one graduate student who would represent the class at the annual meeting of the College Art Association by giving a paper on some art-historical subject. To my surprise Professor Sachs, who was then the chairman, chose me for this honor. He explained that I could select any subject I wished and suggested that I let him know my topic in a week or two. I immediately blurted out, "I know exactly what I want to talk about: the relation between photography and painting in the nineteenth century." Professor Sachs was so taken aback that I had chosen a subject so unconventional and unexpected, he had to sit down. But he consented, and I gave my lecture at the Metropolitan Museum in March 1934. It was published that October in the association's magazine, *Parnassus*, with the title "Photography and the Artist." I received a second Carnegie Art Scholarship in 1934 to attend the summer school of the Courtauld Institute of Art of the University of London. This was an intensive presentation by several professors of British art. Classes were held in the mornings, and in the afternoons we were free to visit museums, galleries, and historic buildings. I spent much of this time in the library of the Royal Photographic Society. Founded in 1853, over the years it had acquired, largely through gifts, a great many books on photography. The society was then located in a townhouse on Russell Square, and I was made welcome by James Dawdle Johnston, since 1923 curator of the permanent collection of historical photographs.

Since the books were on open shelves, I could freely browse among them. It was exciting to read manuals of long-forgotten processes written by Fox Talbot, Daguerre, Scott Archer, and the other great pioneers. Thanks to the hospitality of the R.P.S., I began serious research into the history of photography in its library. J.D.J., as Mr. Johnston was familiarly called, was a most generous and genial man. He frequently invited me to join him in afternoon tea, when we would talk together about the history of photography.

❖

Nancy

At this time I met Nancy Wynne Parker. She was living in Swampscott, a town adjacent to Lynn, where I resided in the family home. We soon discovered that we had a strong common interest in art, and we saw each other frequently.

Born in Swampscott on December 15, 1908, Nancy was my junior by six months. She was an only child, and her parents, like mine, were descended from early settlers in New England. Her father was a dealer in automobile tires. For most of her youth Nancy lived in Portland, Maine, and Newburyport, Massachusetts. Before entering Smith College, she was a brilliant student at several private schools. At Waynefleet Latin School in Portland, she was at the head of the class of 1926. She was art editor of the school's student magazine, *Now and Then*, to which she also contributed poems she had written in English and in French, as well as a rhymed translation from Virgil's Latin. She was a gifted writer. She recalled in 1962, "I think back to my mother reading me Shelley instead of nursery rhymes; even if at age two or so I didn't get the complete meaning, I did get the sound and the style, and I cannot remember learning to read. I just did. There it was. And I read everything I laid hands on from then on." She wrote poems at the age of seven, and when she was eleven she contributed a poem to *St. Nicholas* magazine.

At Smith College Nancy concentrated on art, writing, and drama. Again she became art editor, this time for the *Smith College Monthly*. She made woodcuts, and illustrations printed from her blocks often appeared in the text and on the cover of the magazine. The periodicals also published her poems. Upon graduating from Smith in 1930, Nancy studied painting at the Art Students League in New York. She especially admired the portraits, figure studies, and landscapes of Leon Kroll, and from him she gained mastery of portraiture. Already her paintings were winning praise. Her first one-person exhibition, at the Grace Horne Galleries in Boston in 1933, was favorably reviewed in the *Boston Herald*. The critic wrote: "Not only does the young artist show command of her medium…but

Nancy Wynne Parker, c. 1937. Photograph by Beaumont Newhall. (Courtesy of Scheinbaum & Russek Ltd., Santa Fe, New Mexico)

she also shows an amazing sureness of touch. She draws exceedingly well. She is capable of filling a small canvas with brilliant sunshine without resorting to obvious tricks. Her shadows are vibrant with illumination."

In his review of art exhibitions in Gloucester and Rockport, Massachusetts, the art critic of the *Boston Evening Transcript*, William Germaine Dooley, wrote on July 21, 1933:

> The only surprise of this reviewer is to see several examples of the ultra-modern "Middle Western School" already penetrated to the fastnesses of Gloucester. This group of self-conscious young Americans have turned their backs on the Paris of the moderns, and face the native scene with a grim determination to paint their country in its common everyday aspects, with as bald and bare a treatment as may be expected of their countryside. For them the city slums, the accidental placement of industrial buildings, the carnival of plain American genre subjects make strong appeal, and they translate them into a "back to the earth" movement that tries to stem from purely national art, after the lead of Benton, Curry, Wood, and others. Of very recent origin, it is remarkable to see its acceptance at Gloucester so quickly, even in a liberal summer exhibition.

With the review was a reproduction of Nancy's painting *The Scrub Game*, captioned "The New Native American 'Middle West' School, Aiming to Report on the Contemporary Scene in 'Scrub Game' by Nancy Wynne Parker, at the Gloucester Society of Artists." Nancy was indeed captivated by this "Middle Western School" and in particular by Thomas Hart Benton, under whom she studied at the Art Students League. She wrote an enthusiastic biographical essay about him in the April 1934 issue of *The New Frontier*, a periodical of which she was art editor. She opened the essay with a stirring paragraph:

Thomas Hart Benton is perhaps the most compelling and significant figure in American art today. He has hacked a clear trail through the decadent jungle of European art. He has broken new ground and sowed the seeds of an art as basic as the corn fields, as twentieth century as a dynamo, and as American as gosh. It embraces the scope of our existence and is stated in our own idiom. It reaches us with the impact of personal experience, startlingly clear because isolated and expressed by a great intelligence through the science of form and color.

To Nancy painting was a passion. She wrote me in December 1935 that she had just finished

one of the best day's painting in my life. It seemed as if the touch of the brush brought to life the latent picture in the canvas. Why? Why should I paint better today, when I cared not whether I lived or died, than I do on other days? There is a mystic quality to painting. When I am bad, I am puzzled and hurt and in my own way. When I am good, a current from some vast power seems to flow through me. Some things are good from the first brushful of paint to the last, some struggle horribly, some are foredoomed. I keep finding things in my memories of the Bible—"that virtue has gone out of me" (Luke 8:46)—as well as the familiar haunting of "Take no heed what ye shall eat, nor what ye shall wear, only have faith, and all these things shall be added unto you" (Matthew 6:31–33).

During those years in New England, Nancy and I saw a great deal of each other, and very soon our friendship turned to love. Nancy was then studying sculpture at the Art Students League, and I was in New York researching French illustrated books of the early nineteenth century for an exhibition at the Fogg Art Museum that was part of my graduate studies at Harvard.

We became engaged on January 1, 1935. Nancy used to take delight in telling that we first kissed on New Year's Eve in Times Square, precisely as the time ball dropped and the crowds cheered, and every other couple, it seemed, also kissed. We decided that we would not marry until I had a permanent, well-paying job.

That month I was appointed assistant administrator of the art project of the Emergency Relief Administration of Massachusetts. Later called the Public Works of Art Project (PWAP), this was one of Franklin Delano Roosevelt's New Deal work-relief programs to provide employment to artists and craftsmen during the Depression years. I helped judge the artistic abilities of the numerous applicants and found work for those we had selected that was congenial, useful, and of aesthetic value. I also persuaded community leaders to raise money for the purchase of the artists' materials. As certifying officer I signed the payroll checks of about sixty artists working throughout the state. The average salary was twenty dollars per week. With so many artists steadily at work, the project produced a surplus of paintings and sculptures. We asked the press to write about the availability of these artworks for permanent display in public buildings. I enjoyed working on this project, for I met many artists and craftsmen and traveled extensively through Massachusetts. But my salary of $28.80 per week was minimal, even in those days of the Depression, and I felt that I should spend more time than the job allowed studying for the Ph.D. oral examination at Harvard, so I resigned in July 1935.

My ideas about art were profoundly altered during my brief sojourn at the Philadelphia Museum. Fiske Kimball, the director, was a wonderfully dynamic and enthusiastic individual. While I worked there I was invited to attend his informal and completely voluntary seminars, held in his beautiful house in Fairmount Park, not far from the museum. One evening he explained, *viva voce*, the twenty-nine-page booklet *Das Erklären von Kunstwerken* (The Interpretation of Works of Art)[5] by the Swiss art historian Heinrich Wölfflin, which brought to me an entirely new and stimulating approach to art history, based on visual analysis. I also found the writings of Wilhelm Worringer deeply inspirational, particularly his books *Form in Gothic* (1907) and *Abstraction and Empathy* (1916).[6] The first book, translated from the German by Herbert Read, was very helpful in preparing my talks on the museum's medieval collection. Worringer explained that spiritual aspiration and artistic volition drove the cathedral builders to thrust the spires heavenward. His theory was that Gothic philosophy was the need to prepare oneself on earth for the eternal existence in heaven, and that this concept of the infinite was expressed in Gothic architecture.

5. Heinrich Wölfflin, *Das Erklären von Kunstwerken* (Cologne: E. A. Seemann, 1940).

6. Wilhelm Worringer, *Form in Gothic*, translated with an introduction by Herbert Read (London: G. P. Putnam's Sons, Ltd., 1927); *Abstraction and Empathy*, translated by Michael Bullock (New York: International Universities Press, 1953).

> If we cast a glance at the Gothic cathedral, we see only a kind of petrified, vertical movement from which every law of gravity seems to be eliminated. We see only an enormously strong upward movement of energies in opposition to the natural downward weight of the stone. There are no walls, no mass, to procure for us an impression of fixed material existence, only a thousand separate energies speak to us, whose substantiality we are hardly conscious of, for they act only as vehicles of an immaterial expression, as bearers of an uncontrolled upward movement. Vainly we seek for that indication of the relation between weight and energy which our feelings demand: weight does not appear to exist; we see only free and un-

controlled energies striving heavenward with an enormous *élan*. It is evident that stone is here entirely released from its material weight, that it is only the vehicle of a non-sensuous, incorporeal expression, in short, here it has become dematerialized.

This Gothic dematerialization of stone in favour of a purely spiritual mode of expression answers to the de-geometrization of the abstract line, as we have seen it occur in ornament, in favour of the same purpose, that of expression.

Spirit is the opposite of matter. To dematerialize stone is to spiritualize it. And by this statement we have made clear that the tendency of Greek architecture towards sensuousness is in direct contrast to the tendency of Gothic architecture towards spiritualization.

The Greek architect approached his material, stone, with a certain sensuousness and therefore allowed the material to express itself as such. But the Gothic architect approached stone with a desire for purely spiritual expression.…The sight of a Gothic cathedral does not impress our minds as being a display of structural processes but as an outburst of transcendental longing expressed in stone. A movement of superhuman force carries us up with it into the intoxication of an endless willing and craving: we lose the feeling of our earthly bonds, we merge into an infinite movement which annihilates all finite consciousness.

Every nation in its art creates ideal possibilities for the liberation of its sense of vitality.…The beauty of the finite was sufficient for the inward exaltation of Classical man; Gothic man, dualistically driven and therefore transcendentally disposed, could only feel the thrill of eternity in the infinite. The culmination of Classical architecture lies therefore in beauty of expression, that of Gothic in strength of expression: the one speaks the language of organic being, the other the language of abstract values.[7]   7. Worringer, *Form in Gothic*, p. 104.

My colleague and friend Paul Vanderbilt suggested, very tartly, "Why don't you read the man from whom Worringer got all of his ideas, Alois Riegel?" The author of a book titled *Stylfraggen*, meaning "style questions," Riegel developed the metaphysical concept that there is a spirit that guides creative artists in the same direction at the same time, no matter where they are: the zeitgeist, which inspires the artist's "will to form." I found him very stimulating as well, although the book had not then been translated into English, and the German text was difficult. This book became a bible for the German Expressionist painters—one of the few times I've discovered an art historian who really affected creative artists. It was Worringer, however, who was to have the more profound effect on my thinking.

When I had returned to Harvard for graduate work, I immediately expressed my new enthusiasm for Worringer and Riegel to my advisor over lunch at the Harvard Club. After I'd spoken enthusiastically for about fifteen minutes, the good professor pointed up to the chandelier overhead, a fake colonial piece with four candlesticks and a sphere, and said, "What you said is all fine, but I could tell you that chandelier points to the four rivers of Paradise, and you couldn't gainsay me." In other words, you can't prove these things: there's no evidence. Not only was this pure theory, it was spiritual theory. Although I got slapped down at Harvard, these writers remained an inspiration to me. I hope what I learned from them is reflected in my writing.

I took my orals in the fall of 1935. To my amazement and embarrassment, I did not pass. My growing lack of interest in conventional academic art history had become exasperation at the factual emphasis, the archeological approach. One of the typical questions I was asked has stayed with me: "What artist worked for two royal houses?" For good or ill, I was unable to muster whatever was required to care about the answer.

❖

The Museum of Modern Art

In 1935 my friend Henry-Russell Hitchcock, Jr., told me that the Museum of Modern Art in New York was looking for a librarian to replace Iris Barry, who had been appointed the curator of the museum's new film library. Russell was closely associated with the museum. As an architectural historian he served on the advisory committee of the influential exhibition "Modern Architecture," and contributed several essays to the catalog.

I applied for the position at once. I already knew the museum, for I had frequently visited its exhibitions whenever I was in New York. And I had met the director, Alfred H. Barr, Jr., in 1929 while he was teaching the history of modern art at Wellesley College—the first such course offered in any university. Like myself, he was an alumnus of Paul Sachs's museum course at Harvard. However, I knew nothing about modern art at all—I was taught at Harvard that the history of art stopped just before Cézanne. I did know a little bit about library work because I had cataloged books as an undergraduate .

I was not the recommended choice of executive director Thomas Dabney Mabry, Jr., who wrote to Alfred in Europe: "Tomorrow Mr. Walter P. Chrysler, Jr., is going to see Mrs. Holzhauer who until today had been marooned in a tree at Woodstock for a week because of the great flood thereabouts. Russell Hitchcock recommended a guy named Beaumont Newhall, to whom I have written. I am beginning to lean toward Mrs. Holzhauer because I think we need someone really efficient as a *librarian*, who can build it up."[8] But to my delight Alfred hired me, at an annual salary of eighteen hundred dollars, which came out to about thirty-four dollars a week, and I reported for work on November 1, 1935. When I entered the museum I asked Mr. Tremp, the genial receptionist, to direct me to Mr. Barr's office. "Mr. Barr is on the second floor, sir, installing the van Gogh exhibition," he replied. So I climbed the staircase and there found Alfred sitting on a campstool, surrounded by a blaze of sixty-eight of van Gogh's brilliant canvases and fifty-eight of his drawings, watercolors, and prints. As we shook hands I asked, "Where's the library?" He answered, "Oh, forget about the library. Take off your coat and help me hang the van Gogh show."

8. Thomas Mabry to Alfred Barr, July 11, 1935. Letter in Museum of Modern Art archives.

Installation view of the van Gogh exhibition, November 4, 1935–January 5, 1936, The Museum of Modern Art. Photograph by Beaumont Newhall. (Courtesy of Scheinbaum & Russek Ltd., Santa Fe, New Mexico)

Like so many of Barr's exhibitions, this one was extremely innovative. He had painstakingly selected and negotiated the loan of these paintings and drawings from museums and private collections in America and Europe. More than half the pictures were lent by V. W. van Gogh, the artist's nephew, and by the Kröller-Müller Foundation. To Alfred the purpose of a museum exhibition was not only to provide aesthetic enjoyment for visitors, but to elucidate and explain as well. His wall labels were unusual, for in addition to giving the title, date, and lender of each of the paintings and drawings, he added quotations from van Gogh's letters describing the circumstances surrounding the very picture in front of the viewer. One of these labels had on it a photograph of *The Good Samaritan*, a painting by Eugène Delacroix that van Gogh had copied. Alfred noted that the copy was laterally reversed. "Isn't it strange that this is a reversed image? Van Gogh must have painted it with a mirror," he said. I suggested that perhaps van Gogh worked not from the original, but from a lithograph of it by Jules Laurens that appeared in the magazine *L'Artiste*. This would have reversed the image. Alfred asked, "How do you know that?" I told him that I had seen one of those lithographs in the print room of the Metropolitan Museum. He said, "Take the Fifth Avenue bus up to the Metropolitan and bring it back." Which I did—taking a bus both ways. I at once realized that I was not just a librarian, but a member of a team, one that at that time numbered thirteen. Of course it would be impossible today simply to borrow something from the Metropolitan, or any other museum, so casually, on a moment's notice, as if it were a lending library. One would need to go through five committees, plus negotiate insurance, crating, loan forms, shipping, and all this would take months.

Working with Alfred Barr was a great experience, for he *was* the Museum of Modern Art. He set its pace and he shaped its style. He had intense energy and a devotion to the promotion and understanding of the avant-garde art of America and Europe. He demanded high standards for himself and his curatorial and executive staff. My twelve staff colleagues in 1935 were: Thomas Dabney Mabry, Jr., executive director; Ernestine M. Fantl, curator of architecture and industrial art; Dorothy C. Miller, assistant curator of painting; Frances Collins, manager of publications; Elodie Courter, secretary of circulating exhibitions; Sarah Newmeyer, director of publicity; Ione Ulrich, assistant to the executive director; Dorothy Dudley, registrar; John Ekstrom, superintendent of the building; Ernest Tremp, assistant at the information desk; John E. ("Dick") Abbott, director of the film library; and Iris Barry, curator of the film library.

In the early days of the museum, everybody did everything. Not only the employees, but their spouses, too, would descend on the museum the night before an opening, and probably work all night on it. Indeed at some exhibitions Alfred wore a green eyeshade and crept around putting things up at the last minute. Nancy used to call our group an early Christian task force: we all believed so fervently in the cause of modern art, and worked so hard to establish the museum as an institution to spread the good word, it reminded her of the founding of the early Christian church.

We were all very young, very optimistic. Alfred was in his twenties when he became director, and I was too when I came on board. Once when an insurance salesman came to our offices to offer us a pension plan, we all got together to consider it. We were told that when we reached the age of sixty-five we could begin to collect on our contributions to the plan. "Sixty-five?" someone said incredulously. "Nobody over fifty should be allowed to work at this museum!" The insurance man was staggered by that reply. We went back and forth discussing it, and finally a deal was struck: we could retire at age sixty. Today I receive, every month, a pension check for $31.50.

Alfred H. Barr, Jr.
Photograph by Ansel Adams.
(© 1992 by the Trustees of
The Ansel Adams Publishing
Rights Trust. All rights
reserved.)

It is seldom that a learned scholar is simultaneously a brilliant showman. Take the case of the banner. At the time of the van Gogh show, Alfred hung a huge yellow flag with the artist's name emblazoned on it in vivid red letters high over the front door of the museum. Within a few days we were visited by a delegation from the Fifth Avenue Association and informed that the Association prohibited banners on the avenue.

"But we're not *on* Fifth Avenue," one of us said. "This is Fifty-third Street."

"The rules of the Association cover fifty feet east and fifty feet west of the avenue," a representative retorted. I rushed to the museum's workshop and came back with a hundred-foot tape. We measured the distance from the curb of the avenue to the museum door. It was more than fifty feet. The banner was not furled.

The van Gogh exhibition was a popular success—or as Alfred liked to describe any major installation that filled the whole space, it was a "Big Top" show. Attendance was so great that the police had to control admissions for fear that the building would be crowded beyond capacity.

❖

The Museum of Modern Art was then at its present location, 11 West Fifty-third Street, but housed in a nineteenth-century, five-story private mansion of conservative design that in 1932 was leased from John D. Rockefeller, Jr. The four lower floors of the residence were converted into exhibition galleries by installing ceiling lights focused on the walls and by boxing in the fireplaces and closet doors with wallboard. For each exhibition the rooms were freshly painted, usually white, but often in lively colors. The fifth-floor rooms were used for staff offices. The penthouse, formerly the nursery, became the library. The adjoining bathroom, stripped of its plumbing fixtures, was the office of the museum's director of publicity.

In 1931 Lillie P. Bliss had bequeathed her private collection of art to the museum on the condition that a sizable endowment be raised within three years to maintain it. When I arrived the library was being used as the temporary headquarters of a fund-raising committee, whose chairperson had appropriated the librarian's desk. But until I knew what books we owned I had no need for a desk, so I put the two-drawer card catalog on an empty typewriter stand and worked my way around the shelves, checking each book. There were between fifteen hundred and two thousand volumes, most of them the gift of A. Conger Goodyear, the museum's president.

I was particularly impressed with the amount of ephemeral material that had already been collected, such as the extensive documentation of the now famous Armory Show of 1913—the spectacular exhibition of abstract, expressionist, and other schools of modern art then considered radical. There were catalogs, newspaper clippings, and even lapel buttons worn by the exhibiting members of the Association of American Painters and Sculptors, Inc., who had organized the exhibition. I was equally impressed by two fine collections of Surrealist publications, one from Paul Éluard, a leading member of the group, and the other from Dr. Camille Dausse, a physician who exchanged his services for books, catalogs, and art documents. I described in the museum's *Bulletin* for May 1936 the library's mission as an archive for the museum's collecting and exhibiting activities.

As librarian it was my duty to catalog the books and to shelve them by subject matter. I devised a classification that was somewhat unorthodox. I grouped the books by schools of art, such as Impressionism, Expressionism, Cubism, Neo-Plasticism, and so on. These were given shelf numbers. Monographs had codes consisting of the initial letter of the artist's last name, followed by numbers of the second and third letters. The numbers were derived from the telephone dial. Thus James Thrall Soby's book on Georges Rouault had the shelf number R68. If the book was a catalog, the shelf number was followed by "X." This enabled the library staff to locate any of the books quickly. I also had all paperback books rebound in cloth, always in the color of the original, at the request of Alfred Barr. He would phone for "that red book on Matisse." In the late 1980s I visited the museum and met the librarian. I asked him if the library still used my classification. To my surprise he said that they did indeed.

The next exhibition I worked on was the highly controversial "Cubism and Abstract Art," which opened in March 1936. It was a major show that filled the four floors of the museum with 386 works of art, most of which were almost unknown in America. The catalog of this exhibition, like those of all the museum's "Big Top" shows, was a hardbound book, with 223 illustrations. The scholarly text was written by Alfred. I contributed the bibliography, which listed 444 titles.

In addition to library work I took installation photographs of each major exhibition and made publicity prints. The museum paid me two dollars a negative. In order to process the film and make the prints, I converted the men's room—formerly the bathroom in the servants' quarters on the top floor—into a darkroom. Anyone making use of the john had to crouch under my sink, and under the clothesline I strung up for drying the wet negatives. That's how the museum knew I was interested in photography. They couldn't help but notice.

One series of installation photographs I made was of a group of nineteen abstract sculptures sent from Europe for display in the "Cubism and Abstract Art" exhibition that included works by Henry Moore, Georges Vantongerloo, and Archipenko. Normally museums could import works of art duty-free, but the customs inspector who examined these pieces insisted the museum put up a bond for these "outlandish" works because he considered them to be not art but garden ornaments. We had arranged them in the front hall for the customs agents to examine, and Alfred suggested I photograph them. With his wonderful sense of publicity, Alfred sent copies of my prints to art periodicals and newspapers along with a press release headed "U.S. Says Not Art."

Although Alfred Barr had included photography in his preliminary plans of the museum's collecting and exhibiting policy, little had been shown beyond the exhibition "Murals by American Painters and Photographers" (1932) and a small show of Victorian houses by Walker Evans, arranged by my classmate and benefactor of the arts Lincoln Kirstein (1933). It was therefore a great surprise to me when in the spring of 1936 Alfred Barr stopped me in a corridor and casually asked me, "Would you like to put together a photographic exhibition? The trustees have approved it and we have a grant of five thousand dollars to cover expenses."

"I sure would!" I answered. "What kind of show do you want?"

"It's not what *I* want," he replied. "What would *you* like to do?"

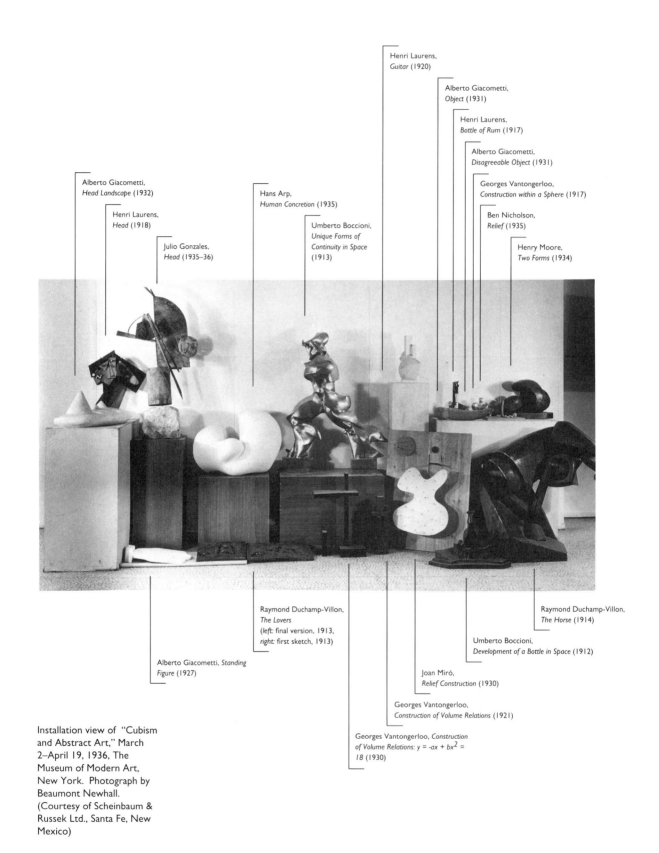

Henri Laurens,
Guitar (1920)

Alberto Giacometti,
Object (1931)

Henri Laurens,
Bottle of Rum (1917)

Alberto Giacometti,
Disagreeable Object (1931)

Georges Vantongerloo,
Construction within a Sphere (1917)

Ben Nicholson,
Relief (1935)

Henry Moore,
Two Forms (1934)

Alberto Giacometti,
Head Landscape (1932)

Henri Laurens,
Head (1918)

Julio Gonzales,
Head (1935–36)

Hans Arp,
Human Concretion (1935)

Umberto Boccioni,
*Unique Forms of
Continuity in Space*
(1913)

Raymond Duchamp-Villon,
The Lovers
(*left*: final version, 1913,
right: first sketch, 1913)

Raymond Duchamp-Villon,
The Horse (1914)

Umberto Boccioni,
Development of a Bottle in Space (1912)

Alberto Giacometti, *Standing
Figure* (1927)

Joan Miró,
Relief Construction (1930)

Georges Vantongerloo,
Construction of Volume Relations (1921)

Georges Vantongerloo, *Construction
of Volume Relations:* $y = -ax + bx^2 =
18$ (1930)

Installation view of "Cubism
and Abstract Art," March
2–April 19, 1936, The
Museum of Modern Art,
New York. Photograph by
Beaumont Newhall.
(Courtesy of Scheinbaum &
Russek Ltd., Santa Fe, New
Mexico)

I said, without hesitating, "For the museum's first major exhibition of photography I think we should have a historical overview."

"Fine," said Alfred, and then he asked me, almost as an afterthought, "Of course you'll need to go abroad?"

I quickly said, "Yes, of course."

Although I was floored by the corridor conversation with Alfred, I had already grown very interested in the history of photography, and was quite confident about accepting his challenging offer. With my training as an art historian I could handle research in French and German and had developed a sense of stylistic analysis. I had been reviewing books regularly for the *American Magazine of Art*. Nevertheless, I was very enthusiastic about the subject.

In 1935 I had reviewed a book entitled *Making a Photograph: An Introduction to Photography* for the *American Magazine of Art*.[9] The author was Ansel Adams. It was a staggering book. There had been a decadent pictorial trend in most photographs made during the 1930s and intended as "art": these were soft-focus, sentimental, with retouching and bromoils and other technical aspects that allowed for a great deal of handwork. The technique was very poor, weak and ineffective, and in the 1930s this type of "artistic" work was being shown in camera clubs and reproduced in magazines. Lincoln Kirstein, writing in the catalog of the 1938 Walker Evans exhibition at the Museum of Modern Art, described it: "In the swampy margin of the half-arts, the wallowing of painter-photographer and photographer-painter has spawned probably the most odious and humorous objects in the lexicon of our disdain."

9. Ansel Adams, *Making a Photograph: An Introduction to Photography*, with a foreword by Edward Weston (New York: The Studio Publications Inc., 1935). My review appeared in the *American Magazine of Art*, vol. 28 (August 1935), pp. 509, 512.

The reaction against this work was a movement known as "straight" photography, and in *Making a Photograph* Ansel had set himself the task of indicating "the basis of 'straight' photography, and what may be achieved by simple and logical procedure of unmanipulated negatives and prints." He expressed the ideas of this new movement very eloquently. I was only twenty-six at the time, and I was absolutely bowled over by the school of straight photography. Adams's photographs reproduced in this book were astonishing—each one was tipped in, and they were so superbly printed that today many mistake them for original prints. However, I was not totally praising of the book, describing Adams's compositions as "all obvious," and adding, "like Stieglitz, Mr. Adams approaches his subjects as if they were still-lifes, and his work has an extraordinarily static quality, which is not necessarily a criterion of pure photography."

Ansel sent a copy of his book to Alfred Stieglitz. The following is a letter Ansel wrote Stieglitz thanking him for his response:

Nothing could have made me happier than the letter I received from you today. It was wonderful to hear from you and to know that you approve of the book.

Frankly, I was doubtful that you would like the book. Not that I did not have faith in what I was writing about, or faith in you that your criticism would be just. I felt that you might react to it as just more *writing* and not enough *doing*. I hesitated when asked to write the book; I thought "It is comparatively easy to write about photography—there is too much written already—and not so easy to make good photographs. Should I spend the time and energy required on the book in making photographs?" And then I figured that someone should write on photography in a simple and direct way and try to give some conception of the straight simple photographic approach. So I tried it. I know I could have done much better if I had not been distracted with many things to do. But the book is released and I am more than pleased at its reception.

These photographers were very strict. Focus and clarity were important: everything in the picture must be sharp, the negative must be printed on glossy paper, and no retouching or other manipulation of negatives or prints was allowed. These ideas reached the level of dogma, particularly among members of the West Coast group known as f.64. I accepted all of it, however, and in fact found it a very refreshing point of view. Indeed in my review I wrote that the book was so exciting because the pictures looked so modern. When I began to make my selection of photographs for the 1937 retrospective exhibition, I treated soft-focus work as an aberration that should be eliminated. And I found a strong affirmation of straight photography in the magnificent nineteenth-century work of Nadar, the Brady school, Hill, and Adamson, among others, and in the twentieth-century work of Eugène Atget, Alfred Stieglitz, and later Ansel Adams, Paul Strand, and Edward Weston.

❖

The opportunity given me that day by the museum to direct what would become a seminal exhibition of the history of photography, and to write and edit a book-length catalog, was the beginning of a lifelong career.

Alfred Barr and I both thought that since the museum had no reputation in the field of photography, and was not known to the photographic community, we should form an international advisory committee to serve as our sponsor. We even had a calling card printed with my title: Director, International Exhibition of Photography, 1839-1937.

The first person I approached to join the committee was Alfred Stieglitz, who was not only a great photographer of international repute but also the founder, in 1902, of the Photo-Secession, a society for the promotion of photography as a fine art. In addition he was the editor and publisher of the journal *Camera Work* and had an outstanding collection of original prints by the photographers he reproduced in that handsome quarterly. At that time he had an art gallery, An American Place, in an office building on Madison Avenue, just a block from the museum.

Although I had frequently visited the gallery, I had not met Stieglitz until 1935, when I went to see an exhibition of his recent photographs. They were for the most part views of midtown Manhattan, taken from one of the windows of the gallery, which was on the fifteenth floor, or from the equally high vantage point of an apartment in the Shelton Hotel, where he and his wife, Georgia O'Keeffe, were then living. I had been greatly impressed by the photographs. They were sharp, fully detailed, and bold in composition. Stieglitz was in the gallery that day, talking to visitors. I had asked him a simple technical question, "Did you use a panchromatic film for this photograph?" He turned on me as if I had insulted him and replied, "Young man, that has *nothing* at all to do with the picture!" and turned on his heel and walked away. He had no use for me, none at all, and was not a bit friendly.

I did not see Stieglitz again until a year later, when I asked him, on behalf of the museum, if he would serve as honorary chairman of the advisory committee of my exhibition. His answer was a firm no. I then asked if we might dedicate the exhibition and catalog to him. This he also declined. I further asked if he would lend us a substantial number of his photographs for the show. This he most emphatically refused to do, saying he thought the exhibition was a terrible idea—terrible for photography; I didn't know enough and couldn't do it, and furthermore shouldn't be doing it at all. He intensely disliked the museum: it was becoming too popular; and also, it was riding on exhibitions of modern art by artists whom he had been the first in this country to show. I proposed showing his photographs, but borrowing them from the Boston museum. Even this was met with icy silence. However, Stieglitz did give permission for the museum to use already published material, and so he was represented in the exhibition only by photogravures from *Camera Work*. I was extremely disappointed by Stieglitz's negative attitude toward the exhibition, the museum, and myself.

The next person I invited to join the Advisory Council was Edward Steichen, then at the height of his fame as the leading portrait and fashion photographer in America. He immediately accepted. The other committee members were C. E. Kenneth Mees, director of research of the Eastman Kodak Company, Rochester; D. A. Spencer, president of the Royal Photographic Society, London; Charles Peignot, editor and publisher of *Arts et métiers graphiques*, Paris; László Moholy-Nagy, artist and former master at the Bauhaus School of Design, Dessau, Germany; Paul Rotha, director of production, Strand Film Company, London; and Alexey Brodovitch, art director of *Harper's Bazaar*.

Our first press release defined the exhibition in concise terms: "The aim of the Museum of Modern Art's first photographic exhibition is to show how photography since 1839 has become an increasingly vital method of visually interpreting man and his affairs. It is the hope of the Museum and of the Advisory Council that this exhibition will enable visitors to understand the principles which have governed photography since the earliest days and that it will demonstrate the capabilities of the camera as a medium of expression."

Nancy was living in a studio in Marblehead, Massachusetts, when I wrote the news of my appointment as director of the photography exhibition. I told her I finally felt established as a staff member of the museum and thought we should marry as soon as possible. She enthusiastically agreed. "You shouldn't pack your letters so full of good news," she wrote me on May 14, 1936. "The rafters of the studio won't stand it!—six weeks together soon, *and* a raise in salary, *and* beyond a doubt enough to get married on *and* perhaps a honeymoon! Can you think of anything else just now?"

We were married in Swampscott on July 1. Nancy's family had generously given her as a wedding present a round-trip transatlantic ticket on the most popular and glamorous ocean liner of the day, the SS *Queen Mary*, and we planned to go to Europe together on a collecting and research trip right after a short honeymoon. But the voyage was postponed because suddenly I fell ill with appendicitis and was operated upon in the Lynn Hospital. My recuperation was very slow, but the time was not wasted, for Nancy brought me from the Widener Library at Harvard College two basic

Our wedding portrait. Photograph © Ernst Halberstadt. (Collection of Beaumont Newhall)

histories of photography: the two-volume *Geschichte der Photographie* (History of Photography) by the Austrian photographic scientist Josef Maria Eder, and the *Histoire de la découverte de la photographie* (History of the Discovery of Photography) by Georges Potonniée,[10] a French collector. In fact, I became so involved in reading these, I resented any interruption, even by my new bride, who was sitting next to my hospital bed. I'd say to a nurse, "Could you find a glass of ginger ale for Nancy?" and return to the text. She never forgave me. These books, even though they were basically technical, gave me a sound foundation for further study in the splendid libraries of the French Society of Photography in Paris and the Royal Photographic Society in London.

10. Josef Maria Eder, *Geschichte der Photographie*, 2 vols. (Halle: Wilhelm Knapp, 1932). Unillustrated translation by Edward Epstean, *The History of Photography* (New York: Columbia University Press, 1945. Reprint, New York: Dover Publications, 1978). Georges Potonniée, *Histoire de la découverte de la photographie* (Paris: Paul Montel, 1925). Unillustrated translation by Edward Epstean, *The History of the Discovery of Photography* (New York: Tenant and Ward, 1936. Reprint, New York: Arno Press, 1973).

We finally did get abroad later in the year. In Paris we met Charles Peignot, who was a member of the Advisory Council of the exhibition. He was not only the publisher of *Arts et métiers graphiques*, a handsome periodical on typography and the design and production of books, but also of the annual *Photographie*. He assigned a member of his staff to make appointments with a number of Parisian photographers to bring their portfolios to our hotel. I chose a few prints from this person, a few from that person, and none from the others. It was fatiguing and difficult and not at all the way to select an exhibition. Still, most of the French work that I selected has since been recognized as classic.

Peignot introduced me to Victor Barthélemy, a private collector who specialized in early French photographs. He was a short man who was intense, vivacious, and enthusiastic about his collection. He lived in a walk-up apartment at the Porte de Clignancourt on the northern outskirts of Paris, and there he showed me his remarkable collection of calotypes—prints from paper negatives—of famous cathedrals taken in the 1850s by Henri Le Secq and by cameramen from the photographic printing establishment of Louis Désiré Blanquart-Evrard. From Barthélemy's rich collection I selected seventy-five pieces. From his friends Albert Gilles and Georges Sirot I obtained the loan of some splendid daguerreotypes, mostly French but, rather surprisingly, several made in America.

Paul Nadar welcomed me to his studio and allowed me to choose for the exhibition a selection of his distinguished father's portraits, as well as some of his own. Born in 1856, he was eighty years old, deaf, and walking with difficulty. He sat behind a huge desk in a vast, cold room, while his daughter Marthe served as interpreter when I found it difficult to make myself understood. He told me that in 1880 he had taken complete charge of the Nadar studio, which had achieved the height of glory under his father in the 1850s and 1860s. Marthe showed me large albums, about twenty by thirty inches, containing the portrait work of the Nadar studio. These great books, ranged in a special cupboard, were so overwhelming I was not able to do more than glance through a few of them. Prints of a very inferior quality were made by the studio from the original negatives, and these were signed by Nadar fils in imitation of his father's hand. I found it difficult to explain that I did not want modern prints, and the few originals I selected to be forwarded to New York never arrived. In their place were such inferior reprints I was forced to rely on material from other collections.

M. Nadar said, "I should like the honor of photographing you," to which I agreed. His studio—a huge painter's atelier with a lofty skylight—was littered with the heaviest of furniture, deep stuffed chairs, and the bric-a-brac of the turn of the century. The camera was a massive affair with a large, long-focus lens. He seated me on a stool beneath the huge skylight. Lights were turned on, as in late October it grows dark early. As the studio was chilly I kept my overcoat on. I was about to take it off for the sitting when Nadar asked me to wear it, and very carefully folded up the collar to give a dark accent. He pushed my head around, then made an exposure, which was so long a headrest was required.

We went from Paris to Holland, where we were met with great hospitality but found very little of interest. In England we visited Miss Mathilda Theresa Talbot, who had inherited Lacock Abbey, the ancestral home of her grandfather, William Henry Fox Talbot, who, in 1839, invented the first negative-positive photographic process, which he called the calotype. She generously lent ten of Talbot's calotypes. From the Royal Photographic Society's collection we borrowed an important group of classics of Victorian photography: anecdotal "combination prints" made in the 1850s from several negatives by Oscar G. Rejlander and Henry Peach Robinson, magnificent portraits by Julia Margaret Cameron, and impressionistic landscapes by Peter Henry Emerson.

While in London we were particularly glad to meet László Moholy-Nagy. He offered us sixteen prints, including his photograms (made without the use of a camera) and experimental color prints. I bypassed Germany completely, since none of us would go to that country as long as Hitler was in power. In fact, the museum was very active in bringing over refugees from Germany, and I

In Paris, 1936. Photograph by Paul Nadar.

was a sponsor for the first person who really examined the history of photography from an art-history point of view, the brilliant Viennese art historian Heinrich Schwarz. His book on David Octavius Hill is a landmark.[11]

11. Heinrich Schwarz, *David Octavius Hill: Master of Photography*, translated by Helen E. Fraenkel (London: George C. Harrap & Co., Ltd., 1932).

Around Thanksgiving Day of 1936 Nancy and I returned to New York and I began to collect work by American photographers. Among those whom I invited was Ansel Adams. I had already arranged with Mrs. Charles Liebman, a New York collector, to borrow three of his photographs from her collection, and I now wrote Adams asking if he would lend three more prints "which will preferably show your recent use of the miniature camera." Adams obliged by sending three prints from his recent exhibition at Stieglitz's gallery, An American Place. As an afterthought he offered to lend "a collection of original prints, chiefly by a man named Timothy O'Sullivan, taken in the Southwest about 1870. A few of the photographs are extraordinary—as fine as anything I have ever seen." I accepted the loan with enthusiasm. I had already selected a number of O'Sullivan's Civil War photographs, but I knew nothing about his equally fine photographs of the southwestern frontier.

I also selected five prints from Alexander Gardner's two-volume *Photographic Sketch Book of the War* (1862–65). Each album contained fifty original albumen prints by Gardner and his associates. I had purchased the first volume for fifty cents, while I was a student at Harvard. Several years later, when I was collecting photographs for the Museum of Modern Art, I visited Frank Roy

Fraprie, the editor and publisher of the periodical *American Photography*. He was offering his daguerreotype collection for sale, and I had traveled to Boston to inspect it. On an upper shelf of his office I noted a copy of the Gardner album. The binding was identical to mine, but lettered "volume 2." I told Mr. Fraprie that I had volume one.

"Are you a sporting man?" he asked.

Somewhat taken aback, I answered, "Why, of course."

"Well, I'll sell my copy of volume two to the Museum of Modern Art for twice what I paid for it if you'll do the same with your volume one."

"Agreed," I answered. "How much did you pay for yours?"

"Fifteen dollars," Fraprie replied.

So the Museum of Modern Art acquired both volumes for thirty-one dollars. On April 14, 1989, Swann Galleries in New York sold another set for $30,840.

The exhibition was not purely historical. Many of the contemporary photographers who lent prints are today considered "old masters," including: Berenice Abbott, Ansel Adams, Cecil Beaton, Margaret Bourke-White, Brassaï, Francis Bruguière, Henri Cartier-Bresson, Imogen Cunningham, Louise Dahl-Wolfe, Walker Evans, Florence Henri, André Kertész, Man Ray, László Moholy-Nagy, Martin Munkacsi, Charles Sheeler, Edward Steichen, Ralph Steiner, Alfred Stieglitz, Paul Strand, Brett Weston, and Edward Weston.

The exhibition opened on March 17, 1937. Upon entering the museum, visitors faced a life-size photograph of a man with a miniature camera at his eye, a transparency in a wooden frame that hung from the ceiling of the front hall. On the wall behind the transparency could be seen an enlargement of a mid-nineteenth-century wood engraving of a daguerreotypist taking a portrait with his bulky camera perched on a table. This three-dimensional installation was conceived and created by Herbert Matter.

In the corner of the front hall, right beside the entrance door, we built a huge box camera. It must have been eight feet high by ten feet wide by ten feet deep, for it was large enough that people could enter it. In one side we put a mammoth lens. Inside the camera we hung a framed sheet of ground glass on which was focused the upside-down image of visitors entering the museum. The art critic for the *New York Times*, Edward Alden Jewell, wrote:

> You got inside the earliest camera, which was not a "candid" but a capacious dark room. And Alfred Barr, who is something of a magician himself, has had a "camera obscura" built into the entrance gallery of the Museum of Modern Art as Exhibit A in the show assembled under the direction of Beaumont Newhall.
>
> This dark room is not uncozy, although the sum of its accoutrements is a lens set in the wall facing the information desk....Then, even though Mr. Tremp [the receptionist] appeared upside-down on the ground glass screen in the camera obscura, the basic principle of photography was demonstrated with full splendor. After that you emerged as one who knew, as one prepared for whatever the exhibition might unfold.

The exhibition was very large: 841 items were shown. We solved the problem of framing such a great number of photographs by grouping them on large panels, with cutout window mats. In place of glass we used clear plastic. By using colored mats and various sizes of panels we were able to avoid the monotony of row upon row of frames. Wherever feasible we introduced a few three-dimensional objects, such as cameras on tripods, daguerreotype processing equipment, and a dark tent a nineteenth-century photographer would have used for sensitizing and developing glass collodion-coated plates in the field.

At the opening, Isaac Newton Phelps Stokes, architect, print collector, and author of the six-volume *Iconography of Manhattan Island*, congratulated me on displaying superb daguerreotypes by the Boston firm of Albert Sands Southworth and Josiah Johnson Hawes. "I'm going to buy them for the museum," he said.

"I'm delighted, Mr. Stokes," I said. "Thank you very much!"

"Oh, I don't mean this museum," he replied. "The Metropolitan, of course."

A traveling version of "Photography 1839–1937" was circulated to ten leading American museums from coast to coast. Ansel Adams saw the exhibition while it was on display at the M. H. de Young Memorial Museum in San Francisco. He wrote that it "clearly presented the progress of the medium over a period of one hundred years, and indicated the significance of photography, socially and aesthetically, as a major expression of our time. Few could fail to respond to the revelation of this exhibit. Personal reactions to certain prints, social-aesthetic opinions at variance with some trends of contemporary work, nostalgic regrets in the absence of misty romanticism—all were overpowered by the basic realities of this show."

"Photography 1839–1937" was a great success. The museum's president, A. Conger Goodyear, wrote: "It must be one of the most complete and satisfying exhibitions in the museum's history." As it did with all of its major exhibitions, the museum published a clothbound catalog, which was selected by the American Institute of Graphic Arts as one of the fifty best-printed books of the year. On March 29 *Time* magazine wrote:

> Last week New York's Museum of Modern Art continued its great series of loan exhibitions with the most comprehensive exhibition of photography ever held in the U.S. With 841 exhibits backed by a 225-page explanatory catalog the museum has attempted to present and illustrate the history and development of photography, and also to show a selection of the work of the greatest living photographers.
>
> Organizer of the show and author of the catalog, which was hailed last week as one of the most concise histories of photography available in English, was the museum's librarian, Beaumont Newhall. With prints as well as actual pieces of equipment he has been able to show practically every milestone in the history of photography.

The *New York Herald Tribune* gave the show a leading editorial. However, Henry McBride, art critic for the *New York Sun*, facetiously lamented that the exhibition marked the demise of painting: "They say that if you are lost at sea, you should swim with the tide. I suppose I shall

Entrance to the exhibition "Photography 1839–1937," March 17–April 18, 1937, at The Museum of Modern Art, New York. Installation by Herbert Matter. Photograph by Beaumont Newhall. (Courtesy of Scheinbaum & Russek Ltd., Santa Fe, New Mexico)

have to swim with the modern museum and give up painting—at least temporarily—until this second edition of the dark ages has passed and we shall have been blessed with another Renaissance."

Lewis Mumford, art critic for *The New Yorker*, wrote: "Mr. Beaumont Newhall, who assembled the photographs for the museum, did an admirable job in ransacking the important collections for historic examples; his catalog, too, is a very comprehensive and able piece of exposition—one of the best short critical histories I know in any language." However, he took issue with the fact that Stieglitz was not represented by original work.

> A landscape by Paul Strand or Edward Weston, a building by Steiner or Sheeler, a torso by Steichen, a portrait of Sinclair Lewis by Man Ray, a street scene by Berenice Abbott or Walker Evans are all significant contributions to the art. But to single out these American names from a much longer list is a little invidious, especially because the most important modern photographer, Alfred Stieglitz, is not represented in this show by any of the work he has done during the last twenty-five years. An amazing omission that at least called for an explanation.

Had Mr. Mumford read the preface of my book he would have found my explanation: "At the request of the photographer, the later work of Alfred Stieglitz has not been included."

I enjoyed meeting Edward Epstean, Josef Maria Eder's friend and translator of his *History of Photography*. Epstean was the former president of the Walker Photoengraving Company, who, in his retirement, began avidly collecting books on the history of photography. He later presented this great collection to the Columbia University Library. He translated a great many European books on photography in addition to Eder's work, including the 1925 history by Georges Potonniée. Little did I realize that while I sat in my apartment on Fifty-third Street, reading the original German edition of Eder's quite extraordinary and indispensable history of photography, an English translation of it already existed in an apartment house on Eighty-second Street, just thirty blocks from my home. The manuscript was not published until after the war, in 1945. Although the text was painstakingly translated, the book appeared without any of the illustrations from the original. Epstean gave the following reason: "Most of them have only an ornamental value and are of little practical use to the student." So a portrait of Sir John Herschel by Julia Margaret Cameron is of little use to the student?

At the recommendation of Mr. Epstean, I sent a copy of my catalog to Eder, founder and director of the Graphic Arts School and Research Institute in Vienna. Eder wrote thanking me for "the excellent, superbly illustrated, and historically valuable publication."

Nancy and I became good friends with Mr. Epstean. A generous host and good friend, he enjoyed cooking and would often invite us to an early lunch he had prepared, by arrangement with the management, in the kitchen of the Plaza Hotel. Woe to the waiter who unwittingly distributed menus to his guests! Mr. Epstean would instantly snatch them away—to our astonishment and that of the waiter—and throw them on the floor, for he had prepared his own treats. One day Mr. Epstean came into my office with a manuscript that the publishing house of Macmillan had asked him to read. He dumped it on my desk and said, "You do it! They'll pay you fifteen dollars." It was titled *Photography and the American Scene*, written by Robert Taft, professor of chemistry at the University of Kansas.[12] I found it a well-written, meticulously documented history of photography in America in the nineteenth century. I was not surprised that the author had gone over much of the same ground that I had researched, so much so I felt compelled to ask the publisher to send me a confirmation that the manuscript had been sent to me after my book had gone to press. In my five-page reader's report I wrote that the scientific information was thorough, but the closing section on photography as art was quite weak, and might be omitted. I urged Macmillan to publish the book, which they did in 1938.

12. Robert Taft, *Photography and the American Scene* (New York: Macmillan, 1938. Reprint, New York: Dover Publications, 1978).

After one year the three thousand copies of the catalog of my exhibition were sold out, and the museum decided to publish a second edition. We replaced the now-obsolete checklist of the exhibition with concise biographies and bibliographies of each photographer discussed in the text, which we reprinted without change. We gave the book a new and more accurate title: *Photography: A Short Critical History*.

I wanted to dedicate the new book to Alfred Stieglitz and, if I could possibly obtain his consent, to reproduce one of his recent photographs as a frontispiece. At that point Stieglitz couldn't even remember my name: he used to write Ansel, "That nice young man from the museum came in today." I enlisted the assistance of Mumford, who had been so critical of my not including any of Stieglitz's recent photographs. Since Mumford was a long-standing friend of Stieglitz's, I wrote him of my plan. He sent my letter on to Stieglitz with a note: "A single photograph by you as the frontispiece of the revised volume would have an elegance and an authority that would put the emphasis of the volume exactly where it ought to be."

Stieglitz was gravely ill when he received Mumford's letter. However, my request was so much on his mind that Georgia O'Keeffe telephoned me.

"Would you please do me a human favor?"

"Well certainly," I replied. I didn't know her a bit then.

"Alfred is sick in bed. He's not well at all, and he can't talk about anything but 'the Museum of Modern Art wants to use my photograph.' Please go over and let him talk it out with you. Of course, he won't let you have it," she added, and hung up. With that happy welcome I met Stieglitz in his sickbed. The room was dim and he was very weary and weak physically, but not in spirit. I stood at the foot of the bed and told him that I wanted to reproduce one of his photographs as a frontispiece.

"Well which one do you want?" he asked.

"I would like the choice to be yours, sir," I replied.

"That is *not* an answer to my question. What picture do you want to use?"

I quickly responded, "I very much like your photograph *Grape Leaves and House, Lake George.*"

"Very well," said Stieglitz. "Go over to The Place and ask Andrew to let you take that photograph home. Also choose two others. Live with them for two weeks and then come back and talk to me."

So I went over to An American Place and told Andrew Droth, the caretaker, that Stieglitz said I could borrow three photographs for two weeks. I do not remember what else I chose except that Lake George house. That photograph grew on me. After two weeks I returned. Stieglitz was convalescing, sitting up, and we began to talk about photography. I told him that I still wanted to use the picture as the frontispiece to my book. He agreed. I thanked him, then added, "I would like to dedicate my book to you."

"That is not necessary," Stieglitz replied. "It's your decision," he added.

Of course we printed "To Alfred Stieglitz" on the page opposite his photograph.

This was the first sign of friendship that Stieglitz showed me, and after that everything changed. I think Alfred had a way of testing people's sincerity. As his health improved I visited him regularly. I even brought him some of my own photographs to look at. While he was hardly enthusiastic about them, I think he was favorably impressed by the seriousness of my efforts.

I anticipated his further cooperation with the Museum of Modern Art. It then was our hope that he would allow us to help him organize a major retrospective exhibition of his photographs. He finally agreed. However, he kept postponing the task of selecting the prints; it was too much for him to undertake at his advanced age and poor state of health. From his summer home at Lake George, he wrote me in 1940: "It is too bad that my condition is such that getting ready for the planned exhibition of my prints is impossible.—When I arrived I soon realized it would have been worse than suicidal to have made the effort to get ready. I know you fully understand."[13]

13. Letter from Stieglitz to Newhall, July 27, 1940. Author's collection.

❖

Ansel Adams, 1944.
Photograph by Nancy
Newhall. (Courtesy of
Scheinbaum & Russek Ltd.,
Santa Fe, New Mexico)

The new building of the Museum of Modern Art that replaced the Rocke-feller mansion at 11 West Fifty-third Street opened to members and invited guests on May 10, 1939. It was not only a functional building, it was itself a museum piece, for it was designed by Edward Stone and MoMA trustee Philip Goodwin in the International Style of architectural design that the museum had already made famous by the exhibitions and publications of its department of architecture. For the first time we now had enough space to show a generous sampling of all the arts with which we were concerned: painting, sculpture, architecture, industrial design, photography, and film.

Although officially I was still the museum's librarian, Alfred Barr asked me to curate the photographic section of the inaugural exhibition, "Art in Our Time." I chose fifty-three prints by seven American photographers: Berenice Abbott, Ansel Adams, Harold Edgerton, Walker Evans, Man Ray, Ralph Steiner, and Brett Weston. I partitioned the allotted space into seven small gal-leries, one for each photographer. I had the walls of each of these galleries painted a different color.

I chose dull red for Walker Evans. He objected strenuously to showing his photographs against this color. Only through a third party was our needlessly acrimonious dispute ended. "Mr. Evans," I was told, "will exhibit his photographs only on condition that he be allowed to hang them himself, but not in your presence." I agreed to these conditions and told the night watchman that Mr. Evans had my permission to enter the museum after closing and hang his photographs in his allotted space. Next morning we saw the result: Evans had dry-mounted each of his photographs on a large piece of white cardboard. When placed edge to edge, the mounts completely covered the offending color.

❖

Nancy and I met Ansel Adams for the first time in 1939, when he came east to attend the opening of the museum's new building. We knew him only through his voluminous and lively correspondence over the past several years. We arranged to meet in front of the building. I saw this tall man marching down the street, using an enormous tripod as a cane. We invited Ansel to lunch with us nearby at our favorite restaurant, the Café St. Denis, on Fifty-third Street, just off Fifth Avenue. Nancy and I liked him immensely right there and then, not only for his great appreciation of photography as an art, but also for his good humor.

After lunch we went back to the museum. I took him on a quick tour of the new galleries. He was greatly impressed by the "Art in Our Time" exhibition and was pleased that I had included eight of his prints. However, he did not like my installation of this "mini-exhibition" at all. He felt that my use of color was unsuitable for the most effective presentation of photographs. My defense was that I had chosen colors to emphasize the individuality of each photographer and to eliminate the monotony of hanging fifty-three photographs on conventional off-white walls. This argument Ansel did not find convincing.

We then looked at some of the photographs I had acquired over the past two years for the museum's collection. There were not many, and these were stored in my crowded office in the museum's library. We had a group of West Coast photographs that Albert Bender, a San Francisco patron of the arts, had presented to us at the suggestion of his friend Ansel. This gift included several photographs by Ansel as well as prints by Edward Weston, his son Brett, Imogen Cunningham, and other contemporary California photographers. The U.S. Department of Agriculture's Farm Security Administration (FSA) had given us a liberal selection of documentary photographs by Walker Evans, Dorothea Lange, Arthur Rothstein, and other members of its photographic section. I was particularly gratified by James Thrall Soby's outright gift of 104 prints by Man Ray, although I admit that at the time I was not an ardent supporter of the Surrealist school of photography.

❖

I never asked Alfred Barr, nor did he tell me, how the museum had suddenly received five thousand dollars for a photography exhibition. It wasn't until forty-one years later, when I was a houseguest of Ansel Adams on the occasion of his seventy-fifth birthday celebration, that David H. McAlpin, investment banker, lawyer, and generous patron of the arts, quietly admitted to me that he had been the benefactor. A grand-nephew of the Rockefellers, he was a man of great wealth who kept a low profile. This was the first of many gifts he would make to the Museum of Modern Art to advance photography as a fine art at a time when the museum was not particularly receptive to the idea.

Once I received a check for a thousand dollars from David McAlpin through the mail. I called him up right away. "That's for photography. That's for you to spend," he told me. I took the matter up with Barr, who said we had to take him to lunch to see what he wanted. As it turned out he didn't want anything. I later discovered he sent the same amount, under the same circumstances, to the Metropolitan Museum, then sat back to see what would happen.

David H. McAlpin, New York City, 1941. Photograph by Edward Weston. (© 1981 Center for Creative Photography, Arizona Board of Regents)

Well I spent half the money in the next few days. I went down the street to the Delphic Studio galleries and bought the entire one-person exhibition of some fifty photographs by László Moholy-Nagy for five hundred dollars. These were, for the most part, made in the mid-1920s, while he was teaching at the Bauhaus. Moholy-Nagy defied the conventional rules of perspective by pointing the camera now upward, now downward. He made negative prints in which the shadows were light and the highlights were dark. His most abstract photographs were made without a camera, by placing objects on photo-sensitive paper that was subsequently exposed to light. In addition to these photograms, as Moholy-Nagy called them, there were fantastic, often humorous, and sometimes sardonic photomontages, or assemblages, of cutout photographic images, often combined with words.

That collection, plus the work I later acquired for George Eastman House, constitutes the greatest collection of Moholy-Nagy in this country. McAlpin liked the way I spent his money, I guess. The Metropolitan husbanded theirs over the years.

❖

In the early years of the Museum of Modern Art the curatorial staff had little concern about how the museum was run. We left all matters of management and policy to the director, Alfred Barr, and the executive director, Thomas Dabney Mabry, Jr. But when Nelson Rockefeller became president in 1939, we came to feel that we were working for a commercial company rather than an educational institution. We never thought that we would undergo surveillance by an efficiency expert.

Shortly after the opening of the new building, there was need for a photograph of the library. We had none, and the simplest way to solve the problem was for me to take one. So I took off my shoes and stood on a table with my camera on a tripod and focused on the library stacks. I had no synchroflash for my camera, so I asked each of my two assistant librarians to hold a flashgun and to press the button on its side at the count of three. I needed another flash to light up the stacks nicely when a very well dressed young man carrying an attaché case entered the library. I spotted him as a bookseller. Somewhat curtly I put a flashgun in his hand, pointed it where I needed more light, and asked him to press the button along with the others. I counted aloud to three. All went well: the three lamps flashed brilliantly. I jumped down from the table, put on my shoes, thanked the visitor for his help, and asked, "What can I do for you?"

"Mr. Rockefeller has asked me to look into the efficiency of this department," he said.

I hastily ushered him into my office and explained what we were doing with the library. His visit was short, his questions few. Certainly he could hardly expect the librarian to be the museum's photographer as well. I never saw him again, but I was pleased when the budget I submitted for the library was accepted without cuts.

We on the staff were greatly alarmed when Mabry, executive director, and Frances Collins, manager of publications, were summarily dismissed by the trustees, headed by Nelson Rockefeller, while Alfred was hard at work in Paris selecting paintings by Picasso for the forthcoming exhibition. We did not know if Alfred was aware of this action or not. In our concern for our jobs, we wired him. We sent the cable from my apartment—which was a few doors away—because we were afraid the museum telephones might be tapped. Alfred wired us to sit tight until his return. He later told me, "It had to be done. I couldn't do it." He did not give me any explanation for this cryptic remark, nor did I ask for one.

In the summer of 1940 Nancy and I took our vacation on the West Coast. Neither of us had been there, and we looked forward to sight-seeing and visiting relatives in Los Angeles and Medford, Oregon. On our arrival in San Francisco we told the taxi driver to take us to a hotel. There we showered after the long ride of five days cross-country in a tourist-class train. We then called up Ansel Adams to say hello. He greeted us warmly, then asked where we were staying. I told him, and he at once exclaimed, "Oh my God! Stay right where you are and I'll come and get you!" It seemed that the taxi driver had chosen to take us to a somewhat notorious hotel in the middle of the red-light district. Ansel found us a more respectable lodging.

Ansel became at once a most hospitable guide and host. He introduced us to his friends and drove us through the surrounding country and north on the coastal road running along the ocean. We went with him to see "A Pageant of Photography," an exhibition he had organized for the Golden Gate International Exposition on Treasure Island. The show was large, filling nine galleries of the Palace of Fine Arts. The main exhibition was a handsome collection of about a hundred pho-

Ansel Adams, Bolinas, California, 1940. Photograph by Nancy Newhall. (Courtesy of Scheinbaum & Russek Ltd., Santa Fe, New Mexico)

tographs, from early daguerreotypes to contemporary prints. In addition to this, Ansel presented small temporary shows.

To our delight, Ansel invited us to drive with him and his wife, Virginia, to Yosemite National Park. After a long ride across the torrid San Joaquin Valley we arrived at the park. Nancy wrote eloquently of her first impression:

> Then, suddenly, the mountains humped huge. Firs appeared among the oaks. We passed massive boulders that could crush a house, and, at Arch Rock, drove actually between and among them. The cool shadows of great heights fell upon us as one by one the cliffs loomed and receded above, unfolding now and then to reveal the long sparkling shimmer and rainbow mist of impossibly high waterfalls. The exquisite fragrance of the Valley!—pines, firs, incense cedars, oak leaves, ferns, moss, meadow grass, alpine flowers. I could not believe my eyes, nor indeed, any of my senses.

We drove directly to the studio that Virginia had inherited from her father, Harry Best. The sprawling one-story building almost at the foot of Yosemite Falls was now both a second Adams family home and a shop specializing in the finest of silver jewelry and other crafts of American Indians, as well as cameras and film and exquisite photographs by Adams of Yosemite Valley.

During the long drive we discussed our shared passion. Ansel was very enthusiastic about forming a museum department of photography. In the introduction to *Making a Photograph*, he had accurately cited the state of confusion in photography at that time, and the inadequacy of the salons, camera clubs, photography schools, and books to assist the serious student. He expressed a need for a photographic museum:

> What is required above all else is a number of centralised institutions which combine competent instruction in theory and practice with library and Museum features. Repositories of the most significant photography, past and contemporary, are sorely needed. The understanding of photography as a form of art implies much more than a knowledge of physics and chemistry and a superficial education in the aspects of painting and other media. It is necessary to study photography itself—to interpret the medium in its own terms and within its own limitations.[14]

This was a new idea at the time. The majority of the schools emphasized the commercial aspects of photography, treating it as a craft, not an art. Inspired by this statement, I had written Ansel, in March 1940, asking what he thought of the idea of a museum department of photography. His reply was enthusiastic: "You have a magnificent project—and you have the 'plant' to physically effect it. And you have the enthusiasm to innovate it. What you are beginning now may grow into one of the most important undertakings of its kind. I cannot conceive of any serious photographer not wishing it a vital and complete success."

14. Adams, *Making a Photograph*, p. 14.

It was a long and hot ride to Yosemite that day, but the more we talked the more excited we got. By the time we reached the Adamses' house, right in the valley, we were all fired up. We sat on a porch next to a manzanita garden and had a drink. Then Ansel stood up and threw his ice out of his glass and into the bushes, saying, "It's time to call Dave." He got on the phone to his friend McAlpin in New York. In that phone call Adams interested McAlpin in the project. David in turn gathered support from the other Rockefellers on the museum's board of trustees. It was there, in Yosemite, that the first department of photography in any museum was conceived.

Ansel and Virginia insisted we stay with them on our brief visit. Every day we made excursions, by foot or by car, to view the spectacular scenery. At night we would often listen to Ansel playing classical music on his piano. I'll always remember him seated at the keyboard; he seemed to belong there. Relaxed and with sympathetic friends, he played on and on. Sometimes his technique was bold and smashing; at other times he played soft passages with great delicacy.

We returned to San Francisco with Ansel. He told us that Edward Weston was in town attending a photographic conference, and he had promised to drive him to his Carmel home. Ansel suggested that we might like to come along. We enthusiastically accepted his invitation and soon we were driving south on the coast road. Edward was polite and cordial. We arrived after dark.

Left: Nancy in Ansel's backyard, Yosemite, 1940. Photograph by Beaumont Newhall. (Courtesy of Scheinbaum & Russek Ltd., Santa Fe, New Mexico)

Right: In Ansel's backyard, Yosemite, 1940. Photograph by Nancy Newhall. (Courtesy of Scheinbaum & Russek Ltd., Santa Fe, New Mexico)

Left: Edward Weston looking out of his darkroom at Wildcat Hill, 1940. Photograph by Beaumont Newhall. (Courtesy of Scheinbaum & Russek Ltd., Santa Fe, New Mexico)

Right: Charis Weston and Nancy, Wildcat Hill, 1940. Photograph by Beaumont Newhall. (Courtesy of Scheinbaum & Russek Ltd., Santa Fe, New Mexico)

Edward's wife, Charis, greeted us warmly and invited us to stay for dinner. Afterward we looked at some of the photographs Edward had taken on his travels with Charis during his Guggenheim Fellowship. These had been chosen to illustrate the book *California and the West* that Charis was writing.

Almost immediately we became friends. We abandoned our original plan of visiting relatives and traveling to Oregon and the Canadian Rockies; instead we stayed in the nearby Highlands Inn for about two weeks. Every morning we walked down to the little one-room house in which the Westons lived with their cats. Edward and Charis aptly named their place Wildcat Hill: their place was swarming with cats. At one point in 1943 Edward wrote us there were sixteen cats in residence.

Sometimes Edward would invite us to go photographing with him on Point Lobos, a peninsula that is now a state preserve a few miles south of Carmel. On this piece of land are windswept cypress trees, cliffs plunging down to the sea, beaches littered with storm-tossed kelp, and rocks eroded into sculpture by the tides. Edward used a large view camera for 8 x 10-inch sheet film. It had an accordion-pleated leather bellows fastened at one end to a lens board and at the other end to a frame containing a sheet of ground glass exactly the size of the film. When in use, the camera was mounted on a heavy tripod. By covering his head, shoulders, and the back of the camera with a light-tight cloth, either white or black, Edward could study in detail the image formed by the lens on the ground glass. Although the image was upside down, Edward maintained that it showed him exactly what the final print would look like. He then replaced the ground glass with a film holder and made the exposure.

Edward would often invite those with him to look under the focusing cloth at the image. Comparing it with what was in front of the camera offered a lesson in seeing. I felt bashful with my 9 x 12-centimeter folding-plate camera and made only a few exposures of Point Lobos, for it seemed to me that Edward had photographed everything. I was so strongly influenced by his vision that I found myself imitating him. I decided instead to make a number of photographs of the outside and interior of their Wildcat Hill house: the stove, the Victorian coffee grinder, Charis's typewriter, Edward's darkroom.

Edward very generously invited me to use his darkroom to develop my negatives. He showed me how he worked, and even gave me the formula for the pyro developing solution he favored. When I had developed my exposed film, he found the negatives satisfactory, and asked, "Aren't you going to print them?" and showed me how he used the light of a plain overhead lightbulb for the exposure. So I made a few prints. He looked at them critically. "Why didn't you dodge them?" he inquired, suggesting the process of shading areas of the image that were weak so as to maintain detail in the print. "Why *dodge*, Mr. Weston?" So he took me back into the darkroom and taught me how to do it. It had never occurred to me that it was "ethical" in the canon of straight photography to dodge a print. Weston, it turned out, dodged his prints heavily, and also "burned in" dense areas that required more light, and he stood next to me as I tried it. He taught me more than any other photographer I have known, for he demonstrated to me—rather than just telling me about—his brilliant technique. Edward loved music, and Bach was his favorite composer. He once told me, "When I can hear Bach in my photographs, I know I've succeeded."

When Edward showed us his prints, he had a regular ritual for it. He set up an easel, which he lit with a floodlight. He would stand with a pile of his prints next to him, and place a photograph on the easel without saying a single word. We would look at it and offer comments. When he thought we were ready to move on, he silently put up a new photograph. He made no attempt to explain the circumstances of each photograph, or to offer an interpretation, or to have us look at it in the way he wanted it to be seen. However, if we asked him a question, he readily answered it. Weston gave Moholy-Nagy a viewing in this manner. Moholy-Nagy jumped up at one point and moved to the easel. "Oh, Mr. Weston, can I put this photograph upside down? It's more beautiful this way." Edward didn't say a word, but he was absolutely fuming, Charis later told us.

Edward's dignified presentation was in stark contrast to the way Moholy-Nagy showed me his work when I visited him in Chicago. He held each print up for my inspection, and never stopped talking, telling us what we should be seeing. There was no opportunity for us to comment. Then he casually threw the photograph on the floor. At the end of the viewing he looked down at the pile of prints at his feet for several minutes. "Oh, Beaumont, this is so beautiful this way," he said very thoughtfully, tilting his head and looking at several images sideways, then upside down; "I never saw this before."

On that visit to the Westons, Nancy and I looked at a great number of Edward's photographs and read much of his journal, or Daybook. Our visit led to the Weston retrospective exhibition of 262 photographs at the museum in 1946, which Nancy organized, and to the publication of his Daybooks in two volumes, which Nancy edited.[15]

15. Edward Weston, *Daybooks*, vol. 1, *Mexico* (New York: Aperture, 1961); vol. 2, *California* (New York: Aperture, 1966).

❖

The Department of Photography

The success of the photography exhibition that I had directed for the museum in 1937, in addition to Ansel's enthusiasm and the support of David McAlpin, led us to propose the establishment of a department of photography. I envisaged a collection of photographs old and new, a library, a study room, and a program of frequent exhibitions.

The first move toward the realization of our dream was made by McAlpin, the anonymous sponsor of the 1937 exhibition. He gave the museum a thousand dollars to found the department. I wrote Ansel, "We are indebted to you for putting Mr. McAlpin on our track. He is a delightful man, and I look forward to getting to know him." He came to know Stieglitz quite well and collected his work. At a later point he gave the museum a thousand dollars with which to purchase photographs from Stieglitz's *Equivalents* series.

Within a short time Dave became a good friend and an energetic colleague. He presented my proposal for departmental status for photography to the museum's then president, Nelson Rockefeller, with the result that the board of trustees, at its meeting on September 17, 1940, approved the formation of a department of photography, and named me its curator. They also appointed McAlpin the chairman of the Photography Committee, a position he said he would accept only if Ansel Adams would serve as vice chairman. Ansel agreed to come to New York for several weeks; McAlpin agreed to underwrite his travel expenses and a consultation fee.[16]

Ansel arrived in New York in mid-October 1940, and we began at once to make plans for the announcement of the new department and an inaugural exhibition of sixty photographs, selected largely from the museum's collection, which already numbered over seven hundred prints.

16. The other members of the Photography Committee were John E. Abbott, the museum's executive vice president; Alfred H. Barr, Jr., the museum's director; Dr. Walter Clark, assistant director, Research Laboratory, Eastman Kodak Company; Archibald MacLeish, poet and Librarian of Congress; Laurence S. Rockefeller, business executive; James Thrall Soby, art critic and collector; and myself as curator.

In the museum *Bulletin* of December 1940/January 1941 McAlpin explained: "In the introductory exhibition we aim to draw attention to some of the significant examples of photography as a medium of artistic interpretation, thereby to stimulate and sharpen our imagination and perceptions, and to encourage photographers to express simply, sincerely, and effectively some of the qualities of their experiences and of the world about us." Alfred Barr stated in the same issue: "By exhibitions both in the Museum and throughout the country, by increasing in size and scope the photographic collection and reference library, by publications and lectures, it is hoped that the Department will serve as a center for those artists who have chosen photography as their medium, and will bring before the public work which, in the opinion of the curator and the Committee, represents the best of the present and the past."[17]

Eight of the photographs in the exhibition were reproduced in the *Bulletin*. All now well-known classics, they indicate the range of photographic vision covered by the show.

17. "The New Department of Photography," *Bulletin of The Museum of Modern Art*, vol. 8, no. 2 (December 1940–January 1941), pp. 2–14.

Alfred Stieglitz: *New York—Night*. 1931.

David Octavius Hill: *Spindle Rock*. c. 1845.

Henri Le Secq: *Stair Tower, Chartres.* 1852.

Henri Cartier-Bresson: *Children Playing in Ruins, Seville, Spain.* 1933.

Eugène Atget: *Street Musicians.* 1898-99.

Dorothea Lange: *Pea Picker Family, California.* 1936.

Man Ray: *Rayograph.* 1923.

László Moholy-Nagy: *From the Radio Tower, Berlin.* 1928.

Ansel and I selected this first show, "Sixty Photographs," together. We were not always in agreement. One of the most striking of the photographs that I chose was Moholy-Nagy's bird's-eye view, looking straight down from the great height of the Berlin radio tower onto a snow-covered circular terrace on which a path had been cleared. I found it a strong abstraction; however, Ansel didn't like Moholy-Nagy's work at all, and particularly disliked this photograph. He felt it was too poor a print to exhibit. I suggested that Moholy-Nagy, who was then teaching in Chicago, might possibly lend us the negative so that Ansel could make a better print. Moholy-Nagy graciously obliged. I stood in the museum darkroom while Ansel made the new print. It was full of details and textures not found in the original print—but it was no longer an abstraction. We both agreed that the original was the print to show and we tore up Ansel's print while it was still wet.

The exhibition was installed in one spacious gallery on an upper floor of the museum, and was on display for less than two weeks at what was in those days a poor time of the year for visitors—from December 31, 1940, to January 12, 1941. We were pleased that *Time* reported: "Manhattan's pioneering Museum of Modern Art last week announced that it would give photography a large, permanent place alongside its departments of painting, sculpture, architecture, industrial design. As curator of its new department, the Modern Museum appointed its librarian, scholarly, gangling camera expert Beaumont Newhall."[18]

18. *Time*, January 6, 1941.

The review in *U.S. Camera* magazine, however, was so negative and full of misunderstanding that it was upsetting. The unsigned writer pointed out there were three photographic exhibitions on display in the museum at the same time as "Sixty Photographs": a tribute to the film director and producer D. W. Griffith, a retrospective of the architecture of Frank Lloyd Wright, and a photojournalistic reportage by Thérèse Bonney of Finland at war. These occupied "vast areas of floor space. The 'Sixty Photographs' exhibit is a gem of another character—very choice, very small, very ultra." The writer apparently had forgotten that our show was in a museum of modern art, for he complained that "undue regard and space is given to the ultra-modern in photography."[19] Had he read the articles in the *Bulletin* by Barr and by McAlpin, he might have realized that the intention of the exhibition was to introduce the new department with a visual review of various aesthetic uses of photography.

19. "Museum of Modern Art Photo Department," *U.S. Camera*, vol. 1, no. 14 (February 1941), pp. 28, 82.

Ansel had returned to California on the opening day of the exhibition. I wrote him:

> About 500 people showed up—which was very good considering that the exhibition was not a major one and that it occupied only one gallery. The room was crowded from 5 to 7 with people eager to see, not one another, but the pictures; they actually formed a queue right around the wall, which slowly progressed from picture to picture; seldom have I seen such interest in pictures at an opening....
>
> Stieglitz came to see the show with Dave [McAlpin], and spent about half an hour in the gallery, looking at every print....He thought that we had made a beginning, a fine beginning: "Mistakes, yes; not the way I would have done it, but sincere and fine. What Barr has written is very important. He has committed the museum to photography. More important than he knows, or you. You have a lot to fight for. So long as you do the things you believe in, so long as you can please yourself, all will be well. You'll be criticized. Correct only the misstatements, the falsifications."
>
> ...Here was praise more generous than I had hoped for. And I wished that you could have been present to hear it. These words don't begin to convey that feeling of sincerity, that placing of confidence, that belief, which passed between us. Dave was delighted, and, I think, as surprised as I that Stieglitz was so very pleased and so very cordial and receptive.

The most unusual of the new department's exhibitions was "Image of Freedom," which opened October 29, 1941, and was on display for three months. Ansel had suggested that positive statements by photographers about America and its people would reaffirm faith in our country during the critical and difficult war years. He proposed a dramatic competition: one hundred of the submitted photographs would be chosen by a jury for purchase by the museum for twenty-five dollars each. As many as five prints could be purchased from one photographer.

A prospectus was needed, and our first thought was to ask Archibald MacLeish, then a museum trustee, to write it. He agreed, but asked for an outline. At our request,

Nancy wrote and submitted what she considered a draft. When MacLeish read it, he told me that he thought Nancy had written a superb statement which certainly should not be edited by him or anyone else. He congratulated her on it. Nancy wrote:

> PHOTOGRAPHERS: Let us look at these United States...now, in these critical days, when our lives and all that gives them meaning are threatened:
>
> What gives our lives meaning? Why do we feel that, with all its faults, this is the place we want to live? Why do we feel that the foundations of our national life are not only unshaken but capable of supporting a greater, more human structure than any nation, or combination of nations, has yet built?
>
> In this immense panorama, what, to you, most deeply signifies America?
>
> Can you compress it into a few photographic images? Not with the hysteria and jingle of superficial patriotism, with the bitterness of protest, but profoundly, simply, with insight and emotion?
>
> In the belief that you, photographers of America, can through photography express and confirm our faith...you are invited to enter a competition...IMAGE OF FREEDOM.

The jury of the competition consisted of three staff members: myself, Barr, and Monroe Wheeler, director of exhibitions; and three members of the Photography Committee: David McAlpin, Ansel Adams, and James Thrall Soby. The photographs were not signed but simply numbered, and not until the end of the judging, when the numbered entry blanks were matched to the prints, did we know whose work we had selected. Among the sixty-six photographers a few were familiar, notably André Kertész, Eliot Porter, Charles Sheeler, Aaron Siskind, and Brett Weston. Some, like Minor White, were as yet unfamiliar.

In 1942 Ansel and I arranged the exhibition "Photographs of the Civil War and the American Frontier." One of the people whose work we included was William Henry Jackson, the nineteenth-century frontier and Indian photographer. We had discovered that Jackson was, at the ripe age of ninety-eight, living in a midtown Manhattan hotel room a few blocks away from the museum, and so we borrowed several photographs from Jackson himself. It was fascinating to talk to a photographer who had actually worked the wet-plate process, and I visited him often. Ansel and I invited him to the opening, which he enjoyed very much. Alfred Barr was a Civil War buff, and that night was amazed to find that Jackson had actually been in the Civil War. Jackson was a humble man and could have told Alfred any story at all. Instead he said, "I didn't see the fighting at all. I was in Washington, guarding the baggage." As Ansel escorted him around the galleries, Jackson stopped in front of a mammoth print of Taos Pueblo, taken with a formidable view camera that used 20 x 24-inch plates that Jackson and his mule had lugged on photographic expeditions across the Territories in the 1870s. He looked at it for a long time without saying a word. "That's a pretty good photograph, Mr. Adams. Who took it?" he asked.

"Why, you did, Mr. Jackson."

"Oh, so I did. And I took it with that big camera. Look, Mr. Adams, I can make better photographs now with this little camera," Jackson replied, and he triumphantly pulled out of his hip pocket a small amateur Kodak Bantam camera. "And in color too!"

Jackson died several weeks after this exhibition.

Henry Ford had purchased Jackson's Detroit Publishing Company for his museum, but was storing Jackson's photographs in a steam tunnel between buildings. Ansel was horrified at this, and went out to Dearborn, Michigan, to bring the situation to the attention of the company. Following our advice, the single trustee of the Ford Museum sent all their photographs of the West to the Denver Historical Society; those not of the West were sent to the Library of Congress.

One of my goals was to begin to assemble a permanent collection of photographs for the department—not an easy assignment, as the funds for purchasing work were scarce. In those days I did not make studio visits, as is a common practice today, and there were no galleries. Rather, photographers made an appointment to come to my office with their portfolios, to ask advice and in the hope that I would make a purchase. I was aided in this by Alexey Brodovitch, the legendary art director of *Harper's Bazaar*. Among those he sent over was the young portrait photographer Arnold Newman, who came up from Florida, where he had a portrait studio. Philippe Halsman was another visitor. Helen Levitt and Berenice Abbott also brought their work by frequently. As the department became increasingly well known, more photographers found their way to us.

Earlier I had the opportunity of meeting another pioneer, the documentary photographer Lewis Hine. He came to the museum with a portfolio of his photographs of the construction workers building the Empire State Building. The workers were up on iron girders, dozens of stories above street level, and Hine and his large view camera were right up there with them. Then in his seventies, Hine had been photographing for about fifty years. However, I had not heard of him, as he worked with social reform groups and was not a regular member of the then very small photography community. Although he had developed a reputation earlier in the century for his beautiful work on immigrants, in 1940 his work was not being reproduced anywhere, nor was it being exhibited. Hine's photographs were a great discovery for me. I knew he was having financial problems, and although I was unable to buy photographs, I wrote an article about this amazing series for *The Magazine of Art*, the journal of the Art Association of America, and gave him the fifty dollars I was paid for writing it. I got to know him quite well. When Hine died suddenly in 1940, his son gave his entire estate to the Photo League. One of the most important things the League did was to make prints from his negatives and make a portfolio available. With the demise of the Photo League in 1951, all of this material was turned over to George Eastman House, of whose collection I was by then the curator.

❖

2

MILITARY INTERLUDE

In Bari, Italy, 1944.
Photograph © Paul Bates.
(Collection of Beaumont
Newhall)

On December 7, 1941, 439 Japanese airplanes bombed the United States naval base at Pearl Harbor in Honolulu. Five of our major battleships were sunk and three were damaged beyond commission. One hundred forty-nine airplanes that were grounded were completely destroyed, and the toll in human life was terrifying: 2,403 sailors, soldiers, Marines, and private citizens were killed, and an additional 1,178 men and women were wounded. The following day President Roosevelt declared war on Japan.

Our friend Edward Weston was traveling with his wife, Charis, toward the American South, making photographs to illustrate a new edition of Walt Whitman's *Leaves of Grass*. They had left us only one day before Pearl Harbor, and Edward wrote inquiring what the reaction was. I answered on December 16:

> There has been a change during the past ten days, and you are right in feeling that it was lucky that you were in New York "before the deluge." With fake air raid alarms and with a general hysteria, the city has not been pleasant during the past week. Furthermore, I hear that many photographers have been stopped from working in the city, and that alien photographers have been prohibited from working in the city. Poor Sunami, the Japanese photographer who did most of our work, was put under the ban first thing Monday morning, and probably now is in a detention camp....I hear that *Life* is having a very tough time, on account of the preponderance of alien photographers on their staff.

There was great concern in museums and art galleries for the safety of the art in their collections. Francis Taylor, of the Metropolitan Museum of Art, was certainly the boldest of the museum directors. He leased an unoccupied private country mansion that contained 150 air-conditioned rooms and was located on a large estate about twelve miles from Philadelphia. In February 1942 Taylor shipped ninety van loads containing fifteen thousand works of art to the country house for safekeeping for the duration of the war.

BASIC TRAINING

I never expected or desired to wear the uniform of a soldier. With the declaration of war, I wanted to serve my country, of course, but I had received a lottery number for the draft and did not want to become simply a foot soldier. Steichen told me he had done photoreconnaissance work during World War I, and suggested I try to do the same. I decided to take a leave from the museum and enlist. In August 1942, while a houseguest with Charles and Musya Sheeler, I received my commission as first lieutenant in the Army Air Force, with orders to proceed to Miami Beach for Officers' Training School.

My sudden orders almost resulted in the museum management "putting the department on ice until the war [was] over," in the words of Executive Director Dick Abbott. The main issues were: (1) was the photography department important? and (2) was Nancy qualified to take my place at the museum? The political factions in the museum, which would become more involved with the photography department while I was overseas, asserted themselves. The continuation of the department, and Nancy's and my role in it, was defended by Alfred Barr, Jim Soby, and David McAlpin. Nancy was reluctantly appointed acting curator.

All of Miami Beach was then a military camp; everywhere were men in uniform. We lived in the luxury hotels, two or more of us to a room. We got up before dawn, had a hasty breakfast, and then, out on the street, we formed in groups, four abreast. One of us acted as leader and we marched to the drill field, about fifteen minutes away. We marched everywhere. It was the quickest way of getting around town, for all traffic had to stop for us and only the leader was required to return the salutes of the dozens of enlisted men we passed.

On the drill field we joined our platoon and stood at attention while the group commander received the attendance report of each unit and read the orders of the day. Then we marched and marched around the drill field for about an hour, until we went to our first class: the organization of the army. This lecture was followed by physical training. After lunch more classes until retreat, when we marched again, this time with a band, and then stood in formation, at attention, while the American flag was ceremoniously lowered. In the evening we studied for the frequent examinations—not in our rooms, for a total blackout was in effect, but in a study hall. As I wrote Nancy, "March, march, march. It seems as if all I see all day long is the neck of the man in front of me!"

The most unexpected instruction was survival swimming. Since the majority of us would certainly travel overseas by ship, there was the possibility that our troopship might be torpedoed and sunk and we might need to swim to safety. So every other day, six hundred men in khaki shorts would gather on the beach and learn to swim with one arm only. We were told that with the other arm we could make huge splashes ahead of us to disperse burning oil on the surface of the sea, an eventuality we hoped would never occur.

The last week of school was a total break from this routine. We spent a whole day learning to shoot. Each of us fired one hundred rounds with a Thompson submachine gun, a pistol, and a rifle. Out of a possible 200 with the rifle I scored 145, little better than average. We were on the range—a desolate, dusty, and blisteringly hot stretch of beach vegetation—from eight until six, with a picnic lunch—an exhausting day. I felt relieved to know at least enough about shooting to load and fire three typical weapons. However, when I arrived in the combat zone five months later, the Colt

In uniform, 1941. Photograph by Philippe Halsman. (© Yvonne Halsman)

.45 pistol issued me in Miami was confiscated by the military police with the remark that I would not know how to use it.

On the final day of classes we had field maneuvers. A stretch of land had been designated an airport and we were taught how to take cover so as to be hidden from the sight of sharpshooters or strafing airplanes. General Ralph Wooten, our commanding officer, flew over us like lightning, hedge-hopping at about fifty feet, trying to spot us. "We seemed to have learned our lessons pretty well," I wrote Nancy, "because of the 1200 men deployed all over the desolate area the general spotted only six foolish fellows who were running across a road."

We had graduation exercises September 19, and the next day we were en route in a special train to Harrisburg, Pennsylvania, to attend the Air Force Intelligence School. This was quite different from Miami Beach. There was little marching and a great deal of classroom work as our instructors crammed into us information about warfare on the ground and sea, as well as in the air. I was always irked when I passed under a huge sign hanging in the entrance hall of the headquarters building that read: "IN THE GREAT GAME OF WAR THERE IS NO SECOND PLACE." Never, for a moment, did I consider that I was being coached to play a game! I was in the army with hundreds of thousands of others to help bring to all people in the world President Roosevelt's Four Freedoms—freedom of speech, freedom of religion, freedom from want, freedom from fear.

We lived downtown in the Harrisburger Hotel, and took a bus to the school, which was housed in a building that had been made available to the Air Force "for the duration." In the first few weeks we learned about intelligence in general, and then we were divided into three sections:

Combat Intelligence, Photo Reconnaissance, and Prisoner-of-War Interrogation. I had already elected Photo Reconnaissance, and was just ready to attend my first class when I found in my mailbox a note ordering me to report to an officer in the headquarters building. I knocked on the door. A voice replied, *"Herein!"* I entered, and found myself speaking German to an officer I had never met. He told me that I had been assigned to Prisoner-of-War Interrogation. I was bewildered, and replied, "But, sir, I'm here to learn to be a photo interpreter—I can't speak German well enough to interrogate!"

"But we're talking German now," he replied. "With a few months of language school…" I interrupted him with an explanation of my background in photography, and my conviction that I could best serve my country as a photo interpreter. The officer relented. "Well," he said in English, "you can be a photo interpreter if you'll run the German table at the mess." So I sat at the dining table on which was a miniature German flag. Eleven other students prattled German in a somewhat desultory way. One day, when the mess hall was crowded, the commandant spied a vacant seat at our table and sat down with us. He was perplexed. "Don't you guys know English?" he fairly barked out. I answered "Yes, sir. But by order of the commanding officer, all student officers assigned to the foreign language tables shall refrain from the use of the English language throughout the meal."

"What order?" the colonel asked.

"This, sir," I replied, and from the pocket of my field jacket pulled out a bunch of folded mimeographed sheets. I gave one to the colonel, who read it and then said, with a smile, "This order is hereby revoked. We're Americans, lieutenant. I'd forgotten that I had signed it."

The U.S. Army Air Force F-5, used for photoreconnaissance. Photographer unknown. (Smithsonian Institution)

Until Harrisburg I had only a vague idea of the military importance of aerial photographic reconnaissance. At the Air Intelligence School we learned that air photographs of enemy territory were proving to be of immense value to the Allied forces, not only in bomb-damage assessment, but for gathering a great deal of other critical information. The strength of the enemy's air power could be estimated from photographs of his airfields and the identification of his types of warplanes. Industrial activity could be determined by a study of the contents of freight cars being loaded and offloaded at factories. Warships were easily identified, and their movement from harbor to harbor plotted. Gun emplacements, radio antennas, and radar installations could be located for destruction.

The appearance of the earth and what lies upon it when seen by the camera of an airplane flying at altitudes of five miles or more differs greatly from the view as seen by ground-based observers. The airplane used by the U.S. Army Air Forces for photoreconnaissance was the F-5, a modified version of the P-38, or Lightning. It had two propellers, one on each wing, and flew at a speed of four hundred miles per hour (well beyond the speed of enemy fighter planes), and an altitude of twenty-five thousand feet (well above the range of antiaircraft fire). The plane was a single-seater. The pilot had neither weapons nor armor plate. On long-distance flights extra gasoline tanks were fastened beneath the body of the plane.

In the nose of the plane three cameras were mounted, each loaded with enough roll film for 250 9 x 9-inch pictures. Two of the cameras had lenses of long focal length (24 or 36 inches). The third camera had a wide-angle lens (6 inches focal length) and so covered a much larger field. These cameras were pointed straight down to the earth; in photo interpreter's lingo, they took "vertical pictures." The shutters and film transport of these cameras were automatically operated by a push of a button the pilot controlled. Depending on the speed of the plane, exposures were made at such intervals that the pictures overlapped 60 percent. This was essential, for the overlapping photographs formed stereoscopic pairs that could be seen in exaggerated three dimensionality with a stereoscope. This was a great aid to the interpreters.

The task of the photo interpreter was to locate geographically, identify, and often measure everything of military significance shown in the aerial photographs, and to make a written report on the findings. At Harrisburg we learned the fundamentals of this technique, but not until we reached the combat zone did theory become operational and practical routine.

Nancy visited Harrisburg to attend our graduation on October 31. It was a beautiful fall day. We students stood at attention proudly in our best uniforms while the commandant gave a short speech. Then a group of fighter planes from a nearby air base flew over us and dipped their wings in salute. As we broke ranks and rushed to greet our families and friends, a great flock of ducks flew over the Schuylkill River in a perfect "V" formation, to the delight and applause of all. But it was also a day of foreboding, for I had just received an order to "proceed to Washington, D.C., immediately, reporting on arrival to the Director of Intelligence Service Headquarters, Army Air Force, for temporary duty pending overseas assignment." The following day I was assigned to the Third Photo Intelligence Detachment, Ninth Air Force, a cadre unit of only eleven officers and eighteen enlisted men stationed temporarily at Bolling Field, near Washington, D.C., awaiting overseas transport. We were outfitted with government-issue combat gear: steel helmets, gas masks, canteens, heavy G.I. boots, puttees, and sidearms—none of which we ever used.

Nancy met my fellow officers, who proved to be congenial comrades. A group of us invited her for lunch at the officers' club. When it came time for her to take the train to New York, I was given permission to accompany her to Union Station. I climbed into a car with her, found her a seat, and kissed her goodbye. Just as I was getting off the train I remembered that I had her ticket in my pocket. I rushed back and gave it to her. She was weeping. I kissed her again and ran out of the car, which was already moving. She wrote me later: "Didn't we have a lovely weekend? And I was happy to meet the gang and see something of what this interlude at Bolling Field is like. I didn't mean to cry when I left, darling; I meant to be gay. A sailor said to me: 'Don't cry lady. Think how good it will be for you when he comes back.'" Neither Nancy nor I then knew that we would not see each other again for two and a half years.

DESTINATION: EGYPT

On December 9, 1942, I happened to be the first to arrive in our room at Bolling Field when the telephone rang. I answered. The voice said, "We have a coded telegram for the commanding officer of the Third Photo Intelligence Detachment." I rushed to the signal office and was given the telegram, which I took to the decoding office. At about 11 P.M. it was put into English and proved to be warning orders for our movement overseas. A few days later we all received orders marked "SECRET" to proceed from Bolling Field to Camp Patrick Henry, a staging area for overseas transportation. It was in a forest of pine trees not far from Richmond, Virginia. Although the camp was not yet finished, troops came piling out of special trains that dead-ended over a freshly laid spur track beside an immense building with a roof of still-bright corrugated iron.

We had nothing to do for nine days while we waited our turn for inspection of this, inspection of that, and the inevitable medicos with needle after needle for shots against small-pox, typhoid, cholera, yellow fever, tetanus—until orderlies had to paste extra sheets onto the official Form for Inoculations. There was nothing to do, except to look at the magnificent pine trees. Most days it snowed, and sitting around the warmth of the coal stove in the barracks we could see the branches of the trees grow heavy.

One night, or rather one still-dark early morning, we were awakened by a shrill whistle, the door flung open, a command. It was embarkation day. Some went to wake up the men, without benefit of whistle, but with their newly acquired voice of command. Others went to look after the technical equipment. Officers and men ate together in the deserted mess hall. Everybody had beefsteak; it was, we had been told, traditional before overseas transport. Then began the long trek to the train that was to take us to the ship, that was to take us we knew not where.

Infantrymen are trained to travel miles with packs. We photo interpreters had neither packs nor training. We had civilian baggage—bulging "flight bags" with Class A dress uniforms inside them. These bags we lugged through the snow a mile or more to the train. They pulled at our wrists, made our fingers numb, chafed the calves of our legs. Some of our comrades, more ingenious than most of us, found broken branches in the woods. They pushed a branch between the handles of two flight bags and, in pairs, slung them over their shoulders. At last we reached the railhead and the immense warehouse. We marched inside, threw our bags on the concrete floor, and waited. The cold penetrated first through the heavy soles of the G.I. boots that everyone was wearing. It went right through the overcoat, the field jacket, the flannel shirt, and the gray underwear.

We waited and we waited. Then suddenly the packed warehouse burst out with a Christmas carol. All of us joined in the old favorites: "Silent Night," "It Came Upon a Midnight Clear," and the one that nobody there would ever hear again without remembering that December morning, a popular ballad, "White Christmas."

The train at last arrived. We all stopped singing and quietly filed into the warmth of the waiting coaches. Soon we were dockside and boarded the SS *Mariposa*, a luxury liner normally in service between Hawaii and the continental United States. The ship had been requisitioned by the army and converted to a troopship. We were told that five thousand soldiers were crowded into the vessel. We eleven officers shared a deluxe stateroom and the adjoining lanai, or private deck, that had been boarded up to contain three bunks. Only when we sailed did we learn that our destination was Egypt.

The voyage was uneventful. After forty-five listless days we disembarked at Suez and were met at the pier by a jeep painted a light sand color, loaded with bags of mail. One of them was marked "3rd Photo." We had a hard time not opening the mailbag at once, but the letters were not sorted, and we had to postpone that until we were in the train that took us to the camp in the desert outside Cairo known simply as "Kilo 13." It was much appreciated that the army had the mail waiting for us. Once aboard we sorted out the letters and read them all while the train was standing at the pier, then reread them. Everyone was pleased.

We finally pulled out just as night was falling. We rode through Suez past cafés, laundries, and shops, their signs in Arabic and French. From a long causeway we had a view of an oil refinery over which floated fifteen barrage balloons, used to support wires or nets as protection against air attacks. Then on to the desert. Nothing could be seen from the carriage windows except flickering fires of native encampments and the lanterns of occasional way stations. About eight-thirty we saw rows of lights in the desert, which we guessed were barracks. The train backed onto a siding, and a jeep sped toward us. An officer crossed the headlights and bellowed "Train Commander!" Our commanding officer, Captain Pollock, answered, and soon we were on the desert with all our gear. Our heavy flight bags were picked up by a truck and we walked through the night to our barracks. We unpacked our mess kits and had a most welcome hot supper. Next day we found we were to be quarantined at the camp for two weeks, as a case of measles had broken out aboard ship.

We join the Royal Air Force   The Ninth Air Force, to which we were attached as interpreters of aerial photographs, had no photo planes and no photofinishing facilities to take and process photographs for us to interpret! We were told that we would be assigned to the Quartermaster Corps. Fortunately our commanding officer convinced the U.S. Ninth Air Force to place us on detached service with the Middle East Interpretation Unit of the British Royal Air Force in Heliopolis, a suburb of Cairo.

On March 1 the officers of the Third Photo Intelligence Detachment were quartered in a villa that had been made available to the air force. It was a one-story bungalow with a fairly large central parlor surrounded by the dining room and four bedrooms. We had a household staff of a majordomo, a cook, and several servants, for we took all our meals in the villa. "It is very pleasant to eat 'at home,' as it were," I wrote Nancy. "We are living in real luxury: white robed servants with turbans and red sashes bring us early morning tea, and serve us at table." Nancy must have been as surprised to learn this as we were to be living in such splendor. We were just as surprised that the RAF Middle East Interpretation Unit, where we worked, was in an apartment house in the middle of the town of Heliopolis.

We did not realize it at the time, but we soon discovered that we were in what the army called "the rear echelon"—where we were destined to remain during our entire foreign service. Located a considerable distance from the front, we were concerned with administrative and supply duties. During my two years of overseas duty, I never saw combat, never heard a shot fired or a bomb explode.

The Middle East Interpretation Unit (MEIU) was responsible for all British photographic reconnaissance in the Mediterranean area. When we joined them there were between fifty and a hundred men and women of the Royal Air Force and the Women's Auxiliary Air Force working at the exacting and challenging task of extracting from thousands of aerial photographs information of military importance. The interpretation was divided into several sections. We Americans were each assigned to work in one of these sections for a week or two, then rotated to another. This was excellent training. The first job I had was working for a woman whose specialty was shipping. She told me to count and measure the ships in Naples harbor. She looked at my work and couldn't understand what I was doing. "The *Conte de Savoie* is not six hundred seventy feet, it's six hundred five feet. How did you get that?" I replied that I did what I had been trained to do: I measured it and applied the formula of the height of the aircraft, and so forth. "How do you know the height of the aircraft?" I told her the pilot had written it down. No, she said, pilots were not reliable. Why hadn't I measured it using a ship I knew the length of, using the catalog of ships she gave me? So they found the height of the plane by using proportion and calculating it mathematically. Photoreconnaissance was a British technique. The RAF thought our system didn't work, while theirs, we discovered, was infinitely more accurate. We used it throughout the war.

Basically there were three phases of interpretation. First Phase was examination of the photographs immediately after their processing. The interpreter noted any change from previous cover—such as the departure of a major battleship from its customary berth, or an unusually large concentration of aircraft on an airfield, or the progress of repair work on a bombed-out railroad bridge.

When it became my turn to work with the First Phase section I went out to the airfield around four in the afternoon with Flight Officer Bill Kerr, an experienced RAF interpreter. A Spitfire reconnaissance plane had just landed with film exposed over Crete, and the darkroom crew was already processing it. We escorted the pilot to the briefing room. He sat down wearily, pulled from his boot some maps, and proceeded to write his report. We then walked back with him to his graceful plane and saw him take off and fly into the dusk to his home airport. In about an hour the film negatives were ready for viewing. They were unrolled for us over a light box and Bill used a china marking pencil to indicate the frames he wanted printed. They were ready for him in about fifteen minutes. From them he made an interpretation of movements of shipping in harbors and the types of planes in airports. Meanwhile the darkroom crew wrote in ink on the margin of each frame of the entire sortie the serial number, date, name of the flying unit, and plane altitude at the time of the exposure. From these negatives two prints were made, one for plotting and the other for Second Phase Interpretation.

Plotting was an important part of photo interpretation. On maps of the land over which the pilot flew, rectangles were traced on transparent overlays of the exact area covered by each photograph. Thus all the cover of a certain area could be quickly retrieved from the vast quantities of prints stored in the MEIU library. This was essential, for photo interpretation was to a large extent a comparative study of photographs taken over a period of time.

Second Phase was the interpretation of all of the photographs taken during one day. This could demand the examination of upward of six hundred photographs per sortie; on a good flying day, with a cloudless sky, as many as eight sorties were not uncommon. Teams of interpreters began to study the photographs as soon as prints were available, and continued through the night. It was routine to count all aircraft parked at an airfield, to identify all shipping, and to assess bomb damage to railroads, highways, bridges, and industrial plants. If possible, the locations were plotted of antiaircraft, wireless, and radar installations and—especially toward the end of hostilities—launching sites of rocket bombs.

These Second Phase reports were in the nature of newscasts. They formed the substance of the daily morning briefings of the commanding general and his staff. So important was photoreconnaissance to the high command that failure to obtain photographs held up military operations. On one occasion a staff officer of the Fifteenth Air Force, on being told by the Senior Interpretation Officer that cloud cover prevented the photographing of an important target, exclaimed, "Goddamnit, man, do you realize we have fifteen hundred aircraft and thirty thousand men sitting on their damned asses because your photo planes can't get pictures? Get sorties off the ground at every hour on the hour until you can bring me some kind of a photograph we can fly by!"

Third Phase was a reexamination of photographs, mainly for special purposes. One of the most detailed in which I was involved was the study of Crete, then occupied by Germany. In utmost secrecy a few of us studied the topography of the island, in preparation for a proposed invasion by Allied forces. I was ordered to produce "goings" maps, on which I marked roads and bridges passable by tanks and large six-wheeled trucks, and those that could be used only by much smaller vehicles. We helped craftsmen build exquisite scale models of the landing beach, complete with every shoreline tree in its proper position for study by the Allied invasion troops planning the attack. To my knowledge, no such invasion ever took place.

Another service offered by Third Phase was the corroboration of reports by secret agents of enemy activity. Without photographic evidence the agents were not paid. The Corinth Canal divides the mainland of Greece and the peninsula of Peloponnesus. It was crossed by a railroad bridge, which was destroyed by the Allied forces. But during the German occupation supplies were still getting through to the peninsula by rail. A secret agent informed British forces that a pontoon bridge capable of supporting railroad tracks, a locomotive, and a train of cars had been put across the canal by the Germans. The British Royal Engineers, when consulted, stated that the report was obviously false, for a pontoon bridge, they said, could not possibly support a locomotive. However, by studying photographs and referring to a technical manual, I was able to prove the report was true. When the commanding officer of the MEIU asked me to send him a short note describing how I did this, I wrote, in my best military style:

> A ground report was submitted to this interpreter by the Senior Intelligence Officer for checking from air photos. This report stated that a pontoon company with 30 pontoons was stationed at the canal. A sketch was appended, showing a cross-section of a typical pontoon with the roadway suspended from pyramidal supports at either end of the pontoons.
>
> It was recollected that U.S. War Department Technical Manual (No. 3-450), "Handbook on German Military Forces," contained a description of pontoon equipment. A copy of this manual in the headquarters of this detachment was consulted, and it was found that the specifications of the Herbert 24-ton pontoon bridge equipment tallied exactly with the ground report.
>
> From the manual the length of the pontoons and the width of the road were obtained. It was found that the 30 pontoons visible in the air photos agreed exactly with these dimensions. The general appearance conformed to the description. It was, therefore, concluded that the pontoon bridge photographed at the Corinth Canal was identical to the Herbert bridge.

I was pleased that during this first year of military service I was promoted to captain.

TOURISTS IN UNIFORM   On our free days, which were infrequent, we took long hikes across the desert, or we would go to Cairo, which was a short streetcar ride from Heliopolis. Of the glories of the Egypt of the Pharaohs we saw but little. Several of us rode the streetcar to Giza, bargained there for camels, and on their swaying backs made the pilgrimage to the Great Pyramid and the Sphinx. However, all the museums were empty, and every movable relic of the ancient past had been put in the immense, bomb-proof caves of Mokkatam, through which railroads ran and where the British General Staff planned to seek shelter from enemy action before the miracle of El Alamein turned

the desert campaign to its triumphant westward course. I saw almost every mosque in Cairo and discovered an art little known to the Western world. The enjoyment of seeing these splendid monuments was spoiled by the everlasting "Baksheesh! Baksheesh!" of the shoeshine boys, or the chatter of dragomen who insisted on showing us the sights, and were difficult to shake off. And so, like most Americans and most Britons, we sought in Cairo that which was of the West. We had French food at Groppi's, steak and chips at St. James's Bar, martinis in the back bar of Shepheard's Hotel—and wished we were back in the States.

One of the most unusual and delightful wartime institutions in Cairo was a theater-like club called Music for All—so named because its principal purpose was to provide instruments for soldier musicians to play and for soldier music lovers to enjoy. When I visited the place with some fellow officers, a string ensemble, in shirtsleeves, was playing light music. We sat down at a table in the auditorium and enjoyed delicious pastries and French coffee. There was a restaurant off to one side of the foyer, and opposite it a shower room, where for the equivalent of fifteen cents one could enjoy the blessings of a truly hot bath—a real luxury to those front-line troops who were in Cairo on furlough, enjoying a respite from field conditions.

The love of music by soldiers was, to my amazement, matched by the number and quality of poems written by so many of us. Our newspaper, the *Stars and Stripes*, had a poetry section. Here is a poem that so deeply touched me that I sent a clipping of it back to Nancy.

> The wind swept in from the hills last night,
> Through the streets of an ancient town.
> Banging at windows, twisting the vanes,
> Romping and playing the clown.
> The wind sang soft as it passed me by
> Of village lawns turned green—

Lilacs and tulips—sweet lazy days,
Hours of sun with showers between.
A message I gave to the wind last night,
A message meant only for you—
"Carry it safely and quickly," I begged,
"Over the land, an ocean or two.
Say that I dream of a spring that is past
And hope on one yet to be"—
Did you hear last night, my love,
The wind's little message from me?

Sgt. Virgil Scott

I have never met Sergeant Scott. If he reads this, I hope he will accept my thanks.

THE JERUSALEM EXPRESS   In the summer of 1943 I had an attack of what was diagnosed at the field hospital as sandfly fever, a tropical disease that sends one's temperature to alarming heights and then drops it back to normal in a few days, leaving one exhausted and listless. After a short hospital stay I received seven days' leave for recuperation. I chose to visit Israel, then called Palestine. I wrote the following account in my journal.

On an August afternoon I was seated by the window of a first-class railway carriage in Cairo Main Station, looking out on the crowded platform. A local had just pulled in beside the waiting Jerusalem Express, and now the passengers, mostly Egyptian fellaheen, were piling out in frantic haste: swarthy men in gownlike caftans and women in black, their faces masked, their eyes outlined with black kohl, balancing on their heads baskets filled with eggs and vegetables, carrying by bound legs live chickens. A fellah led a white horse through the milling crowd. A wave of uniformed men opposed them, all bound for the Express: Eighth Army New Zealanders in shorts and black berets, Royal Air Force officers in snake-blue tunics, a handful of American soldiers in faded khaki. And then came the peddlers, selling oranges, "gazooza" (soda pop), figs lost to sight beneath swarms of black tenacious flies, glittering wrist watches, fly switches, and swagger sticks. Long before the Express was due to leave every seat was taken, and through every window the peddlers thrust their wares, cripples displayed their maimed stumps, flies buzzed in the close, hot air of the carriage and passengers stumbled over baggage piled high in the corridor.

Sitting there in the railway carriage, impatient to be on my way, with nothing to read and nobody to speak to, I fell into an introspective mood. "What did you do?" I was sure I would be asked when I returned home. I thought I would answer evasively, making a mystery of it, "Intelligence. It was all secret: interpreting aerial photographs." And then I asked myself, What *do* I do? And I answered, "I send destruction on its way. I put a sharp-pointed pencil on the photographs and say, "There, there…Unload your fiercest bombs on this target. There it will hurt the enemy most. There his hide is sensitive." And after the heavy bombers have returned I pore over the photographs of what had been an intact thing until our planes came out of the southern skies. I write on my report: "One oil tank, approximately 100 feet diameter, totally destroyed. One oil tank burning." Five miles above the earth even the eye of the camera cannot see people—cannot see workers trapped by that flood of burning oil. Photographs are mute; they do not record the wail of the air raid siren, the terrifying explosions, the answering, insistent, desperate ratatat of flak. These are not on the photograph. I make no note of them. I write down with my sharp-pointed pencil what I see through my stereoscope. "Central span of five-span through-truss two-track railway bridge, approximately 500 feet long, destroyed. Locomotive lying on side beneath bridge. One passenger car in water." I cannot see, and thus cannot describe, the bodies piled on one another in that fallen railway carriage. I cannot tell what happened to the engineer when the boiler of his locomotive burst apart. It is not my job to tell. I am an expert in destruction: this bridge is cut; it is unserviceable. Enemy trains cannot go across it for at least a month. Then one day I'll see on a photograph that the bridge has been repaired. Out will go my report: "Five-span through-truss bridge now serviceable." And the cycle will be repeated.

What do I do? Behind guarded doors I sit planning the invasion of Crete, 500 miles away. I know the surface of every road, its every turning, its every bridge, its every culvert. This way tanks can go; there gliders can land. Commandos will find cover in the cove. Enemy defenses can rake that beach with deadly fire. "Avoid it," I warn. And if I overlook a hidden pillbox? Nobody knows how many British troops may die on the beach—because I didn't use my eyes. Those tank drivers passing by on the platform depend on my "goings" map. If the bridge they plan to cross is wooden and not masonry, as I wrote in my report, their tank would crash through it and they might be killed.

Now the Jerusalem Express started. It was not so much the motion that woke me from my gloomy introspection, but the mad rush of last-minute arrivals, who tried to climb aboard the already overcrowded train. I looked around the compartment. My companions were all military and all were officers. I fell into conversation with the British officer sitting opposite me, a captain on his way back to a lonely desert outpost after ten days' leave in Cairo. His talk reminded me of the talk I had heard from other men who had lived and fought in the desert. The captain hated the isolation, the loneliness and the feeling that he was "not part of the show." Yet there was something about the desert that brought these men great satisfaction: its immensity, its beauty, the brilliance of the nights. Later I was to meet in Italy soldiers who were homesick for the desert: they contrasted the muddy wallow of the Italian spring with the clean desert, the slow advance from town to town with the swift, panther-like sweep of tanks across the endless plains.

The train rushed through Zagazig, a name that seemed to me right out of the *Arabian Nights*. Late in the afternoon we crossed the Suez Canal. It looked like the Cape Cod Canal back home; a huge ditch with piles of sand on each side reaching as far as the eye—the human eye, that is, not the camera eye—could see, with many derricks busy pumping out the channel. At El Kantara we stopped for almost an hour. I walked beside the squalid town, which had been fenced off for miles with barbed wire and posted: "Out of Bounds to All Troops." One lonely Coptic church was all of El Kantara I could see: in the setting sun it looked better at a distance than close by, when its slovenly work-manship and crudity became apparent. We had a dinner of sorts at a hut bearing the strange word "NAAFI," which stood for "Navy, Army, Air Force Institute," a welfare organization for the British armed forces.

When night fell, the lights of all the cars of the train were blacked out. There was nothing to do but to try to get some sleep. I couldn't curl up the way the others did—at 6'3" my legs were too long, and the seats too crowded. At Gaza there was a long halt. Everyone rushed out onto the dimly lit platform and stood in line for hot, bitterly strong tea, ladled out from a ten-gallon can, and tasteless dry muffins, gingerly handed out one at a time by white-gloved natives.

I thought of home. I tried to imagine what it would be like to suddenly return. I had now been overseas eight months. They had gone quickly enough and yet they seemed interminable. Time is a strange measure: its pace is never uniform. Was it only eight months ago that I had last seen my wife? I looked up at the sky and the brilliant stars. Maybe Nancy is looking at that sky right now, I thought. And then I realized that she now looked out from the other side of the world at another sky. Home seemed more remote than ever. When will I return? When, when, when—oh Lord, when will that be? I asked myself. The train rushed on through the night. My companions slept. I alone remained awake.

The U.S. Photographic Reconnaissance Wing

In October 1943 the Third Photographic Intelligence Detachment was ordered to Tunis, to work with a newly activated Photographic Reconnaissance Wing commanded by Colonel Elliott Roosevelt, the son of the president. I was sorry to leave my colleagues in the Middle East Interpretation Unit. They had been my mentors in the techniques of photo interpretation and had become my friends in the few months that I had spent with them. I had even been elected to their officers' mess, which in the RAF was more than an eating place, it was a club.

While waiting for the four C-457 transport planes that would fly us to Tunis, I walked to the edge of the desert and watched the clouds. We did not often see clouds in Egypt, and I photographed them. It seemed an optimistic sky; the clouds were not threatening but were swift and fleeting, scudding through the air as I hoped we would soon be doing. When it came time to take off they had all disappeared and we had a flight I have never forgotten: a whole day watching the North African desert unfold beneath us, a terrain I had seen so often in air photographs that I knew it in exact detail. It was a strange experience—one that every photo interpreter who flies has undergone—discovering that the earth and what is on it conforms to the photographs!

After a few days of utter confusion in Tunis, where we were billeted in the basement of some public building, we were assigned quarters in two pleasant villas high above the Mediterranean in the suburb of Sidi Bou Said. We worked in the top floor of a huge monastic building within walking distance of our living quarters. Our photographic interpretation was for the most part routine. I was ordered to Third Phase, and became a specialist in the communications section. My responsibility was to report the condition of all roads and railroads visible in photographs of enemy territory in Italy. Of particular concern was bomb damage to bridges, for they were major targets for the Allied bombers. We studied freight yards (or, as the British called them, "marshalling yards"), where heavy concentrations of freight cars ("goods wagons") were often to be seen. These we counted almost daily: if the cars were open gondolas we would, as far as possible, identify the contents, particularly if it appeared to be miliary equipment.

In November 1943 we were told that there would be a review of all personnel and that we must wear dress uniforms. A schedule had been worked out for transporting the men to La Marsa airfield that morning. We had no idea who was to review us. As we were breakfasting, resplendent in our blouses and pinks, word was passed around that the review was canceled, but we were to remain in formal dress for a routine inspection of the lab by General Carl Spaatz. Just after lunch, while I was working in the lab, our commanding officer burst in, all breathless. "The review is on!" he shouted, and ordered me to round up all hands.

It was late in the afternoon when we finally got lined up on the airfield, four deep. We waited and we waited. A staff car came by with a general in it. "All this bull for a general!" we said to each other. But nothing happened and still we waited. Finally a jeep came slowly down the airfield. Plainclothesmen were huddled around a shortwave transmitter. Their eyes were glued to the road. We couldn't follow their glance because we had been called to attention. A second similar jeep followed and a two-ton covered truck, filled with military police armed with tommy guns. And then, sitting in a jeep beside the driver, wrapped up in a Navy cape, wearing a light-gray hat, the President of the United States, Franklin Delano Roosevelt, rode up to greet his son. Everyone stiffened, came to a more precise attention. It was absolutely silent until the jeep stopped beside the colonel. We saw FDR shaking Elliott's hand and heard him say, "Son, you've got a swell outfit here!" Then the jeep and the entourage slowly drove past the lined-up men and back again. It was all over in ten minutes.

FDR looked very tired and old, worn down by care and anxiety. Only later did we learn that he was on his way to the Cairo conference with Winston Churchill and Chiang Kai-shek. The officers were ordered front and center and instructed to tell their men that the utmost secrecy must be preserved. The security was remarkable. On Sunday, the day after the review, a British officer of the RAF who was having a glass of wine with me in my billet said that his men had heard a wild rumor that the president was in town.

SAN SEVERO   The Wing began its move to Italy in December. As the Italians had surrendered and the Germans had been forced back, it now was considered safe to set up headquarters there. The bulky and heavy photofinishing equipment, capable of developing aerial film automatically and making hundreds of prints daily, was loaded on trucks, together with thousands upon thousands of photographs that had been interpreted, indexed, and filed as "back cover" for future reference. Other trucks carried tents and field kitchens for encampments en route. Yet others carried personnel. The convoy went overland from Tunis to Bizerte, where the trucks were loaded on landing craft that crossed the Mediterranean under naval escort to Taranto. From there they proceeded to the Wing's new headquarters in San Severo.

I did not travel with the Wing's convoy, for I was detailed to fly to Italy with the secret files. I was assigned a jeep, a sergeant, and a C-47 transport plane with crew. Somehow we managed to squeeze the jeep on board the plane, which, except for the files, was otherwise empty. I wore, for the first and last time, a loaded pistol on my belt. It was an easy flight and we soon landed at one of the airstrips around Foggia, a city on the flat plains surrounding the base of the Gargano peninsula, the mountainous promontory jutting into the Adriatic that is often called the "spur" of the "boot" of Italy.

We drove north on a road ripped up by tanks and six-wheeled military trucks to the quiet city of San Severo. In the fall of 1943 the Germans had left all in a hurry and the British and Americans had entered. Allied trucks, ambulances, guns, tanks, and all kinds of military vehicles rolled through the cobbled streets, which were declared one-way by the military police. The procession seemed endless. Some vehicles went farther north, others parked in the public squares. Overnight the city became a garrison. At one time there were enough ammunition trucks to have blown up the entire city if it had been bombed. But strangely, San Severo, although at one time only twenty miles from the front, was never bombed during my stay there of almost a year.

Our living quarters were in one wing of the palatial mansion of the mayor, and soon we set up a kitchen and had all our meals there. The photographic laboratory, the vast library of maps and photographs, and work space for the photo interpreters were all in a large school building in the middle of town.

One day I saw hung up beside the door of a home just around the corner from our billet a sign in English: "Italian lessons, 25 lire an hour." I rang the bell. "In groups of four," said Professor Giuseppe Fiore.

"Will you take me alone if I pay you one hundred lire?"

"Certainly," he replied.

The professor was a tall, gray-haired man racked with rheumatism, so that for him to write was painful. He was a schoolteacher who had been bombed out in Naples and moved to San Severo to be near his son, who was in a military hospital there. He made my enforced stay in the barren town unforgettable, for he introduced me to the beauty of Italian literature. Every night I had a lesson in Italian. The hour became two, then three, and finally I left my teacher at ten, only because that was the hour of curfew.

He didn't teach me what I had come to him to learn: enough Italian to be "useful." He was not going to let me off with a smattering of the language he so loved. When I asked him how to tell our houseboy, "Shut the door to keep the flies out!" it became "Close the door in order that the flies may not enter." And he was determined that I learn to speak Italian without an American accent. He would have me read an Italian text out loud and would join in, shouting in my ear, beating the cadence with his maimed fist, urging me to speak quickly and to cut the final vowels short. One night, in desperation, after having corrected me again and again, he pushed back his chair and blurted out, "You speak Italian just like Mayor La Guardia." He was referring, of course, to the Italian-language shortwave radio broadcasts then being made by the mayor of New York City, who was of Italian ancestry.

Professor Fiore had me translate English into Italian. There were no bookshops open in San Severo, but fortunately I had paperbacks of my favorite authors: Thoreau, Melville, Thomas Wolfe. But these, to the professor's mind, were of little value—the style was too simple. So when the bookstores did open I bought at his request an Italian translation of Charles Dickens. There, the professor said, was a man who knew sentence structure; there I could use the subjunctive, relative prepositions, subordinate clauses. There was a test!

Each lesson began with a page of Dante, which he would read aloud. Then, without translation or even explanation, I read aloud with him. Then a reading and a translation of a passage from Alessandro Manzoni's *I Promessi Sposi* (The Betrothed), a novel Italian schoolchildren were required to learn by heart. This was followed by my reciting paradigms (I had to learn all the conjugations, and all the rules of grammar). Then at last we came to the part that was, to me, the most stimulating: reading the great Italian writers, Giacomo Leopardi, Giosuè Carducci, Giovanni Verga.

Leopardi's poetry shone more vividly in San Severo than it ever has since: in the stuffy room, hunched over a charcoal brazier, with the single electric bulb flickering and sometimes going out, we read together some of the greatest lyrics ever written. Just as I had become comfortable reading Dante, the professor suddenly left town to return to Naples. I never saw him again.

❖

The monotony of routine interpretation of roads and railroads was relieved by occasional trips to other photographic reconnaissance units. In March 1944 the commanding officer of the Wing ordered me to visit various headquarters to find out what I could about the use of our reports and how they could be improved. I welcomed this chance to travel. I took along with me one Lieutenant Haden, who had been working with me. We became good friends and I could not have found a better companion.

I was assigned a jeep and we left San Severo at 10 A.M. for Caserta, a town not far from Naples. The ride over the Apennines was beautiful, and getting out of the plains of Foggia was a relief. We climbed up and up through picturesque hill towns and passed terrain that was strangely familiar to me from my study of air photographs. The Allied headquarters of Caserta was in the massive Royal Palace, where I found our liaison officer. He greeted us warmly and offered us a place to stay on the top floor of the huge 830-foot-long building. We counted the steps up to our room: exactly 234.

We began by going to the Air Room, a conference room with a long table and chairs, its walls covered with maps. A couple of one-star generals arrived, and a young captain walked in front of the large map of the European theater of war, came to attention, then gave an excellent "newscast" of military operations during the past twenty-four hours. The rest of the morning I visited some of the photo interpreters who used the reports. I was pleased that so many found our work of value.

Next day Haden and I started off from the command post of the Fifth Army. North of Caserta the roads had been chewed into a slushy mixture of mud and snow. Every bridge was a temporary one, for those we had not bombed were blown up by the Germans and Italians in their retreat. At Capua we crossed the Volturno; ruined houses became more frequent, and we could see the ugly splash of machine-gun bullets on the whitewashed walls of homes. Along the road were encampments, one after another. Piles of stores stood unprotected in the open fields. Every so often a dispatch rider whizzed by on his motorcycle. At the end of a dirt road we swung into an encampment in an olive orchard, as neat as a garrison in the States. A white-helmeted military policeman pointed out the photoreconnaissance trailer, actually two large trucks with boxlike bodies parked back to back. The print library and maps occupied one, the interpretation desks the other.

We next visited the Third Photo Reconnaissance Group in Pomigliano d'Arco, a town at the northern foot of Mount Vesuvius, which was then erupting with a violence not seen since 1872. After supper a group of us drove up the side of the mountain to the town of San Sebastiano. Parking the jeep, we joined the crowd watching the flow of fiery lava.

The houses had been vacated by the townspeople, who were moved out by the Allied military government trucks when the threat of an eruption became apparent. Now the main street was crowded with civilians and G.I.s who were held at bay by a couple of military policemen. I stood on a terrace beside the road, watching the lava slowly pile up against a church and the building near it. The pile was ninety feet high. Every few minutes a piece would break off from the top and go tumbling down into the street to smash into pieces that were white hot; rivulets of molten lava ran like quicksilver out of the broken mass, but soon cooled and turned dark. The crowd, fascinated and strangely quiet, hushed by the weird drama of the phenomenon and by the realization nothing could be done by man to stem the tide, waited to see the church crumble. Then, as if brushed by an immense, unseen hand, the walls of the building gave way to the lava, and fell with the unreality of a slow-motion movie. A cloud of dust rose up, and when it cleared there were hot flames dancing over the exposed wooden beams. I walked through somebody's garden right up to the edge of the fiery lava. Tomato vines had been planted, and carefully tended. Plants and the weeds, shrubs, and trees were devoured by the lava, which spread in falling masses. It was more terrible to witness at close hand this destruction of the land than the destruction of the buildings.

Then we did a crazy thing. We walked through the deserted town, looking for a vantage point from which to see the vastness of the lava flow. Our footsteps and our voices resounded through the empty streets. It was getting dark. Underfoot we felt the crunch of the cokelike dead lava. We looked around the corner. There, not twenty-five feet away, was the live stuff. The building next to us might at any moment have toppled. We ran on the double to a safer place and climbed onto a roof a distance away.

We soon realized that what we had witnessed was but a minor and unimportant part of the terrifying show. From the hillside above the town we looked out over the lava bed, which stretched out in a crescent shape. A thousand bonfires, it seemed, were flickering in the valley. The lava was a quarter of a mile in width. As far as we could see it had enveloped the land. In front of us the church, still standing, was burning fiercely; the windows were crimson, and it seemed as if a great festival were being held inside. If I had heard mighty organ chords I would not have been surprised: it would have been fitting. We were waiting for the church to collapse. It was still standing when night came on, and we walked with the crowd back to our jeep. I realized the full force of the opening lines of Leopardi's poem "Here on the arid backbone of the terrible Mount Vesuvius the destroyer."

On March 23, 1944, we left Naples for San Severo. We had done our business and wanted to get back to the Wing. It rained before we had gone far, and as we climbed the foothills it became cold. The Naples-bound convoys were covered with snow, and we prepared for the worst. Soon we were in the thick of it. The sky was so overcast and the snow so heavy that we turned on the headlights. We fairly crawled up the mountain passes. There was a seemingly endless procession of convoys, some eastward bound, others westward. More than once we came to a halt, shut off the motor, and waited patiently while great guns, as well as huge lorries with bodies as big as freight cars, came slowly down steep grades. When the road was again clear and we started off, the wheels spun the slush snow and we slid across the road. Once we passed a platoon of Scottish troops in full field equipment marching in a column of twos, headed by a pair of bagpipers. All along the route a stream of ill-clad and poorly shod civilians were trudging in the direction of Naples, carrying heavy sacks upon their shoulders. Some were pushing bicycles, across which they had thrown their sacks. At one steep hill, horses were pulling long ropes that men and women grasped to ease the hard uphill climb.

Suddenly we dropped down into a green valley. Looking back, I could see the storm enveloping the summits of the mountain. Later the sun broke through the storm, and the Apennines, so grim a few hours ago, now gleamed with fresh white snow.

PIGGYBACK IN AN F-5   In October 1944 I was assigned to the Fifth Photographic Reconnaissance Group stationed in Bari, Italy, as Group Photo Interpreter. It was my duty to relay the needs of the Fifteenth Air Force headquarters to appropriate photoreconnaissance units. One morning I was summoned to the office of Major General Nathan Twining, the commanding officer of the Fifteenth Air Force. As I walked to his office I tried to remember what I'd been taught in Miami about military courtesy. Once in the general's office, I came to attention, held my cap under my left arm, and raised my right hand in salute. I managed to say, "Sir?" The general was studying a map lying on the table. He looked up. "Cut out that stuff! We've got a war to win! Come in and help."

The general explained that he planned to strike at low level a number of enemy bases. The planes would fly "on the deck"—that is, just off the ground. He needed photos showing the exact height and location of every possible overhead obstruction surrounding the airports, such as towers, water tanks, radio antennas, flagpoles, trolley wires, and so forth. "We need these pictures right away, Captain."

"Yes, sir," I replied. "We can do that in San Severo at the interpretation unit."

"But that's ninety miles away!" the general remarked. "Can't you do that here in Bari?"

"No, sir. You see, we don't have the photo library here, with the negatives and prints of these airports."

"How long will it take to get annotated pictures?"

"Well, sir, I'd say perhaps a week."

"No sooner?"

"I don't know how much coverage we have. If we have to fly new cover it will take a day or two before interpretations can be made. I don't know how much work the interpretation unit has in hand, General. But I can tell the commanding officer to put the job on the night shift, if you wish."

"We'll fly you to San Severo in an F-5. Try to get me pictures as soon as possible." The general rolled up the maps and gave them to me.

A sergeant drove me in a jeep to the Bari airport. The F-5 was already on the runway. It had one seat only, for the pilot. It was possible, however, to squeeze a passenger into the narrow space behind the pilot. You sat on a ledge, with your legs straddling the pilot's seat, and your head just above his, your hands on his shoulders. You were all but clinging to the pilot, so it was called "flying piggyback."

It was a real question whether I could fit my six-three frame into the crowded space. The pilot stood on the starboard wing and the mechanic on the port wing, telling me where not to step, for fear of breaking a pipe or an electric line. When they told me that Gary Cooper had done it, I was determined to succeed. Suddenly I slid into place as slick as could be. The mechanic handed me a set of earphones to wear to shut out the roar of the motors. The pilot climbed in nimbly, cranked up the window, and we lumbered along with great effort to the runway. When the pilot opened up the engines the entire plane came alive and shook as if impatient to get aloft. He released the brakes and we streaked along the runway. I could feel the plane airborne as we banked easily to starboard and headed for the coast, which we followed, skimming over the water "on the deck"—at a height of between fifty and one hundred feet. We flew so close to seaside towns I could identify the Romanesque cathedrals, could see the people at their many tasks, could even see the rigging on a fishing craft. We were so low the sensation of speed was terrific. What was even more remarkable was the feel of the plane. I was part of this graceful, shiny metal object, and had the illusion that if I leaned just a bit to port, the plane would swing in that direction. I became aware of every action the pilot made, for I was all but breathing down his neck, and came to anticipate the plane's response. We soared like a sea gull, only we didn't need to break our glide by flapping our wings. We followed the indentation of the beach, easily curving to right and to left. Then we headed inland, over the tiny farms and the earthbound traffic, which seemed to crawl.

I felt the pilot's shoulders against my chest, and a second later we were streaming straight up, climbing fiercely. My ears cracked painfully, my head was light, my heart was pounding with excitement. We were heading straight for a cloud. I held my breath; it seemed that we would shatter it asunder, but its apparent solidity vanished into soft, soothing mist. The roar of the engines seemed deadened, and we were alone in space, then out into the blue sky on top of the clouds, which seemed more beautiful. We turned sharply, with one wing pointing almost directly down. My body moved with the plane—I had become part of it. I did not feel jostled, nor did I sense I was falling, but a great weight seemed to be pressing down on the back of my neck. Below us stretched the landing strip. The pilot called the control tower from a tiny microphone, then we dove straight down, shattering the air at terrific speed. The field was not clear so we flew out at low altitude across the country and circled lazily, then down again, straight as a plummet, with the brown length of the landing strip standing vertically above the nose of the plane. Somehow we slowed down as we approached the ground and leveled out. Now we could feel the wheel touching the ground; a couple of light bumps and we were on the earth again. The pilot zoomed one engine and we wheeled around, with much fuss and roar, as if the plane considered it an indignity to travel on earth. We parked off the runway, I climbed out and put on my shoes—which I had removed, as they were too large to fit beside the pilot's seat—unbuckled my parachute, and slid off the aft edge of the wing to the ground.

This flight gave me a feeling I was flying. It was effortless, yet I felt I was participating; it was an active, not passive experience. As to General Twining's request, I have no record of what action was taken. I assume he was satisfied, for I did not hear from him again on this assignment.

❖

The end of the war was in sight, but had yet to come.

On his relief of the command of the Allied Mediterranean Photographic Reconnaissance Wing, Colonel Karl Polifka sent each of us who had served under him the following message: "The scope of your combined efforts have risen so rapidly and volume of production has increased so much, that during the month of August 1944, 1,250 sorties were flown and 3,000,000 prints were produced, totals exceeded in this one month more than was flown and produced during the last three months of 1943." We were proud of our record and appreciative of his commendation.

LONDON

In the last few months of the war Hitler bombarded London heavily with his dreaded *Vergeltungswaffen* (vengeance weapons): the V-1, a flying bomb, and the V-2, a supersonic rocket. We in the Mediterranean theater of war knew nothing about these missiles, so when the Allied Central Interpretation Unit in England asked if we had discovered in our photographs any sites for these weapons, we could only say that we did not know. It is a maxim held by photo interpreters that you cannot identify an object unless you know what it looks like from the air.

General Twining ordered me to fly to England and learn all I could about V-bombs: their launching gear, and other paraphernalia, such as fuel tankers and ammunition supply stores. What I learned was unbelievable. I was taken to an underground conference room. On one wall there was a huge map of greater London with all of the buildings destroyed by bombing marked in red. They told me that on the average a hundred bombs fell every twenty-four hours! Defense measures were only partially successful; the V-1 "buzz bombs," as Londoners called them, could be shot down by antiaircraft weapons or fighter planes before they reached the city. Barrage balloons were some protection. But there was no defense at all against the huge V-2 rockets. These were forty feet long, and weighed fourteen tons, including a ton of explosives. Upon lift-off, the rockets, traveling at a speed faster than sound, reached altitudes of sixty miles. From the tremendous height of their trajectories they plunged straight to earth and exploded.

It was easy to spot the launching ramps of the flying bombs; one hundred were discovered by interpreters on the north coast of France—all aimed at London. These were made useless by Allied bombers. But the sites of the V-2 rockets could not be discovered, because each of these huge bombs was hauled on a special trailer to any convenient paved area, such as a highway or a tennis court, and set up vertically on its fins, fueled, and launched. Further bombs would be launched at other locations. On my return to Italy, I briefed our photo interpreters in both the V-1 and V-2 weapons. We searched our photographs with care, but found no launching sites or other evidence of the use or existence of either of these missiles.

HELMUT GERNSHEIM The unexpected trip to London was important to me personally because it was there that I met Helmut Gernsheim, who, at my urging, became a pioneer collector and historian of photography. I had not heard of him until one day in the summer of 1943, when I was in Egypt, I bought a book of his titled *New Photo Vision*, published in 1942.[20] It was a collection of thirty-two of his own excellent photographs accompanied by a stimulating historical text. The photographs were well seen and the text well written. I sent the book to Nancy in New York and gave it no further thought. A year later Nancy forwarded to me a letter from Mr. Gernsheim, in which he wrote that he was in agreement with my statement: "Not through the technique at his command, but through his vision of the world, does the photographer create pictures of significance and lasting value." He did not mention where this statement

20. Helmut Gernsheim, *New Photo Vision* (London: The Fountain Press, 1942).

appeared, but I was able to trace it to *U.S. Camera 1937*.[21] I at once acknowledged his thoughtful note and explained that I was stationed in Italy in the Fifteenth Air Force and that if ever I came again to England I would surely look him up.

Soon after I arrived in London on my military mission I telephoned Mr. Gernsheim. He at once invited me to have dinner with him and his wife. After dining on excellent venison in a restaurant, we went to their apartment near Regent's Park and had coffee. It was delicious, and I remember congratulating Mrs. Gernsheim as I accepted a third cup. "Why do you find it so good?" she asked. "Is it the cream?" And then I realized that I had not tasted real dairy cream for two years.

I had leisure time between military appointments to explore London bookshops. I was delighted to find a few classical photographic books: the folio volume *Pictures of East Anglian Life* (1886), with thirty-two photographs by Peter Henry Emerson, and his charming book *Marsh Leaves* (1895). For these I paid, respectively, five guineas ($26.25) and seven shillings sixpence ($1.88). Today these books fetch thousands of dollars each at auction. A few days later I joined Helmut and Alison—we had already become friends—for dinner in their apartment. Our conversation was, as always, on photography. Many years later Helmut described these visits:

> The most important thing is the change brought into my life by the first book that I published, *New Photo Vision*, [in which]…I sought to "modernize" British photography, my one most important goal to fulfill. That is, until I came across Beaumont Newhall, or I should say, Beaumont Newhall came across me. Beaumont bought my book when he was in the army in Cairo—in '42 or '43….[He] showed up in London during Christmas 1944. He stayed some 14 days—days which in a way transformed my life. Every day he would come to me with stories of things he had bought—of how marvelous and cheap they were. He thought he made my mouth water with these stories, but actually he did not intrigue me, since at that time I simply was not interested in the history of photography as a collector—yet! Not at all! I told Beaumont that I simply hadn't got the cash to start another thing. I was already collecting African art, German Expressionist woodcuts, and Greek terra cottas. I just didn't have *any* money to spare for photography. He said, "Well, give up these other things—you can get them later on—but *now* you should concentrate on photography—stuff is just lying around, wasted, and people don't know what to make of it. It should be preserved!"

21. The statement appeared as an introduction to a portfolio of photographs I selected from my museum exhibition at the request of magazine entrepreneur T. J. Maloney, who published the annual: "The first fifty years of photography saw the technique developed from primitive daguerreotypy and calotype to the modern gelatino-bromide dry plate and film. Within the half-century 1839–1889 every phase of photography was anticipated, if not mastered. Color processes, miniature cameras, enlargements to twelve diameters or more, successive instantaneous exposures, pictures from the air, by flashlight, and of the invisible rays—the germs of all these triumphs of modern technique were sown decades ago. In the past few years these prophecies have been realized; the tool has been made sharper, easier to use, surer in result. Yet the old photographs reproduced on the following sixteen pages show that there has been no corresponding advance in quality. Every one of the pictures was made with equipment which the merest tyro would scorn today and under handicaps which would discourage the most expert technician. May they remind amateur and professional alike that not through the technique at this command, but through his vision of the world, does the photographer create pictures of significance and lasting value." (T. J. Maloney, ed., *U.S. Camera 1937* (New York: William Morrow & Co., 1937), p. 9.

In the foreword to *New Photo Vision*, Gernsheim expressed a similar idea: "Neither camera, nor lens, nor film determine the quality of pictures; it is the visual perception of the man behind the mechanism which brings them to life. Art contains the allied ideas of making and begetting, of being master in one's craft and of being able to create. Without these properties no art exists and no photographic art can come into being."

I was still not excited about the idea. But on a trip to Hampton Court—where I had been doing photography for six months for the National Building Record—I happened to pass by an antique shop and saw a bundle of pictures. I said to myself, "I've probably passed these a hundred times without noticing them." Beaumont's comments made me open my eyes. I went inside and inquired about them. Their condition seemed to be good—including a number of interesting American views, and I bought them thinking, "These will make a nice going-away present for Beaumont."

Beaumont came over and I said, "These are a gift, either for you [to keep], or you can give them to the Museum of Modern Art. I don't care." Beaumont flipped through the pictures and said, "No. I won't take them from you. They should be the foundation stone of *your own* collection."

Wasn't that amazing? That is exactly what [ultimately] happened! I still didn't want to collect because of lack of cash, but Beaumont urged me to "wait and see."

I thought about it overnight and asked Beaumont, before he left, "How would I begin? How would I go about collecting photographic material? I know about collecting other things—not photographs." He said, "You go down Charing Cross Road, where there is one book shop after another and ask: 'Do you have any photographically illustrated books?' Maybe they have one, maybe not. Then you go into another shop and inquire about photographs or photographic journals. *Buy whatever you feel you want to have.* As for daguerreotypes or ambrotypes, you have to go into the lesser antique shops, or the better junk shops—and ask!"[22]

As I look back I think I was not quite as aggressive as Helmut recounts. I recall that I gave a reason for not accepting his going-away present. I pointed out to him and Alison that in the group of stereo cards that he had bought there were several that were exceedingly rare, especially some "instantaneous" views of pedestrians and traffic on Broadway, New York City, taken in 1859. They were too valuable to risk either mailing in wartime or to keep in a footlocker in the combat zone.

Helmut at once began to acquire photographs and books on photography of all periods. By 1964, when he sold his collection to the University of Texas at Austin, he had 35,000 photographs, 4,000 books, and 350 pieces of photographic apparatus. He also wrote an encyclopedic *History of Photography*, originally published in 1955.[23]

❖

When I returned to Bari from London the commanding officer of the group called me into his office and, with a rather stern

22. Transcript of a talk Gernsheim gave October 30, 1984, at George Eastman House in Rochester, New York, to the members of the local Photographic Historical Society. Published with the permission of Helmut Gernsheim and of the International Museum of Photography, George Eastman House. For a complete transcription, see *Image*, vol. 27, no. 4 (December 1984), pp. 2–9.

23. A third edition is being published in three volumes by Thames Hudson. The first volume, *The Origins of Photography*, appeared in 1983; the second volume, *The Rise of Photography, 1850–1880*, in 1988. The third volume is forthcoming.

face, told me that there was an important order for me at the adjutant's office and that I should get it at once. I was puzzled and a bit uneasy. It proved to be my promotion to the rank of major.

At that time I received this letter from Nancy:

My dearest heart,

I have been looking at two photographs of you. The one Philippe Halsman made just before you went away and the one made a month or so ago when you were standing on the shores of some Italian town. Looking at what two years and more have chiseled on your face. It seems sparer, finer, more luminous than ever. And once again it strikes me like a blow how strange it is that you whom I so love, the touch of whom is still intimately in my lips and fingers, in my bones and heart, should all this long while, through interminable days and nights, have been living in places I never heard of, with people I never shall know, sleeping, dreaming, talking, worrying about things I cannot share. I do not know where you are now—not even the nation, nor whether on sea or air or land. You do know about me—you know all that I write you, often better than I do. You know the people and the places, the ideas and events. You know that I am safe and busy and loving you. In a few minutes I shall listen to the news, and hear what happens in Berlin. They tell us not to celebrate when Germany falls, that the war is only half won. But I for one shall feel like a skyrocket—and then probably go burn candles in St. Pat's, if I can get in the doors, praying this victory brings you home.[24]

Written in February, Nancy's letter was more prophetic than either of us had known, for on April 9, at long, long last, I received orders to return to the United States for "Rehabilitation, Recuperation, Recovery." This was neither a leave of absence nor a permanent change of station, but a duty assignment. It carried with it the understanding that I would return to the Group after fifty-two days.

24. Nancy Newhall to Beaumont Newhall, February 4, 1945.

The ocean crossing on the SS *West Point* was uneventful, but our reception at Newport News was quite unexpected. As soon as we stepped off the ships's gangplank we were hustled into the coaches of a waiting train. After a short ride to the staging area we piled out onto a warehouse platform. Over a loudspeaker a Voice ordered us to fall into a column of fours. At this we grumbled. "Well we're back now to the Z.I. [zone of the interior]," I heard someone say. Then the Voice again: "Welcome! There is a band forming now at the head of the column [murmur of surprise]. You are going to march to a theater, where you will attend a meeting ordered by the War Department. Then you will march to your barracks. We have a hot meal ready for you [murmur of approval]. We positively guarantee it will not consist of C-rations [shouts of joy]—you can leave your mess gear in the barracks [shouts]. Carry on, men!" The band struck up, the leader twirled his baton, and away we went in delirious excitement.

The next day I led a group of men to the replacement center at Fort Dix, New Jersey. There we found a lot of outdoor telephone booths. Every so often an operator called over the loudspeaker, "Sergeant Jones, Boston calling," or "Lieutenant Pasquale, Brooklyn calling." There were perhaps hundreds of us milling around, waiting for our names to be called. Finally I heard "Major Newhall, New York calling." I rushed into a booth, and heard Nancy's voice. But I was so choked with emotion I couldn't talk, and could only blurt out, "Tomorrow, darling!"

On May 2, I opened the door of our apartment and we embraced. Nancy had planned a Welcome Home party for me for May 8. Neither of us ever expected the war in Europe would be over that very day. V-E day! So our party was a double celebration.

We decided that on my leave we would go to California. Ansel Adams and his wife, Virginia, generously invited us to come to Yosemite. On hearing that I was at last back home Ansel telegraphed: "We have a little private cottage which we welcome you to stay in any time after the tenth of May….It would be good for a second honeymoon. Let me know when you are coming."

Ansel met us at the Merced railroad station, the closest to Yosemite. We joyfully embraced and fairly danced to the nearest bar. It was mid-afternoon. The young bartender said to Nancy, with a smile, "I can serve the lady." To Ansel he said, "I can serve the gentleman." And to me, in my uniform, he said with a grin, "But I can't serve the major." Just out of the army himself, he explained that servicemen could not drink publicly in California in wartime until six o'clock.

The eleven days in Yosemite were delightful and relaxing. We wound up our California visit in Carmel with Edward and Charis Weston. This was partly business, for Nancy was already selecting photographs for the 1946 retrospective exhibition at the Museum of Modern Art.

Since the war in Europe was over, when my "Rehabilitation, Recuperation, Recovery" duty was up, I was ordered to report to Army Air Force Redistribution Station No. 1 in Atlantic City for a new assignment. Just as I was wondering what lay ahead of me I received a telephone call from the Washington office of the Commanding General of the Army Air Force. The Assistant Chief of Air Staff-Intelligence, Major General E. R. Quesada, asked me if I knew anything about the production of maps on which were overprinted aerial photographs of potential targets. "Yes, sir," I replied, "I originated exactly this type of visual report in Italy." He then asked me to serve as Photo Interpretation Specialist with his Joint Target Group. I was assigned to that highly secret unit in July.

The general wanted target map-photos of Japanese railroads as soon as possible. Although headquarters regularly received aerial photographs from the Pacific, they had no photo interpreters to report on them—and I could not do the job alone. Fortunately we were able to obtain the services of half a dozen or so interpreters from the Royal Air Force.

There was a serious problem about printing the maps. In Italy we had a mobile photolithographic press in a trailer and could produce several maps a day. But in Washington the Army Air Force had no such press available. The only way we could get the desired map-photo reports printed was by a commercial press—and that took several days because, incredibly, each one had to be sent out to several presses for bids! So it was proposed that I train some interpreters, somehow find a mobile printing press, and set up a photo interpretation unit in Guam. I was not enthusiastic about this plan, but of course had to obey the general's order.

With the surrender of Japan on August 14, 1945, the proposed interpretation unit was never activated. There was no further need for photoreconnaissance, and although we dutifully reported to our office in the Pentagon, there was no work to be done. We wrote letters, read books, played cards, and otherwise killed time until our turns came for "relief from active duty."

On Thursday, September 20, 1945, upon arriving in the Pentagon I found on my desk a red-pencil note from a fellow officer. "Major Newhall: Go to the Adjutant General's Office, Room 2550, at one o'clock Thursday and you are as good as out of the Army." I was very pleased to receive, a few months later, a personal letter from General Quesada expressing his regret at my separation from the Army Air Force. "While assigned to the Joint Target Group as a Photo Interpretation Specialist on railroad and railway targets, you demonstrated great keenness, enthusiasm and cooperation in the fulfillment of your duties. Your civilian experience in the field of photography was of considerable value to the military organization in which you served. Upon separation from this organization you take with you my best wishes for the greatest possible success in your future."

❖

With Edward Weston,
Carmel, California, 1940.
Photograph by Nancy
Newhall. (Courtesy of
Scheinbaum & Russek Ltd.,
Santa Fe, New Mexico)

3

PORTENTS

By Edward Weston, 1940.
(©1981 Center for Creative
Photography, Arizona Board
of Regents)

THE PHOTOGRAPHY CENTER OF THE MUSEUM OF MODERN ART

During the years I was in uniform Nancy took my place at the Museum of Modern Art. To my surprise the trustees showed little interest in her appointment. The museum's executive director even said, "Let's not argue; take Nancy on till the end of the year and then end it." Fortunately James Soby and David McAlpin backed Nancy, and she was appointed assistant in charge of photographs, and later acting curator of photography. Under her leadership the department was greatly expanded and solidified within the organizational structure of the museum.

During her three-year tenure Nancy curated, almost single-handedly, fifteen major photographic exhibitions, increased the collection, and managed a short-lived and almost forgotten Photography Center. She accomplished this proud record because of her passion for photography and her capability as a curator, and not solely out of loyalty to me. Her voluminous correspondence chronicles the strange and little-known history of the museum's Department of Photography from the summer of 1942, when I joined the Army Air Force, until my return in 1945.

Nancy was greatly surprised to learn one day in April 1943 that the trustees, without consulting her, had offered the vacant position of director of photography to a good friend of ours, Willard D. Morgan, publisher of classic photographic manuals and editor of the colossal ten-volume, 3,600-page encyclopedia *The Complete Photographer*. "Herc"—as his wife and friends called him because of his Herculean stature of six feet seven inches—was not only a publisher, but also the organizer of photographic exhibitions. The most notable of these was the first exhibition of the work of the photographers of the government's Farm Security Administration, held in the Grand Central Palace in New York in 1938. Unfortunately, although he had published excellent books on the techniques of photography, he had no real understanding of the art of photography.

Nancy learned about the museum's offer from Herc himself over luncheon in the museum's penthouse restaurant. He told her, as she recollected, "Well, the museum has asked me if I'd consider being director of the Department of Photography, and I said I would if it was all right with you and Beau. He will continue as curator, of course, and you'd become acting curator in his absence. They're even talking about raising the pitiful sum they call your salary. Well, what about it? Maybe we can get the department on a good, strong financial footing by the time Beau gets back."

At first Nancy was shocked that she had not been consulted about the appointment of Morgan. She knew that Herc had little interest in art. But she also knew that he had energy, initiative, and executive experience. She wrote me while I was in Egypt: "I feel that the thing to do

Willard D. ("Herc") Morgan, 1949. Photograph by Beaumont Newhall. (Courtesy of Scheinbaum & Russek Ltd., Santa Fe, New Mexico)

is to incorporate Herc, expand the department and make it very powerful and independent. Herc and I want your opinion on what we are doing. Would you cable us how you feel?" I wired Nancy: "Expansion of department and appointment of Morgan have my approval. Love."

Another completely unexpected piece of news was that space had been allocated for a Photography Center in two adjoining mansions at 9 and 11 West Fifty-fourth Street, which the museum had leased as an annex from Philip Goodwin, a trustee, and his brother. The second floors of both buildings were joined together by a connecting doorway and turned over to the department. The largest room contained the photographic collection, a library of books on photography, and an "experimental gallery." The other rooms served as offices and a darkroom.

James Thrall Soby, a trustee, director of the Department of Painting and Sculpture, and acting chairman of the Department of Photography during David McAlpin's absence in the navy, wrote me on May 10, 1943: "The general idea is that the department will be greatly expanded, both in personnel, function, and place in the Museum's activities. I feel that the department, given this support and encouragement, can become a center for photography in this country and can rapidly become one of the most important and active departments in the Museum."

The new Photography Center opened on November 3, 1943. Nancy reported: It was a great success. Not only that, but the whole atmosphere was different from Museum openings. It was warm with hope and attention and enthusiasm— and absolutely jammed—with photographers, members, everybody. The place looked lovely—no light except on the photographs—brilliant white walls leading you close to see. There were more of our friends per square inch than you can imagine, and everybody said, "If only Beau were here! Wouldn't he be proud and happy!" The whole thing surprised the Museum—they had expected a crowd— but not this kind of crowd.

Shortly after receiving this jubilant letter, I was shocked and deeply saddened at the unbelievable news from Nancy that Alfred Barr had been terminated as director of the museum. Stephen Clark, the chairman of the board, had in October 1943 abruptly and rudely demoted Alfred to the position of advisory director at half pay and with the assignment to write a definitive book on Pablo Picasso and a popular guide to the appreciation of modern painting. He was stripped of all executive authority and curatorial responsibilities. Even the use of his own office was denied him. Instead, one-third of the already much too crowded reading room of the museum's library was blocked off with a partition wall to serve as his study.

It was hard for me to believe that the trustees should have approved of this summary demotion of the brilliant founding director who had conceived, planned, organized, and installed the astounding exhibitions that had already made the museum internationally famous. Nancy called a meeting of what she referred to as "the old guard" to protest this action. Only a few came: Soby; Dorothy Miller, curator of painting and sculpture; and Dorothy Dudley, the registrar. The

Photography Center Print Room, Library, and Experimental Gallery, The Museum of Modern Art, 1944. Photographer unknown.

"I love the place. It isn't perfect for what we want—a highly imperfect darkroom in a shoestring-shape pantry & so on, but the space & the quiet & now the color, in rugs & chairs & walls, are lovely. And people seem to like it too. Wait till we really begin to operate. The books are now on shelves each side of the Print Room fireplace; one of our big low tables with collapsible legs has arrived. The little Artek chairs look like black and white butterflies—especially against the sea blue wall" (Nancy Newhall to Beaumont Newhall, October 17, 1943).

attempt to reestablish Alfred's position came to nothing. Nancy wrote me, "Alfred asks only that all of us continue to do our utmost to forget him." With his dedication and determination Alfred stayed on, writing in a corner of the library and offering advice and counsel to those staff members who sought him out. The situation was somewhat ameliorated in 1944 when it was announced that Alfred had been appointed director of research in painting and sculpture.

In 1947 Alfred was appointed director of collections, and remained connected to the museum until the 1960s. It is largely his great knowledge of modern art, his impeccable taste, his persuasiveness, and his constant enthusiasm to which the permanent collection of the Museum of Modern Art owes its distinction.

It was mystifying that the trustees announced that no one was to be appointed to fill Alfred's place as director. In a half-page article headed "Museum without a Director" in the *New York Times* for January 30, 1944, art critic Edward Alden Jewell explained that the governing of the museum's artistic activities was in the hands of departmental committees responsible to the executive committee, while the administrative side was under the jurisdiction of the executive vice president, Dick Abbott, who was also director of the Film Library. He was, in Mr. Jewell's opinion, "the chief administrator" of the museum. Nancy had a difficult time. She wrote me on February 4, 1944, "Lacking Alfred, I have nobody I can turn to in the Museum. Jim [Soby] doesn't seem to be worth much. To hell with it! I'm getting blue again, and having to remind myself that what I stand for (you, Stieglitz, and creative photography) is more important than my temporary stymies—and that without it the Center, which is becoming the gleam of light for all photography, may miss and go out, and what we want to do will be harder than if I stick it out and overcome the obstacles."

"The American Snapshot," an exhibition curated by Willard Morgan, opened in the museum's main building on March 1, 1944. It featured photographs from a collection culled from the Eastman Kodak Company's photofinishing plant by one Wyatt Brummit. The idea, of course, was to show the "folk art" of untutored users of the simplest of cameras. I felt this was also an attempt to "popularize" photography at the museum, to widen the audience by appealing to the millions of amateur photographers, and at the same time to bring in financial support from the commercial sector. Nancy described it:

> A lively, sentimental show, corny, full of babies and puppies—with perhaps twenty good pictures in its approximately four hundred. It's queer, but I don't think the Museum realizes that the fight is not for photography but for *good* photography. The American public loves corn, would be delighted if the Museum showed Norman Rockwell and Howard Chandler Christy and the Petty girls. Is Willard's formula the right one?—corn and good stuff, like *U.S. Camera*—but never with passion, with an edge, with a trumpet call? Is the past—beyond the last fifteen years—dead or obsolete? I say he's utterly wrong—Jim [Soby] knows it, so do the old guard. And yet—there were possibilities in the snapshot idea. At times I get very depressed, then I grin at the mess, then I get my fighting courage up and always behave as if carrying on endlessly. Don't be prejudiced by what I write, dar-

ling. If you were here you might feel differently. At any rate, if Herc is called in to use his talents and experience in promoting the department, I suppose he must promote.

The exhibition, unfortunately, was not a success and injured the department's reputation for maintaining the highest standards. The mistake had been in allowing Kodak to select the pictures; had Nancy been allowed to make the selection, a wonderful show could have resulted. But Morgan didn't see fascinating pictures, he saw only popular pictures. Both the staff and the trustees were shocked at what they considered the poor taste, and although Eastman Kodak covered all expenses, it was not moved to make any further financial contributions to the photographic activities of the museum. Shortly after the show closed, Herc Morgan accepted a job at *Look* magazine. But he remained a part-time administrative consultant on a retainer. "The new arrangement with Herc works very well so far," Nancy explained. "He comes in about 5 and we spend half an hour or so together. I'm the responsible head of the department, expected to consult with Herc on directional and administrative problems. It suits me to have Herc's solid sense and strength and experience when I need them."

D-DAY LETTER   Nancy wrote me the following letter about D-Day, June 6, 1944. Ansel and I went to see Stieglitz, Ansel nearly impaling the crowds on that Museum tripod and me with your Egyptian photographs under my arm. Stieglitz and Dorothy were sitting on the couch together, in the deepest gloom. I said hello and backed out again, while Ansel set up tripod and camera. They came after me, and things began slowly cheering up. Stieglitz felt your photographs. He greeted a number with "very good!" and said they had "lovely feeling." The one he liked best

Alfred Stieglitz and Nancy, An American Place, New York City, 1944. Photograph by Ansel Adams. (© 1992 by the Trustees of The Ansel Adams Publishing Rights Trust. All rights reserved.)

was the dark little tree in the curl of a huge shouldering dune [page 81]. (Ansel was very moved by them. So was Paul [Strand], who came in late in the afternoon.) Then I gave Stieglitz your May 26 letter to read—the lovely one telling of perfection, of expression in museums and history. Stieglitz kept being moved by it to expound on your utter correctness. He said the letter had the purity of an O'Keeffe—and felt it was itself a photograph, showing an even greater development than the photos themselves, made, in some cases, about a year ago. Ansel photographed like mad. Got at least one beauty, which I saw through the ground glass, of Stieglitz and the O'Keeffe [sketch] he loves best. He took some of Stieglitz and me for you....[After dinner] Ansel and I drifted into St. Pat's, which was still open and crowded. Masses of votive candles burning. We lighted some too. I don't know that the prayers and candles do any good, but we felt better.[25]

Here is the letter Nancy read to Stieglitz.

25. Nancy Newhall to Beaumont Newhall, June 7, 1944.

I am proud of the feeling which you have given the show, and if it will seem too precious, too prejudiced, too arty by the general public, to those whose judgments we have come to respect it will be recognized as sincere, and as right—in the sense that a beautifully played Bach partita is right. The show, and what you have told me of the ideas of [publisher Alfred] Boni and [Edward] Epstean, and the career of Herc, all point up to a study of success versus perfection. The two do not seem to go together. The fight for the attainment of perfection—or to attain the foothills, even of the peak—cannot be waged while compromising. Success, on the other hand, demands a loosening of standards, a catholic point of view, a willingness to submerge one's own philosophy in that of the mass. Herc, blessed with a warm and generous heart, a true and loyal friend, against whom I shall never talk, does not fully grasp the challenge of perfection that has become our guide. He would rather please everybody than go all out for the best. I tend more and more to feel that we should not try to please, not even attract, the masses, but create opportunities for everyone who believes in us, and to push those who carry our thoughts furthest. I would continue to champion Edward, Ansel, Porter, Walker. would willingly accept their equals or even their potential equals. But I would begrudge any space, time and effort that might be given to, say, Fritz Henle or to Sarra. I even wonder if we should attempt to create a museum of photography, if, under the tremendous mass of material the artistic, creative, use of photography might be swamped, and actually harmed. I mean to say that to credit good photos like the LeConte negatives that Ansel printed seems of questionable value. They are good...but so what? They don't say anything. Curious that I should talk down a museum, talk down history. But it is not talking down, it is rather a matter of relativity. The creative side, the production side, seems to me so overwhelmingly important. I want to see a Center that will go far, far beyond the passive Museum, which will be for the creative workers....I write this fully realizing that it is contrary to my ambition to write the definitive history of photography. That now seems to me a last hangover of my art history pedantism. I have delved far enough into the obscure past: the masses of unimportant and mediocre photographs that would have to be unearthed and appraised frightens me. What did Jackson, for all his charm, contribute to the world reservoir of art? Emerson stands head and shoulders above him—so do a hundred workers whose interest was emotional, not factual.

Stieglitz stands out more boldly than ever: *Camera Work* seems of vital importance. Tradition, yes; pedantic history, no. Roger Fry saw the rich past of painting as a challenge and a tradition; [Harvard professor] Chandler Post sees the past of Spanish art as an immense pile of unsorted material to be arranged and put into order—for nobody's use.

So, dearest, keep on the path that leads to perfection, even though the criticism and obstacles you meet will hurt and discourage you. It is the right path for us to take. Keep on until I can join you.

"ART IN PROGRESS"   In 1944, to celebrate its fifteenth anniversary, the museum filled its galleries with a mammoth exhibition, "Art in Progress," which opened May 23 and consisted of eleven separate shows, one for each department. Nancy selected 247 photographs ranging from the very beginnings of the medium to the present. To judge from the catalog, this historical retrospective was most extraordinary. It included calotypes taken in Scotland in the 1840s by David Octavius Hill and his associate Robert Adamson, portraits by Julia Margaret Cameron, landscapes of the American Southwest by Timothy H. O'Sullivan, a selection of animal locomotion studies by Eadweard Muybridge, exquisite platinum prints by Peter Henry Emerson of the English countryside, and other classic photographs of the nineteenth century. Of the more modern photographers, Nancy showed twenty prints by Alfred Stieglitz, twenty-six by Edward Weston, sixteen by Ansel Adams, and two or three prints by other contemporaries. A total of sixty-one photographers were represented. Nancy wrote in the catalog introduction:

This, the first full-scale exhibition drawn mostly from the Museum's collection of photographs, is presented to demonstrate how vitally the collection serves in stimulating creative photography.

For the Photography Center, which is in essence an experimental laboratory for contemporary photography, the collection is the most dynamic part of working equipment. To every individual who comes to the Center, whether with a vague, undefined hunger to know or with a particular problem, the tangible and satisfying answer lies in actual photographs. Many who come here have never held in their hands fine original prints and so seen for themselves the subtleties which add immeasurably to the photographer's impact

Photography Collection exhibition, The Museum of Modern Art, 1944. Photograph by Nancy Newhall. (Courtesy of Scheinbaum & Russek Ltd., Santa Fe, New Mexico)

but which are almost always lost in reproductions. Many, too, have been completely misled as to the living issues of photography. The collection must, therefore, provide answers to their questions, challenges to their misconceptions, inspirations for their future growth. Often the spark which releases in the questioner new sources of power to appreciate or to realize his own purposes comes from work he has never really seen and it may spring as readily from prints a century old as from the pioneering ventures made yesterday by his contemporaries.

I was amazed that almost all of the photographs in this exhibition were from the museum's own collection. To think that only seven years earlier the prints in my "Photography 1839–1937" show were all loans! Nancy wrote me that she was

> …very surprised and pleased at the number of people of all ranks on the staff who wander through the show, so far as it is hung, again and again; from all sides I hear that it's beautiful and that there are outstanding things in it. My—unuttered— answer is that it ought to be beautiful and astonishing; some of the greatest pictures in the world are gathered cheek by jowl. I don't say it, because I think they're getting from it by themselves a little of what we've been trying to tell them for years. These are beautiful prints, made with love and selected with love, and exhibited with all the love and care I could squeeze through a wartime world. And to anyone with an ounce of feeling for quality it should be worth more than all the spectacular idea-shows ever inflicted. If it fails, it can only be my fault. Not many

people have had the privilege of such rich material to work with in photography. And the quality is unencumbered by historical accuracy or representation. But that so many people should feel the quality in a show not yet finished tickles me![26]

26. Nancy Newhall to Beaumont Newhall, May 31, 1944.

The museum's chairman of the board, Stephen Clark, wrote Nancy: "The photography section of 'Art in Progress' does honor to the Department. It is well thought out and excellently installed. On behalf of the trustees I wish to express our appreciation and to thank you." And David McAlpin wrote Nancy, "Heartfelt congratulations. The Exhibition is swell. I enjoyed it enormously and was stirred with the way you made it come to life. It should have an important effect in many directions—a great deal has been accomplished when you think back to the introductory show!"

In midsummer of 1944 the Department of Photography had to vacate the Fifty-fourth Street houses because they were being sold by the Goodwin brothers. The trustees proposed to rent a store on Fifth Avenue for the Center, and Nancy was working on plans for the alteration of the interior to accommodate a gallery, a library, a small auditorium, and offices, when suddenly the trustees ordered the department to return to its former quarters adjacent to the library in the main building. The move was accompanied by the reduction of the staff to Nancy alone, and the elimination of the Photography Center. This news was most disturbing. The Center had become a highly successful adjunct of the museum during its eight-month existence (November 3, 1943, to June 29, 1944). I was surprised and dismayed to receive from our trustee and friend James Soby, who had so enthusiastically praised the Photography Center, a rather curious letter dated August 2 in which he writes:

> I think that the reduction in size of the Department was the only possible solution. Perfectly frankly I think if we had gone on with the Center, we would have come more and more to depend on Camera Clubs, the photographic industry, and so forth....I would like to say again that I think Nancy has done a fine job. The Photo section of the Fifteenth Anniversary show has been greatly admired and I think will do more to interest and improve good photographers than any amount of pandering to popular taste.

The trustees felt that, after what they considered the fiasco of "The American Snapshot" exhibition, any further attempts to attract contributions from the photographic industry would result in compromise and the lowering of standards. Why they thought that the only source of subsidy was from the manufacturers of cameras and photographic materials rather than from educational foundations, I do not know.

The executive committee decided that the search for a director of photography to succeed Willard Morgan should be held in abeyance. Meanwhile the trustees formed a new Advisory Committee on Photography, with an unusually large membership of thirty, consisting of staff members, photographers, collectors, historians, scientists, librarians, and curators. There were as many laymen as photographers. The officers were Roy Stryker, chairman; David McAlpin, honorary chairman; and Ansel Adams, vice chairman.

John Vachon, Arthur Rothstein, Russell Lee, and Roy Stryker (*left to right*) reviewing photographs in the FSA-OWI Collection at the FSA Historical Section, c. 1938. Photograph by Beaumont Newhall. (Courtesy of Scheinbaum & Russek Ltd., Santa Fe, New Mexico)

Nancy and I both knew Stryker well, as the former chief of the photographic team of the U.S. Department of Agriculture's Farm Security Administration (FSA). He was a brilliant picture editor and director of photographers, but he knew little about and cared less for photography as an art. At the first meeting of the newly formed committee, held on November 16, 1944, Dick Abbott explained that each of the museum's curatorial departments had an advisory committee, the purpose of which was "to give advice and criticism, suggest ideas and projects, and generally supply a broader view than can be maintained by the head of the department alone." He followed this definition of purpose with the warning that "the Committee has no administrative power," and stated that "if an Advisory Committee strongly recommends a project, and the trustees decide against it, the trustees' decision is final. If the trustees decide in favor of a project of which the Advisory Committee strongly disapproves, the trustees' decision again is final."[27] I wondered what the use was of such a powerless committee, one so large that the chairman appointed subcommittees.

27. Minutes of the November 16, 1944, meeting of the Advisory Committee on the Department of Photography.

While I was in the headquarters of the Fifteenth Air Force in Italy, I received a copy of the "Report of the Subcommittee on Policy and Programs," with a request to comment on it. I found the report in general very positive. It stated that the purpose of the Department of Photography "shall be to encourage, develop and integrate photographic expression, use and appreciation" and thus to "reach a broad democratic audience, as well as specialized groups." It went on to state that "the main emphasis should be on living photography." With these goals I was in agreement. But I found the statement that "the Department shall take suitable steps to encourage the widest use and development of photography" far too broad. Such a directive could certainly be recommended for a museum of photography, but it seemed to me inapplicable to a museum of art. I wrote the committee on February 15, 1945:

This report is in accord with my view on what the Department should accomplish, with one exception, which I wish to draw to your attention for possible further discussion and consideration. I found it somewhat surprising that, except for the single word "expression" in the first paragraph, there is no clear-cut statement of what I have always considered the Department's main purpose: the encouragement of photography as an art.

I have always thought of the Department as a place where creative photography can be seen apart from the bewildering confusion of the great bulk of applied photography. A place where the sincere worker can discover the traditions of photography done with the indefinable spirit that distinguishes a work of art from a pedestrian technical accomplishment. A place where photographs can be judged, not as illustrations, but as statements of an individual's vision. Would it not be wise to incorporate in our "platform" a strong statement of our primarily esthetic interest in photography?

Nancy wrote me that when my letter was read to the committee, "Roy Stryker said—unofficially—that in his opinion the Department would die and remain dead until the point of view expressed in [Beaumont's letter] was extinguished."

LETTERS DURING THE WAR

BN to NN
November 2, 1943

It is inevitable that we will be branded for the rest of our lives as "purists" now, with other names later on, because we cannot help viewing photography in a very special way. A comparison with music will make my meaning clear. Music is a great—probably the greatest—popular art. Some never get beyond the appreciation of song-and-dance hits. Others find the "light classics" satisfying. From that point we progress to symphonic music, and finally we end with chamber music. The number of devotees diminishes in each category, and the majority call the minority "purist," using the word "highbrow" or "long-haired." I think that we are in the symphonic and chamber music group, and that Herc is in the light classic and symphonic. It takes some time to find what there is in chamber music that makes its devotees find in it the greatest musical expression of Western man. Once one has found it, it is difficult to judge impartially other less satisfying forms of music. This does not mean that one looks down one's nose at less exalted music, or that one condemns it, or that one wishes to have nothing but chamber music played. But one naturally turns to the string quartet at every opportunity, one spontaneously praises it, and one does all one can to promote concerts and to encourage opportunities to hear the great works of Beethoven, Mozart, Bach, et al. It is not a question of which is better—it is rather a question of feeling so strongly about a thing that it is apparent where one's taste lies.

It is possible for one to accept an enormous number of conflicting and differing points of view intellectually. It is not possible to do so emotionally—not really. Everybody, it seems to me, reacts both intellectually and emotionally. Our problem—the problem of all those who are critics and historians as well as creators—is to keep a balance between the mind and the heart. The mind alone produces sterile Fogg Museum art archivists who know everything about art but don't know what they like. I've been of that number. My release dates from the time I first met you, when a totally new way of looking at art was shown me. You, my dearest, have tended to put too much emphasis on the heart. But you have been balancing that with the intellectual all the time that I have been becoming aware that without feeling art is nothing....

To you and to me there is one type of photography which we feel to be the greatest creative use of the medium, which we consider belongs right beside Rembrandt etchings. Let us not lose this conviction. Let us strive to foster the production of more of that photography, let us make it available to those who want to see it, and let us introduce it to those who will enjoy—enable them, that is, to discover it. This is something that we have a compulsion to do, and I think that it is pretty much our most important responsibility.

But in so doing we will not be intolerant of other types of photography, providing that it is honest and sincere. We'll see that it has every chance of being fostered, that it has a fair chance. Our enthusiasm, our deep-seated belief in Stieglitz's work we cannot, we will not hide, and we are bound to be, because of this, considered either a follower or a worshipper or a defender depending on how our critics feel about Stieglitz. It doesn't matter as long as we are big enough—as Stieglitz is—to admit other points of view, and not only admit them but work for them, hard and with all the conviction that we honestly can.

Do not worry or be disappointed if, in the course of your work at the Center, many of our pet ideas and plans are carried out by others. Give all you can to see that they come as close to perfection as possible. As the Center grows, more and more people are going to consider photography in a new light, and they will be bound to stumble on a lot of our ideas. There is so much to be done that we will always have plenty of scope....Think of the wealth of material to be worked over!

❖

BN to NN
November 15, 1943

If, at this moment, the Museum should disintegrate, and all the work that you and I have done there should disappear, it would be worth what we have put in. For we have started something that is greater than the Museum, greater than any museum or institution. Or rather let me say that we are carrying on a greater thing, for it is not for us to claim the credit of originating, not so long as we believe and respect Stieglitz. Through the Museum we have been enabled to act, and that is what a museum is for. It is not we, however, that owe a debt to the Museum; it is the Museum that is indebted to us. Remember that. I did not value enough my contribution; now I see things in a better perspective....I want you to feel that what you are doing now is not for the Museum, is not to bring in more people, more publicity, some money. It is serving a cause in which we believe, and it is a preparation for something—what I do not know—which will be more solid, more fundamental, more real than the Museum can offer. Something founded on a belief in photography as the most exciting and the most expressive art of our time, as something which is not "sold" through publicity and cheap tricks...but something which is sought for, and which it is our privilege to conserve and foster. A kind of place the success of which will not be measured by the number of people who are cajoled to pass through a turnstile, but by the creative effort which it stimulates, encourages, and gives a home to. Something which is more concerned with living artists than with the fashionables. What a start we've made!...Darling, I know that we are the most genuinely creative people of the Museum! And, what is more, the photographers realize it. And Stieglitz.

So the mad (and mostly needlessly so) hectic Museum life is worth the effort, the patience, and the loyalty we put into it. But it is not the final goal, which we will find together. We can't tell how at this time. But we both know that we will.

BN to NN
December 6, 1943

I can tell from the photos alone that the spirit of the Center is one of friendly welcome, of encouragement, of optimism. The Center is not a place where a visitor will feel ashamed to ask questions, where he may be subjected to a needlessly embarrassing tongue-lashing because he is perhaps ignorant or affected. It is not a place where the welcome comes only after a visitor's worth has been proven. You've been spared much of Stieglitz's sarcasm and bitterness. For years I actually dreaded to go into The Place, for I never knew what kind of whipping boy I might be used for. One of the first times I went in, all eager and trembling with excitement at the New York series (it was 1933 I think), I didn't know Stieglitz then and he didn't know me. He was talking about his things, and Hardinge Scholle [director of the Museum of the City of New York] was there. Hardinge, in all sincerity, said to Stieglitz that the photos were the photos of New York, and he wanted them for the Museum of the City of New York. Stieglitz laughed at him—misinterpreted Hardinge's way of saying that they were swell as a demand for a gift. Then I had to sound off by asking just the wrong question—had he used panchromatic film? I know now—and it has taken me 15 years to know—that it doesn't matter a damn what Stieglitz or any other artist uses—but at that time I was trying to find out what was what. Of course Stieglitz picked up that innocent question and neatly and sarcastically let it be known that it was a damn fool question. I was badly hurt by that episode, and for years couldn't see anything in Stieglitz's work, though up to then I had reacted strongly to what little I had seen —"spiritual America" in 1926 or '27, one of the O'Keeffe hands, and a few others.

❖

BN to NN

December 9, 1943

I've just written Alfred [Barr]. I've tried to tell him how much he has meant to us, and how the Museum and he have been inseparably connected in our minds.... Looking back over the eight years that have passed since I first checked in at the Museum has been reviewing the richest years of my life—my most creative and my happiest. The Museum job brought about our marriage (it would have come about, of course, somehow—but the Museum job was the immediate means), it made possible my excursion into photography and the development of the department up to its present amazing position. It is still incredible that there is a Photography Center! Without Alfred's encouragement and help I might very well have remained a librarian—where I was happy and content but not really giving my talents a chance....Alfred played a vital role in my life. To him I owe a great debt. He helped me to find myself. My respect for him is even greater now that I can no longer share many of his convictions. If he had been the kind that tried to force his taste upon his subordinates, instead of giving them an almost too free hand, I would never have developed beyond being a "Museum worker." I admire Alfred's taste for surrealism just as he respects mine for photography—neither of us seems able to understand the other's mania, but we respect it.

Since the extraordinary adventure of the request for the frontispiece to the second edition of *Photography 1839–1937* I have come to see a different Stieglitz, the Stieglitz you know and whom we love. We know now why he is forced to take the attitude he does toward people who ask him questions that seem foolish—why he is forced to test the worth of every new contact.

❖

BN to NN

December 14, 1943

I had rather anticipated that the meeting of the "Old Guard" would offer little hope of reinstating Alfred. It's too late—not by months but by years. He lost control during the '39 purge....The Museum became no longer his, but the trustees'....It's all bound up with the growth of the Museum from a small group of enthusiastic young people making a place for modern art to be shown and defended into a sprawling decentralized group of unrelated departments, of which the original Museum (the "Old Guard") is one only. I think that Alfred could have kept the rein in his hands at the time of the move into the new building, that he could have remained the C.O. But alas, he didn't, and it's too late now. All we can do is to keep the Department clean and above reproach—no, we could pitch in and perhaps do something about the Museum as a whole, but that would not be possible without making a full-time job of it, to the detriment and possible abandonment of our work with photography, which I believe to be more important than the Museum. Let us profit from what we have observed. Let us keep the Photo Center small in size and in scope. The Museum grew too fast, it became top heavy and unwieldy—yes, unmanageable. Let us not be too ambitious—keep the standards very high—not make the collection the biggest, but the best—our activities outstanding.

❖

BN to NN
December 16, 1943

Bruce Downes's article "Wanted: Critics for Photography" in the October issue of *Popular Photography* impressed me very much. Look it up, I think that you'll agree with me. Downes makes a case for adult artistic criticism of photography. He rightly complains that the present critics "may be masters of the tools of art, but of art itself, its magic and beauty, its profound eloquence, the deep and wondrous things it is capable of whispering or singing or saying, these gentlemen of the juries and photographic pulpits know almost nothing." This is so well put, that I think that Downes feels something the way we do about photography. "When the great critics arrive they will open our eyes to the great photographs, show us the magnificent vistas, the quick transcendent insights, the transforming vision of the creative artist in work that we may have overlooked in our intense preoccupation with technical procedures. The great pictures will prove by turns embarrassing to pictorialist and documentarian alike, for the greatness lies in the vision and insight of the man who made the pictures and who was able to get these intangible qualities into his final print, not in the technical methods used....Photography is a living, vital, modern art, on the threshold of a glorious future. What it needs more than anything else at this moment are mature men to sound the critical clarions." Brave words! And what else is the Photo Center for?

❖

BN to NN
January 21, 1944

I do not feel that Herc will ever feel for photography as do you and I. Few people will. And we must face that fact or else we shall be hurt more than is necessary. Our way is not the popular way. We may and can play an important part in fostering the appreciation of photography. But our quest for perfection, our passion for the expression of feeling in a photograph, are things that in general will be no more appreciated than the great chamber music performers. Therefore a lot of our work will not be appreciated and it may be opposed—not maliciously, but quite unknowingly. And this involuntary opposition is bound to hurt us and to discourage us. But if we do not face it we won't be able to say a thing, for we will be shut up in an ivory tower, and respect for us will be lost. Thus Herc: working loyally, willingly, helpfully. To our eyes blundering at times, and trampling down our carefully nurtured perfect plants which he doesn't even imagine to be growing beneath his feet.

❖

BN to NN

January 27, 1944

[re news of Paul Strand's move to Hollywood]

It must be an almost irresistible temptation to accept the fantastic salaries and promises that are offered. The economic problems of the creative photographer are horrible to contemplate. There seems to be no way for an artist photographer (as opposed to an illustration photographer) to earn a decent salary. Think of Edward selling his stuff for less than the Greenwich Village sidewalk painter! Ansel confused so between pictures for sale and pictures made because he has to. Alas, photography is not recognized yet—only partly—intellectually, but not from the pocketbook. The Guggenheim [Fellowship] is only a partial answer, even were it multiplied a hundredfold—it still is charity, still grudgingly admitting photography in the company of painting, poetry, and pure science. Few have Edward's strength of character to live on nothing in order to be free to create only as he feels is right; for that unusual feat he deserves much credit. One patron alone will not suffice; the Art Center could not answer the problem for more than a few. We must somehow fasten the full financial appreciation of photography, so that a man who creates a score of good photographs a year will have earned enough to live on in reasonable comfort and security....Ansel's letter was fine. I was relieved that it did not contain the complicated, involved arguments of technique that his earlier letters contained, written when he was unhappy at the Art Center School. His simple, clean statement, written in wonderment, of the essence of art was good to read. Of course, Ansel, all that matters in art "is what happens inside of us." And that is why the Stieglitz poplar tree sequence is so great. For all his worship of the man, Ansel never got hold of the heart of Stieglitz's work. A letter like that, without a word of print quality, is good to read.

❖

BN to NN

February 24, 1944

I am amazed at the success of the Center. 140 visitors in one afternoon! It is phenomenal! I do not wonder that you are tired out at the end of such a day, for I know how exhausting and tiring it can be to impart to people one's enthusiasms and to help them really to see....It is inspiring to me that the Center is used, and is appreciated by people, for that is what it is meant for. You are giving people more than any other department of the Museum, for you have the correct formula: informal atmosphere, opportunities to be taken advantage of, and no didactic shouting of principles from the lecture platform or from wordy labels. It is to me immensely gratifying, worth the effort, the compromises that trouble us with the Museum.

The Pictorialist show is a good idea. I'm glad you're doing it, but I do not think that it will make the Pictorialists any less disturbed or that it will help them to see our point of view, because the pictures are not contemporary. They are what the Pictorialists are the epigones of, what they are the decadent followers of. Strong words but, alas, true ones. In Pictorialism they found the formula, and they have not added one iota to it. Not a thing has come out of the organized Pictorial movement since Stieglitz and [Clarence] White made their experiments. Something happened, and it was during the last war. Stieglitz and O'Keeffe, Steichen and his tea cups, Coburn and his vortographs [see p. 212]—a change of attitude, of heart and of technique. I am not wise enough to say what it was that made the leaders break away from group participation and become lone wolves; I can only observe the singular fact that there has been no organization of top notch creative photographers since the Photo-Secession. (No, the Photo League, praise worthy as it was—or is?—cannot be pointed to as an exception, for they are immature and confused between documentation and photography.)…After all the creators got out, nothing was left but the followers, and they have gone on repeating the formula. They couldn't clothe it with flesh and blood and life—all they could do was to retain what was charming, beautiful in an obvious way.…

I got into hot water with the Pictorial Photographers of America years ago, and I have myself largely to blame for creating the distinction in their minds between Pictorial and modern. It was all quite innocent—Ira [Martin] asked me to judge the show, I said I couldn't in fairness to the PPA condemn, as I would have to, the bulk of their work, and so he proposed that the salon be divided into Pictorial and Modern. Let the photographers submit as they saw fit, he said. And I wrote a statement for the entry blanks, describing my point of view. And someone wrote a description of the Pictorial viewpoint. They were identical, so later on Edward (or rather Charis in his name) wrote "I am a pictorialist" and proved it by quoting from that catalog.

What ails the PPA is, after all, a very simple thing. Their members are not creative. And I don't know if there's much that can be done beyond encouraging any signs of individual creativeness.…The majority will be disappointed and left out in the cold. We can't help it for, alas, there can be no democracy in quality.…It is strange how apt musical similes are in photography.…Everyone knows that, from the thousands who play musical instruments only hundreds will be worthy of public recital; of these those who can be called creative will number not more than ten. Yet thousands get fun and pleasure from their own practice, and they become infinitely more appreciative of the few creative ones than the layman.

❖

It is perhaps dangerous for me to give specific advice from this distance about the Museum. I have a pretty clear picture, I think, of what is going on. The general Museum policy I cannot agree with, and I do not like it....Actually, and this seems to me the root of the trouble, there is not one person in the Museum who understands what we are about. The Museum seems to have become a game of attracting people through the turnstiles—as long as a byproduct of the Photo Center is an increase in membership and attendance, we will be favored with the approval of our shows. I wrote "byproduct" because, encouraging as the attendance at the Photo Center may be, it is not the number of people who have visited it that counts, it is how much have the visitors gained? If we can encourage a dozen, or even half a dozen sincere workers to creative effort, if we can lead from the muddles of confused thought a score of photo critics and patrons, we shall have done a year's work. There will be no way to tell others what we have done. We shall know in our hearts, but we cannot prove, which is most important—that 15,000 people saw a show in, say, 1941, or that Wright Morris won a Guggenheim because my criticism so jolted him and stimulated him to push his work farther than imitating Walker? Or that [Arnold] Newman has developed? Or that Walter Scott Shin was fired with the desire to collect daguerreotypes? These are personal facts, not appropriate for annual reports—perhaps forgotten by the people concerned. But no matter. You know, I know, Stieglitz knows, Dave [McAlpin] knows, Dick [Abbott] knows not at all, that what we've done has changed the photographic scene, not radically, but naturally.

The question is if we can continue to influence American photography through the Museum. I believe that we can, as you have demonstrated. We can't do as much as we should like, but we can do a lot, by personal contact with workers, by quality exhibitions, by purchases. I don't like to compromise, and the setup is not ideal. But we cannot do otherwise now. Later on, perhaps, but this is not the time, even were I working with you....There will be times when the negative side of the picture will seem to outweigh the positive, and you will be discouraged. Look, if you can, in those moments at what we have done in seven years, how we have reached out into the whole world of the real photographic artists, have made friends of them, have their trust and respect. Think of what we have meant, in human terms alone, to Ylla and [Philippe] Halsman, to Helen Levitt, to Bill Vandivert, to [Eliot] Elisofon, to Wright, yes and to Stieglitz, for who else but us has even attempted to carry on his grand tradition of informal master, critic, and inspiration? We have managed through the Museum despite handicaps of the most troublesome kind.

❖

BN to NN
March 12, 1944

[on an article by Bruce Downes, "The Museum of Modern Art's Photography Center," *Popular Photography*, February 1944, p. 85]

I'm disappointed that Downes did not realize that we are attempting to forge those very critical standards which he wrote about in "Wanted: Critics for Photography." It makes me realize all the more how important our work is—how what you and I have learned from Stieglitz must be pushed on to fuller understanding. We cannot afford to lower our standards, we cannot afford to compromise—else there is no purpose in the Center. It should be difficult to have a photograph accepted for exhibition or purchase, and it should be an honor to be represented in the Museum. On the other hand it should be easy to submit work for criticism, it should be pleasant and easy to visit the collection. Every chance should be given to the aspiring creative worker, but neither a false sentiment of democracy nor politics should force us to break down our standards—any more than we would expect the Department of Painting to give as much exhibition space to the Greenwich Village artist as to Picasso. I am proud that the people whose work we have most often shown are the best photographers in the world....If the Museum's work in photography under my direction was snobbish, it was snobbish in the sense that chamber music, poetry, and great literature is snobbish compared to the sweet symphonic jazz of Tommy Dorsey, to the jingle of popular poetasters, or to the adventure stories of a Street & Smith pulp magazine. But you know all this. I am thankful that you are there, carrying out our plans, guarding our interests.

❖

BN to NN
March 17, 1944

The fight must be eventually for good, for great photography. I do not believe that our weight can be felt and our message put across through popularizations, through sugar coating the pill with "corn" or "schmalz"—any more than I believe that the Philharmonic should pack its house by playing an arrangement of "Show Boat" in order that 2,000 people may be introduced to a Mozart concerto played at the same time. I keep feeling that the fault of my curatorship was in being too "broad-minded," i.e., too compromising. What does count is the work, as you've so well put it, "with passion, with an edge, with a trumpet call"....Yes, I can see the Snapshot show, and I can share your feelings. I could have had the Snapshot show—you probably know that Kodak asked us for space—but I couldn't bring myself to it. It was not to be controlled by the Museum, and hence was not considered by Alfred, who said that the Museum could not put up a show chosen by others....Either one maintains at any cost, like Stieglitz, a high standard, or one really goes out to meet the amateur. I did neither, and that was not good. I was criticized by Stieglitz and by Tom Maloney. Right now, when taking thought is the extent of my activity, the only road seems to be Stieglitz's one. But that is the most difficult road in the world....Dictation from rich outsiders—be they as close friends as Dave, as impersonal as the Rockefeller Foundation, as realistic as Eastman Kodak—will not allow us to do what we wish. Stieglitz has kept free by his titanic personality, forcing every donor to be grateful for the opportunity. In the complicated social network which supports the Museum the obligations to the supporters have gone too far to make possible the necessary break....In a very real sense, it is not possible to run the Center as we should like. On the other hand, it is not possible for you or for me to play the other game. I can't do it— you know that.

❖

NN to BN

June 4, 1944

It's really touching and flattering that Ansel seems to prefer to be with me, just as he loved living our quiet life two years ago. I think we really are his dearest friends, and even with just me instead of both of us, he gets a feeling of being sustained. He said the other day that the three of us could never really fight, however much we might disagree. There is still a warm flow nothing can interrupt. And so we have a swell time together, and he's being a very great help. He got a salutary shock and surprise the other night. Paul and Virginia [Strand] asked us down to dinner. Paul had asked that Ansel read the lecture he gave at the Museum, and Ansel and I had certain definite ideas about it which raised Paul from his usual apathy. We all had one of those rousing intellectual arguments in which everybody begs to be allowed the floor for "just one minute and then you can say what you like." Finally, Paul brought out his prints—and the Vermont series. Everybody was thunderstruck when it became apparent Ansel had never really seen Paul's work before—just a scattered few and the gravures. The print quality hit Ansel hard— especially when, scarcely six weeks before, he had been teaching Paul what to do to achieve superior results on present-day paper. The rich platinums were a revelation—and the new prints of the last one or three weeks were just as rich and subtle. Ansel felt he and Edward, Stieglitz were all overrated; Paul was the foremost. And the Vermont series *is* beautiful; Paul has really begun the photographing of New England. He hasn't finished it—it's just begun, but the six or eight best have that heartbreaking quality, that pure quality, the granite feeling. There's a little 4 x 5 portrait that is to my mind the best thing Paul has done—a lean, beautiful old Vermonter against weathered clapboards. The white stubble on his chin, the quiet wisdom of his dark eyes, the sumptuous dark tone of the print—it may still go no further than Stieglitz's girl in the hobnail shoes but it goes as far and as deep. Ansel was full of plans for a Strand show in San Francisco and soon. On the way home I attempted to focus his impressions, pointing out that with Stieglitz one never sees the print quality until the emotional impact is absorbed, and that both Stieglitz and I feel that Ansel himself has even more to say than Paul if he'll just get down to it. I didn't want to minimize Paul, who is a great artist. Ansel feels we should have a Strand show this year and a Weston next year, to keep chronology straight. I think he's right. Jim [Soby] agrees. Now, if we can win over the others. Herc has a prejudice against Paul because of his prices and "precious" feeling. I suggested Paul get Herc and Barb[ara Morgan] down there and show them his stuff. They both have real feeling and the Vermont series should reach them if it reached Ansel.

In every review [of the "Art in Progress" exhibition] there has been praise for photography. And, what pleases me more—is that it really helps: Sybil Freed said she's never clearly realized before that photography is a completely personal medium—Frank Vitello, Monroe [Wheeler]'s assistant who helped me install it, got that too—with the additional realization that blowups and reproductions are mere pastiche—totally lacking the impact of an original print. Ansel and I are going to photograph the show together, so this time you'll get a real impression of what it looks like. Another thing, I constantly see Dick [Abbott] and Monroe escorting visitors through the section. Oh darling, imperfect as the show is in many places, something of what we feel—the beauty, the passion, the edge—is getting across! May the conviction remain!—enough to make our task easier. I can forget now the doubts and slights and insults; people now are generous—Dearest, again and again and again, if only you were here!

…You know, as Dave suggested, I think it would be swell if we could make Ansel Field Representative or something—the rivalry you and he had is now, I think, extinct. He, like Stieglitz and Strand and Edward, is now loyal to *us*. In your absence your true stature is more visible than ever, and your unique qualities missed. And the photographers know we're doing a difficult and often amazing job because we love and believe in them and their work. They may disagree with us here and there, but I know they have confidence in us.

❖

BN to NN
July 15, 1944

Have you read Robert Hillyer's "First Principles of Verse"? I find the anatomy of poetry difficult to understand, but worth the effort of study….What he has to say about poetry in general makes me realize all the more that photography as we think of it, as Stieglitz thinks of it, is a form of poetry. "The true poetic temperament is that faculty which perceives the most ordinary events of life as something wonderful and interesting, the most ordinary objects of life as something beautiful or significant. Without for a moment losing sight of that existence which he shares with his kind, the poet will, at the same time, observe it with greater excitement than others and from a larger perspective. In like manner, he uses the same words as the rest of his race, but in rarer and more suggestive combinations."

Is not that a description of what we both feel? Is not photography to us a means of imparting our intense excitement and love for certain aspects of life? And is not the recognition of the miracle of the ordinary, the everyday, our passion? I remember once, years ago now, trying to put into words my growing feelings about photography. I tried to describe the act of photographing as directing vision to an aspect of life that might otherwise pass unnoticed. Ours is the antipode of spot news photography—we are not interested in the unusual, but in the usual seen unusually.

I wonder if there is such a difference between film and photography as we casually believe. Is not the difference perhaps more akin to the difference between sculpture and painting? Each has certain individual characteristics, but both have many points in common—so [the art historian] Wölfflin speaks of painterly sculpture and sculpturesque painting. The Bernini Theresa, that exquisite baroque sculpture, defies all that sculpture should be, and is a three-dimensional painting—Mantegna is two-dimensional sculpture! If I've made a case for the legitimacy of comparing the motion picture camera and the camera, then perhaps I may state the hypothesis that the keynote of both film and photography is directing of the vision. The film does this in the most obvious way, by the magnificent medium of cutting, by putting the spectator on a magic carpet....The cinematographer finds or makes things to be looked at—his art lies in forcing our vision—else the camera could automatically record whatever was interesting. It was found out very soon that the camera could not be passive, and the art of film was born.

Still photography, too, can direct our vision. Usually it does not, but gives us a haphazard record, a substitute for reality. True documentary photography is, after all, a substitute for the real thing. The next best thing to seeing you is to see a photograph of you. If you can't see the statues of Michelangelo, look at photos. There is no art here, only technical skill. But to see you as I remember you, I must have a photo taken by me, and so that charming Queen Mary photo has life that even the beautiful photo by [Lotte] Jacobi doesn't contain for me. Probably those who have seen the great Michelangelo sculptures a hundred times appreciate the Tel picture book photos more than the less fortunate art lover. They do not look at them as a stand-in for the originals—they see them as evidence of new, hidden aspects of Michelangelo's greatness. There's nothing to Strand's mining shack window—we don't want a house like that—we're not interested in the facts. But how wonderful it is to see beauty in what is superficially ugly! How rich nature is! Stieglitz's grass, seen as only Stieglitz can! And the supreme triumph of the interpretive over the documentary—the clouds. Look, says Stieglitz, look at the heavens! All of life is there, if you will but look! Look around you and marvel!

The painter cannot direct our vision in the same way. He creates his own world, if he is a genuine artist. His creation lives within the picture frame. Unless we accept his right, his duty, to create a world, we can never understand what he offers the world. His mission is entirely different from the photographer's. We cannot compare his work with nature. The old Whistler legend: Whistler, painting a sunset out of doors. A lady approaches, looks (perhaps with a half-heard clucking of dismay): "I never saw a sunset like that!" W.: "No? But don't you wish you could?" No approach to Picasso can be made without absolute confidence in his power to create worlds of abstract wonder.

But with Stieglitz, Strand, Weston, Ansel (at his peak), Helen Levitt, Cartier[-Bresson], the point is that anyone can see as they do—can physically, that is. One can at once recognize, and a terrific desire to look thusly at nature comes over me when I see a great photograph. Stieglitz's *Grape Leaves and House* (the frontispiece to the book), with that magic profile of a common, ordinary turned post, so vivid against the black—why a thousand times in a thousand places I've seen those turned posts! How many times have we seen ferry boats, but oh to get just that moment that Stieglitz got! So apparently easy, yet inimitable! "There is nothing here but what I see," the picture seems to say. That is the difference between an interpretive, a creative photo and a documentary photo. "I see a ferry boat crowded with people, snuggling into its slip, the eager, impatient commuters crowding the foredeck—isn't it wonderful?"—that is what Stieglitz says. "Ferryboat, built in 1904, paddlewheel, steam propelled, for 12 vehicles and 150 people. At the time of photograph (12 April 1908) it was nearing ferry slip no. 21, Manhattan. 140 people are visible and 4 teams." That is what the documentary says.

And we can make a similar comparison with films, between the creative and the record, between Eisenstein and a newsreel.

Why is it that this is recognized in films, and that there is a rich and excellent literature on the esthetic of film, while only a handful of us have given serious thought to the esthetics of creative photography?

❖

BN to NN
July 22, 1944

We have fought a good fight for photography. We have gained the intellectual recognition of photography as an art. But we have not found at the Museum the emotional backing, the conviction and the will that must be present before our hopes are realized. That we should have to argue in behalf of Stieglitz, that Edward's work should be dismissed as academic compositions, that Strand's sensitive work should be contemptuously referred to as "those bushes," that Ansel's grand landscapes should bring forth the remark, "Don't *people* live in Yosemite?" are evidences of a complete lack of understanding—indeed an unwillingness. [Their belief] that photographic vision is the starting point of art (*What is Modern Painting?*), that the most important photos are accidental, evocative because of strange combinations of images, is a denial of photography's status as an art form. And I put up with all of this!…

We must find some other way, in which we shall have the force of enthusiasm behind us, and not the dull, grudgingly given "support" of unsympathetic art historians, curators, directors, trustees, advisory committees, and—now—policy committees!

❖

BN to NN
August 1, 1944

I have been thinking more about our own collection. It is very important that we build up one with very high quality. It can be a nucleus for whatever we do in the future. Two years ago I would never have believed that we would own a Stieglitz—who knows what we may own in the future! Let us proceed slowly, deliberately, in Stieglitz's own spirit—not "buying" prints, but helping out those we believe in.…The Philadelphia show catalog has come, and…it gave me the thought that this very personal collection of ours, so bound up with our friendships, so biographical in itself, should be documented as fully as possible, that it should be cataloged in a personal way, for our own satisfaction. I would like to put down on paper the circumstances surrounding the acquisition of each photographer—how we got the Equivalent, the fact that Edward's New York view was made while he was staying with us, that Dorothy [Norman's] gravestone was an exchange for my ship detail, that Outerbridge's Piano was in exchange for my early Exchange Place—all the meaning behind the collection has, to us, an importance comparable to the notes that Stieglitz has on the photographs in the Philadelphia show.…I have a recollection that you bought a Weston nude. If not, we should definitely have one, and a voluptuous one too, in a California setting. Without one, our representation of his work is not complete. I am wondering if Berenice would sell us an original Atget of the famous shop window series at a fair price, if there are any brilliant originals left? Failing that, a new print, as a pair to the Rue Mouffetard. The weak tree I have had best be returned to her—it is neither Atget's nor Berenice's best. A Strand is greatest need just now, and I think it would be fair to offer him what we did for the Museum. Just what one, I cannot now say—a nature study or a Nova Scotia one, possibly. I want to give Walker something, but I can't think what to take of his—possibly one of those evocative Louisiana mansion houses.…What is the best Helen Levitt? I'm divided between the broken mirror and the courtyard with the kids....If there is a choice in getting new photos, of course we should take others than those now in the Museum.

❖

BN to NN
August 5, 1944

I'm made happy by your instant reaction to my letter about setting up our own Photo Center. Everything is tending that way, and it does seem not so much the pipe dream that I need to fear it was. I no longer see it in competition with the Museum, but as a different kind of approach, which can be conducted with the Museum, but not as part of it. We shall not lose the collection; the work we have put into the Museum is in no sense lost or wasted. It is too early to make plans definite enough to estimate the running expenses, but there is no question that we could operate on a much smaller budget than at the Museum. For one thing (if you agree) we would have no forced publicity, and the substantial expenses of handouts to the press would be cut down. We'd aim at a building of our own, but never at a marble palazzo (whether Renaissance or International Style). The staff, even at our greatest expansion, would not be large—as you write, it would be only one step beyond The Place. I would not think of it as a museum, though it will have many of the features of a museum. Now, at present I do not think of it as the place for an historical collection. My reason for reversing what I have so long been wrapped up in is that quality and historical completeness cannot both be satisfied, and our prime motto must be quality. Obviously I'm not so foolish as to cry History is The Bunk—far from it. But, thinking back over my years of study, I see that concentrated research leads one away from the creative aspects. What I should propose is simply an extension of the policy I set up at the Museum—accepting and acquiring a small collection of the great masterpieces of the past, and fostering the collection of works of historical interest alone by other institutions. I would like to stimulate the Metropolitan, for example, to get down to fundamentals. For a few thousand dollars they could lead the field and (here's the point) this money would not be diverted from creative workers, because the Met money is not used that way. In a sense, our role becomes somewhat reversed—whereas during the past years we have been getting to know photographers, persuading them, through their loyalty to us, to play ball with the Museum, now we shall, I think, find ourselves selling photography to museums in general, not alone to the Museum of Modern Art.

The whole proposition raises so many questions of policy and practice, that I can no more than say to you now Be of stout heart and of patience. Our way is clear, and some day we will reach our goal....Personally, we have a clean record, and we have already built a foundation. The Museum record has been clouded over, in spite of us—not frequently, but still too often. With our museum experience, which no photographers can equal, and with our knowledge and feeling for photography, which no museum workers can equal, we are an extraordinary team!

…How we need one another! It is from the interchange of ideas that we shall build something which is greater than either one of us can alone create. There is something about our teamwork that is right, dearest. We are in every sense a pair. Through our blessed union we pull each other up. We continually build—and I know that we shall continue to do so, and that our future will be even more creative, constructive and sound than ever. Every night, in the blissful quiet before going to sleep, I think of you, and I can but marvel at my good fortune in claiming you as a mate—not wife alone, but life partner, co-worker, one who shares everything. And I realize that it was not fortune, or coincidence that brought us together, but some Divine Force. There, in our marriage, is my religion. There is proof positive of a Force.

❖

There is nothing inherent in photography that makes it automatically a force for good. I am more and more convinced that the editor is as important as the photographer, and that our concept of "documentary photography" must include both, that photographic evidence with lying words can be as harmful as photographic evidence with truthful words—and the photographer himself (unless he is also the editor) cannot be a force for good simply by producing superb pictures. And that is why I no longer believe that documentary is a pure medium. For years I thought that [Stieglitz's photograph] *The Steerage* was a "document" of oppressed foreigners hopefully westward bound, and I read into that great picture a sentiment and a meaning which was purely imaginary. For the truth is the opposite: emigrants, not immigrants! Some fascist could with equal, or even greater, truth use that picture to show the failure of democracy, the Return of the Native theme. But the picture is great for itself, simply as a wonderful picture of people crowded on a ship, yearning to get off of it. No explanation is needed; there it is. None of Stieglitz's great photographs needs a single word of explanation; they do not document a particular social problem, but universal humanity, universal problems. That Venetian gamin I can find, fifty years later, outside my door begging a cigarette. He is in Egypt, in Germany. You may run into him tomorrow on Sixth Avenue. Velázquez met him in Spain 300 years ago, and painted him without finding the soul behind those eyes. Would we find this picture eternal if Stieglitz had photographed him as a document? And would even this so obvious portrait survive if, for example, it were presented as illustration to a royalist article showing the unemployment created by the Garibaldi revolution? (Or some such lie, my Italian history of the 1890s is hopeless).

I maintain that even a Stieglitz photograph can be forced into a "non- or anti-human channel"; the greater the photograph, the greater its effect. It is doubtful in my mind if, solely through his photographs, an artist can solve sociological problems. In films? Ah, that is another matter. He is, or has, an editor, and his work is built up into an argument which cannot be misused without obvious and radical alterations....

How a photographer's work is used is something which goes beyond photography. It is up to the critic to judge how well the photographer has said what he has to say...and to estimate his success. If the grandeur of the Sierra Nevadas is what Ansel has to say, he must be judged by that lyric standard which we apply to Cézanne's landscapes (within the photographic medium, of course), not by whether his work is "human." It of necessity is non-human, the human in awe of nature and of God. If what I have to say is the beauty of craftsmanship, of function, of ship details, judge it in comparison with Charles's drawings and photographs—don't look for a symbol of democracy there, for beautiful craftsmanship knows no barriers of creed, race, or time, and my intention was nothing more than to comment, through a single example, on something that is fine in man. If Edward's sand dunes are empty, insignificant, so too must be Persian rugs, Indian fabrics, and Thoreau's description of snow melting in the spring.

The great photograph must have in it something so universal that its message can be grasped at once, with no argument, no caption, no sound track. The documentary is almost at an opposite pole, it is particular, illustrative, meaningless, without words. What we appreciate about the best documentary work is precisely what it contains over and above its definition. What we want to encourage is the development of this recognition of the universal, in whatever field it may be sought. Without it the photograph becomes just a document, an anecdote, an illustration, a record. With it, the photograph becomes truly and unequivocally a work of art.

❖

NN to BN
October 29, 1944

Ann [Armstrong] and I went out for lunch together, feeling pretty good....She told me—final proof of Ann's loyalty—that when Elodie [Courter] told her about coming to help me, she said that later perhaps Steichen might be the Director of the Department and Ann would enjoy working for him. This I heard more about yesterday, at lunch with Tom Maloney, discussing the book. Tom had told Monroe he'd like to back a magazine—a really good one—tops—beginning with photography and eventually embracing all the arts—provided Steichen had something to do with it. (Incidentally, Tom at the moment is at outs with Steichen himself.) Aha, said I to myself, now's the chance to fight fire with fire. So I shall. One encouraging thing is that Dick [Abbott] enjoyed Roy [Stryker]'s tirade against Steichen when his name was mentioned for the Committee, and commented afterward on how swell it was that Roy was so sound on Steichen. Another is that I think the staff as a whole is leery. The truth will be the trustees, to whom Steichen has direct access but to whom I have as yet little or none. I don't think the Museum has yet committed itself. It's my job now to see that they don't. The idea of the fight rather exhilarates me.

❖

BN to NN
November 10, 1944

Your letter was…alarming with the news of the Steichen threat. It had never crossed my mind that he might be appointed director, and the thought of it is most discouraging, for it would mean our complete separation from the Museum. While I envisage a time when we shall want to leave the Museum, I hope that we can do so amicably, cleanly and in a way which will enable us to carry on good relations, and make full use of the facilities which we have created. But if Steichen gets control, such will not be possible, or certainly to a limited extent only. His attitude towards photography is so utterly different from ours, his personality is so self-centered and difficult, his megalomania is so aggressive, that we cannot work under him. The truth is that we cannot work under anybody, for to do so would be to yield prestige to someone who knows less than we do—for we are better equipped for the job than anybody else (with the obvious exception of Stieglitz). The impossibility of finding anybody to take my job, and then your job, when we thought I'd be stationed in Washington, proves that. Herc was not the solution, it was quite obvious. And while I was glad when Herc was made director and given a chance to try his hand, I shall not accept Steichen….Somehow I feel that the threat will not materialize. I sincerely hope it does not. If it does come to pass we cannot compromise, we cannot have anything to do with him, and will have to resign.

❖

BN to NN
November 26, 1944

[re article by Ansel in *American Annual of Photography*]

Perhaps it is because I'm out of touch with photography (except of the record kind) so much that I am impatient with apologia for creative photography, but my interest is turning more and more to that particular use of photography which may be called artistic. I feel less interested in the photograph which happens to be found artistic than in the one which is deliberately made as such. The so-called esthetic of the accident is to me less moving than the successful solution of the self-imposed problem of creating a picture which will move others. It is peculiar to photography that, by the extreme ease of production, many accidentally interesting photos are produced. But a Stieglitz, a Weston, a Strand are deliberate, and show a mastery over the medium that is most impressive. I have yet to see a documentary photograph as moving as a Stieglitz—what I have seen is so *intellectual*. Why is it not possible to recognize the status of the artist-photographer? We should consider Edward, Charles, Ansel, Paul as *artists*. They are not called upon to demonstrate in words their relationships to illustration, abstract painting, manuscript illumination, and the other facets of the painting medium. It seems to me important to make generally recognized the place of the photographer in the world of artists.

I wonder if this is a reaction to handling thousands of record photographs. Each photo is brilliant in technique, yet of no artistic value at all. Once in a while there is a photo which by chance has beauty. But these are rare. I work every day with the proof that what makes a photo interesting is what is put into it by the photographer.

❖

BN to NN
December 17, 1944

The New Workers show is the most important. Perhaps even more than Paul's and Edward's. Theirs will be the greater achievements, but the consequences of the New Workers show will be the one-man full dress shows of the future. I am intrigued by the number of totally new names nominated.

The importance of showing the work of new people came home forcibly to me last night, in looking over the Feininger/Hartley catalog. This handsome book suddenly brought to my mind the whole shelf of books which by now the Museum has published. Our best efforts (we = Museum of Modern Art) have always been with the accomplished, and completed, men. My feelings were mixed as I suddenly met up with a typical Museum of Modern Art one-man show. What painter, what sculptor has the Museum launched? Then look at Stieglitz's record. Look at the procession of them, great names and forgotten names. While it is true that Stieglitz has now made a continued story type of one man show from Marin and O'Keeffe, he has done so logically. They have grown old along with him; their great days have passed with his. But can the Museum so boast? They took that which was accepted in Europe and made it accepted in the States. The insistence that Feininger is an American (what difference does it make?) is one example. Then "Built in U.S.A." seems founded on the premise that although modern architecture began in Europe, it is swell in America, and the Museum's influence is documented. But how much has the Museum done to encourage new and original talent? That should be the mission of the Museum, *plus* shows of accomplished artists. I know we've had several shows of unknown painters—but unless I am mistaken, no artist of very great stature has emerged—nobody like Marin, O'Keeffe, Hartley, Strand. And considering all that the Museum has had to work with, there should be at least one. Our record in the Department of Photography is modest, but I think more promising—and it can and will be more so.

❖

It will be very important indeed for us to examine together the philosophy of photography. I tend to feel that the most important phase of our work will be with the photographers who use photography in a way that can be called artistic. This is a deliberate circumlocution, for somehow the straightforward compound word "artist-photographer" does not connote the right idea. There are etchers and "painter-etchers"—the painter-etchers are the ones in which we are interested. Not that they paint at all, but their attitude towards etching is that of the painter and not the craftsman alone. So we could talk of "painter-photographers" for that is what Edward and Charles and Paul and Ansel are. Only they would hit the ceiling if you said so to them. But their attitude towards photography is precisely that of a painter. They are not illustrators, they have nothing in mind beyond the creation of a picture, and the subject matter itself is something that the picture demands. They do not set out to take a photograph of a building—the building cries out to be photographed. And that is an important distinction....I think that the beauty of accident is definitely secondary to the beauty of recognition. That is badly put: what I mean to say is that the highest point reached by a photographer is when he successfully captures that which he recognized to be a picture....The highest form of photography is in the work of the "painter photographers." All else is interesting, is significant, but is it really creative? I would like to see us admit that the work of the photographers I have named is the greatest work done today with a camera. I would like to separate painting-photographs from illustration-photographs. I feel that documentary photography is very important, very good, and should be carried on and encouraged, just as I feel that journalism and expository writing are important, and a high calling. But there are standards which all writers respect, there is great literature: Shakespeare and Keats and the great prose writers. Everybody who writes learns from these giants. And everybody who photographs can learn from Stieglitz. No matter what field one is interested in, there is something very significant which Stieglitz has done. Documentary, portraits—name it and you will find it in his work. And this is true of Shakespeare; he has something for every writer. That's why I get upset when people claim that we are playing favorites, and that we are only interested in a small group of photographers. I only wish that the group was not so small, and it is my hope that we may be an effective means of increasing the group of significant photographers.

❖

As you probably know, Frederick Evans died recently. A memorial exhibition was held some time ago at the Royal Photographic Society, and the other day I had the privilege of seeing the prints which were shown. I was overwhelmed by them. Evans must be reckoned as one of the great pictorial photographers. Surprisingly, the photogravures in *Camera Work* do not do him justice. It can be no exaggeration to write that his architectural photographs are the greatest of their kind. Because he was able to combine precision of definition with a softness and delicacy of gradation, because he had such an extraordinary sense of scale and of light. His cathedrals are bathed in light. Detail is everywhere—every tracing, every lead of the stained glass windows, is present—yet the result is far from a record—each one is an interpretation. It was a revelation to find him doing landscape as well, and of course his amazing Aubrey Beardsley is famous. He had one view of an attic of an old English house with hand-hewn beams that reminded me of Sheeler. All of the prints were platinotypes, and printed with that beauty which can only be appreciated when viewing the original. Some time we must introduce (or better re-introduce) Evans to American photographers. There is a lesson to be learned from them—that one can be a "straight" worker and yet have delicacy and softness, integrity and yet not the harsh contrasts so characteristic of so much present-day work. The hazards of shipping the prints during wartime precludes any planning of the show now, but sometime we may get a chance to exhibit a selection.

❖

BN to NN
January 29, 1945

While I was in London I visited Helmut Gernsheim, the refugee who wrote to me in praise of my aphorism on the man behind the lens. He has an English wife and a charming apartment. I spent three evenings with them. Once they took me to a restaurant, once Mrs. G. cooked a rabbit stew (not rationed), once I took them to an officers' club for a dandy American dinner of ham with pineapple rings. And every one of these evenings we spent in talk about photography in their sitting room sipping what to me tasted more like nectar than scotch—coffee with real cream. Gernsheim is very much the modern photographer. Too much so, for he is dogmatic about hard sharpness. He and a few other refugees, principally one Hugo van Waynonder, are trying to shake some sense into conservative British camera clubs, and created a minor revolution by throwing out 900 photographs and hanging only 100 at a show of "modern" work at the Hereford or Bristol Camera Club. But their campaign is bearing fruit, and this year they've written to Ansel and Edward and some others to send to a show....My they were nice people—took me in as an old friend, made me feel almost at home. I brought them my candy ration—4 or 5 cheap candy bars—and I couldn't have made more of a hit with 5 pounds of Sherry's best chocolates. So if you would—and can—send them a few hard-to-get things. I'd feel very happy. Mrs. G. would like some red nail varnish, sugar, chocolate and jam.

Here is how I analyze the situation. To my surprise, to my sorrow, and to my intense disappointment, I now realize that the museum was not 100% behind me in the work I have been doing in photography. If it had not been for my precipitate departure from the Museum, and for my intense desire to so arrange matters that the Department could continue, I would not have realized this, for I very much doubt if I would have been summarily fired, and it does not seem to be the policy of the Museum to talk over differences of opinion.

Now of course I am neither so sensitive nor so short-sighted to resent criticism, and I would be the first to admit that I made, or allowed others to make, many mistakes. But I have the feeling that I had been entrusted with the confidence of the Trustees and of the staff. Acting on this assumption I proceeded to conduct the department as I felt best. You know how I feel about photography, and what I believe is the essence of photography. I believe that photographs have a point of view. If some people think that there is an over-emphasis of "purist" photography, I can only answer that more good work is being done in that spirit. The resentment against Edward is something I simply cannot understand—even when it is Stieglitz speaking. Criticism of Ansel I can follow, and it will be noticed that Ansel has not been given any emphasis or precedence in the Museum shows. As to Moholy and Man Ray, I honestly cannot admit either in the ranks of the great photographers. And there, I think, lies one of the criticisms against me. I know that Alfred [Barr] has been disappointed that I did not stage a one-man show of Man Ray when Jim [Soby] gave us his collection. Query: should I have played politics or stuck to the courage of my convictions? There was only one answer that I could make, darling, and only one answer that you could make. There's only one man who knows more about photography as a fine art than I do, and his name is Stieglitz. Why I should be criticized by people who know practically nothing about photography, I cannot understand. Please don't think that I'm complaining, or resenting: I simply had felt that the Museum made me Curator of Photography because I was an expert.

Throughout the Museum, as you have noticed, there is a complete ignorance of photography—almost a resentment of good photography. Alfred means well, but he just cannot *feel* photography; he seems blind to it. Compare Ansel's experience at the Museum and Charles [Sheeler's] at the Met. Ansel, at his own expense, at a sacrifice of time and strength, takes a set of sculpture photos because he has heard that there was a need for them. When I brought them to Alfred, certain that he would be delighted, he found only two or three that he could "use." All the others were not "Museum photographs" because they had shadow areas, or showed (carefully composed) a curving wall, or were made in the garden. And then, in spite of the fact that Ansel had marked them proofs, Alfred wanted to use the two or three that he did like right away—couldn't see why the prints weren't perfect—any fine print would be lost in reproduction anyhow. In fairness to Ansel, I held out for wiring him for either new prints or permission to reproduce from the proofs. I don't believe I told you this sorry tale. It certainly forms a contrast to the carte blanche that the Met has given Charles!...

Let us turn the coin over and look at the other side. What was expected of me that was not given? More spectacular exhibitions, I guess, for one thing. The Steichen show has eclipsed all the little shows that preceded it. Everything I did was in miniature, small, quiet, unobtrusive, in good taste and (I realize it) lost in the shuffle. I didn't fight hard enough, allowed myself to be booted around. I didn't put on didactic shows, marked plainly so that people could read their way through the gallery, because I felt that the photos themselves should tell their own story. I didn't handle the social angle well, didn't get around town, didn't bring in the photographers people were talking about. Another thing: by making close friends of those photographers we believe in, by speaking of them familiarly, I think we have built up a false idea that we're playing favorites!

Of one thing I am very glad. That it was not *you* who held up the decision on continuing the department. Nor could it have been financial, for a *1%* allowance of the total budget would hardly cause such a terrific session of the Executive Committee as there seems to have been. All that I can make of the situation is that the Trustees don't like the Department of Photography *at all*.

If this is a correct analysis, there are two ways to proceed: get out or fight. The die is already cast with your appointment: fight for the recognition of the department. It does seem ridiculous that we have to defend the department now that we have just got into the swing, but there is no alternative; our hands are forced. You'll find all I can give you for the annual report attached, and I think you'll have no trouble in making up an entirely satisfactory account. Once the report is made, then it will be necessary to put the house in complete order. The collection must be cataloged and properly housed. All the passepartout frames must be removed. All odds and ends taken care of so there can be no further criticism of things left undone.

When this has been accomplished, then we can decide what to do next: whether to continue with the Museum or to resign. At least we will have the satisfaction of having created the most important collection of twentieth-century photography in existence, and of having helped many deserving workers. At the present moment, I am ready to say goodbye to the Museum. I foresee little opportunity there to develop photography. Unless there is a remarkable change since I left, the Museum has lost that spirit and that life which made it such an inspiring place in which to work seven years ago. Photography is my passion, not the Museum, and if photography cannot grow in that atmosphere, if it cannot breathe there, then it is time to pull out, as you said—not in anger, but sorrowfully. However the house must be put in order first. I should, I know, have seen to that job myself....

To sum up my reactions: (1) justify the department; (2) put house in order; (3) prepare to jump in the most opportune and advantageous direction, even at the cost of severing all relations with the Museum. Let me know how you feel about this. It is not an easy problem to solve.

But this I do want to say. Despite the fact that at the *moment* I am giving every nerve and muscle and brain cell to the gigantic job I have volunteered to do, photography is still my passion. I love you for letting me deny this, but it will take more than I've been through so far to wipe out my deep interest in photography. At this distance "modern art" does seem a little unimportant, "surrealism" is something we'd tramp over with marching feet, but photography—the spirit, I mean—is *everywhere*: it's precise, lightning-like, clean cut, brilliant, alert. I love you for saying that through your love for me you love photography. Such a wife there never was. I love you for the way you are stepping into problems I originated, carrying on against opposition, working not for the moment but for the future.

❖

4

MY LAST DAYS AT MOMA

AND AFTER

By Henri Cartier-Bresson, 1946. (Courtesy of the photographer)

Paul Strand

I first met Paul Strand in 1936, when I asked him to lend us prints for the 1937 history of photography exhibition and he invited me to his apartment to look at his work. He didn't approve of my doing an exhibition of such great scope, but his attitude was a little different from Stieglitz's. After I described to him my plan for the show, Strand interrupted. "Let's see now. The whole history of photography is what you're trying to do. How many floors in the museum?" "There are four floors," I replied. "Well this is what you ought to do," he said. "The first floor should be all David Octavius Hill. The second floor should be Eugène Atget. Give the third floor completely to Alfred Stieglitz. And on the fourth floor you should have Strand."

He did finally agree to lend his photographs, and I selected thirteen prints; however, he told me that he'd have to hang them himself. One night while Nancy and I were hanging photographs in the main gallery, Strand came in with a friend, who carried a heavy suitcase. It contained bright lightbulbs, which they proceeded to substitute for the regular gallery lights. When he discovered it, Alfred Barr was absolutely beside himself about these lights, as they overpowered everything. I should never have allowed Strand to put them in, and at Alfred's request, they were removed.

In 1942, before I left for overseas, Ansel, Nancy, and I sat down and made a five-year plan for the exhibition schedule. The photography department had not yet sponsored a solo show of an individual's work, and we had all very much wanted Stieglitz to be the first person to be so honored. Initially he refused to show his work at the museum; when he changed his mind and finally did agree, it turned out to be in principle only, for it became clear to all of us that, although willing, he was too old and too frail to see the project through. We then decided we wanted to offer individual shows to three other photographers: Strand, Weston, and Adams. Strand's work became the first seen in a major retrospective at the museum, and the Weston show was the second. Due to unforeseen circumstances, the Adams exhibition would never take place.

In spite of Strand's egotism, which could be trying, Nancy got on well with him, and also became friendly with his wife, Rebecca. Paul wrote me on August 14, 1944, "Nancy has hoped for a good next season of few but important shows. As she has no doubt written you, a retrospective of my work is among them. Of course, I would like that to happen, but the ultimate approvals or disapprovals are not yet in.—As I wrote you before, you can feel very proud of the way Nancy has carried on in your absence."

Paul Strand at Mystic Seaport, Connecticut, 1946. Photograph by Beaumont Newhall. (Courtesy of Scheinbaum & Russek Ltd., Santa Fe, New Mexico)

In January 1945, Nancy wrote me regarding the preparations for the Strand show: "I want so much to put on a show that proves Paul the great photographer he is—dwarfed only by Stieglitz, which is, to put it mildly, an honorable reduction....Paul has told me to go ahead and work out the show my own way. Of course, I shall have him whatever his feeling or his decision or whatever is necessary."[28]

Despite very strong opposition by several committee members to the museum's treating photography as an art form, Nancy organized a handsome retrospective of 172 of Strand's photographs, ranging in date from 1915 to 1944. Until he moved to France, Strand never had his own darkroom; he printed all the photographs for his retrospective in the museum darkroom. The exhibition which opened April 25, 1945, was accompanied by a monograph with thirty-two reproductions and a critical essay by Nancy. Nancy recalled, "I had long known that Strand was a perfectionist who pushes 'superlative purity beyond logic into passion,' as [the critic] Elizabeth McCausland wrote, but I hadn't expected to be called out of conferences and board meetings down to the basement workshop where Paul was working on his show to help decide if a print should be a millimeter higher or lower in its mat or what about this sequence?"[29]

28. Nancy Newhall to Beaumont Newhall, January 17, 1945.

For the ten years preceding, Strand had stopped making still photographs in order to concentrate on documentary filmmaking. In the winter of 1943 he took his cameras off to Vermont, returning to his first love, still photography. One afternoon while his exhibition was up, Paul and Nancy were having lunch in the museum garden and Paul mentioned that he wanted to do a book on New England, but wondered what kind of text to use. "Why not use the words of the New Englanders themselves?" Nancy asked. "Do you need anybody better than people like Thoreau, Dickinson, Melville?" They discussed the idea, and ended by agreeing to collaborate on it, combining photographs by Paul with a selection of writing by New England authors from 1629 to the present day. When it was published in 1950, *Time in New*

29. Nancy Newhall, "Paul Strand: Catalyst and Revealer," *Modern Photography*, August 1969, n.p.

England was the first book to unite text and images beautifully. It was neither a portfolio of photographs nor an anthology with illustrations, but rather an integrated whole in which the text and the images reinforced one another in a remarkable way. It proved a model for books that both would do in the future.

Nancy and Paul were geographically separated, Paul living in Maine with the painter John Marin, and Nancy living in New York. Although one might think that Nancy found quotations to support Paul's photographs, the reverse was true: Nancy guided Paul's photographs so they would elucidate the texts. Functioning much like a film director, she sent him long letters containing detailed lists of the images she sought:

> …an image of peace and established loveliness…might be a common with elms, or rolling countryside with glimpse of town in summer. An image of vast prospects—clouds, horizons…an image to accompany the love of books and excitement of scholarship…nearest I can come to it at present is the closeup of the window with puttied panes, teapot, tomatoes, books beyond, which conveys a quiet and busy life.…The power and vastness of the sea—a violent storm or ragged, clearing sunset without contemporary boats in it, unless they are schooners. What about some keen young men's faces and the sea? Or boys with boats and nautical gear? [30]

Strand, who was radically left-wing in his political allegiance, refused to photograph anything at all in Boston for the book

30. Nancy Newhall to Paul Strand, June 1, 1946.

because the Sacco and Vanzetti executions had taken place there in 1927. And before *Time in New England* was published, his disenchantment with American politics led him to take up permanent residence in France, and so he was not on hand to supervise the book while it was on press. Nancy was not sufficiently knowledgeable in reproduction techniques, and the result was a rather disappointingly printed book. An edition published by Aperture in 1980 is far more beautiful.

Although Strand admired Weston and Adams, his views on photography were quite different, as the following letter illustrates. It was a response to a young photographer:

> Looking at the work of the California School as a whole it appears to me to have a kind of overall antiseptic quality, very clean, very well done as to the negative but lacking a point of view or richness of vision.…Outside of Dorothea Lange, the photographers of the Far West have apparently very little interest in people. On the whole the landscape has been the primary interest.…Mere pattern, textures and a long tonal scale, which are characteristic of the California School, while important as instruments of photographic expression, are not basic ones. In fact, some of the best photographs of the world, viz Hill, Brady and Atget, are very weak in these aspects—but very strong in form and occasionally in movement. On my mantel, for instance, is a small portrait of Lincoln by Brady. The scale is short—flesh tones not all there, no textures. Yet the great monumental dignity of the man is there in the form and contour of the head and body, the use of the hands. It is my conviction that the sense of weight and air in a picture are above all

important. A photograph, like other graphic art, is two-dimensional in actuality but it must give the illusion of a third dimension—allow the spectator to move into it. For the truth of the real work is that no two-dimensional thing exists. Equally true, as science has verified, is the fact that everything is in movement. Thus in a work of art, these two elements are, in my opinion, basic. Without them, the tendency is toward decorative and static things which do not wear well. [31]

While I was in Europe in 1959, I spent a weekend with Paul Strand at his home in Orgeval, a town twenty-four miles from Paris. The following account is from a letter to Nancy.

31. Paul Strand to Mr. Freehe, July 22, 1948. Strand sent a copy to Nancy and me.

A most interesting visit and, if I can convince Kodak to let me have $2500, a most successful one, for Paul will sell Eastman House fifteen prints and give us ten more for this sum. Paul is relaxed, and seemed to me well and not as aged as I had feared. The house is charming—one of the very nicest houses I have seen. It has the simplicity of Edward Weston's, plus solidity, elegance, and great taste. It is hardly more than a cottage set down in the middle of a garden. There are flowers even in the driveway! The front yard is an orchard of pears en espalier—rows of them held up by wires. The town is very small, very rural. Paul seems to know everybody, and they seem to like him. He speaks atrocious French but everybody understands him. He is a happy man, as far as I can see. He grumbles about his age, but admits that he works better than ever; and the staggering amount of work he has done in the past nine years—since he was sixty—certainly shows that he has the energy and strength to match his passion for photography. For that is what it is! He remarked in one of our conversations that he was not going to see cheapened what he has given his life to, and that is his life, actually. I judge that he has no other activity; seldom goes to Paris, and had little to say about anything except photography.

I saw at least five hundred new prints, all mounted, spotted, cased. *The Island of South Uist of the Outer Hebrides, Off the West Coast of Scotland*: a great, though perhaps repetitious, series: landscapes, portraits, details of fishing gear, still lifes inside cottages, beach subjects such as seaweeds, etc., which hark back to Paul's Maine and Gaspé series. Broadly seen, with the touch of the substance, the earth, the actuality in every one. Somber perhaps, but not gloomy; rich prints. He defied me to tell which were enlargements: all of the prints were 8 x 10-inch. I could not. He is full of excitement over his discovery that he can retain in his enlargements the quality of his contact prints. I pointed out that to enlarge from a 5 x 7-inch negative to an 8 x 10-inch print was hardly exacting, but he considers it remarkable.

Portraits. Over a hundred of these, of some thirty-five intellectuals: Pablo Picasso, Georges Braque, Jean Lurcat, André Malraux, Jean-Paul

Sartre, and less well-known writers, scientists, artists. Massive heads, crowding the 8 x 10-inch prints, taken at their workplaces in a matter of minutes—the minutes they could, or would, spare. Competing with Yosuf Karsh! Even bringing his own lights when necessary. And a powerful lot indeed. He had hoped to do a book, but he has abandoned the project for two reasons: 1) the field is so broad that a choice has to be made of subject, and Paul refuses to photograph anyone, no matter how famous, whose face he does not like; and 2) the publishers with whom he has talked insist on a hand in the choice. Also it is too difficult—not too hard work but so annoying to make the appointment, to get the gear to the sitter's place. A pity, for the start was great. I wonder if he ever could have found a publisher, for the portraits are not always pleasing. But strong, revealing—at times massive.

Orgeval. In the garden he loves so well, Paul has made the most exquisite photographs of flowers. His house through the bare branches of the weeping willow tree that stands beside the front door. Ivy on the walls. Little flowers in the grass. A bachelor's button plant against leaves that is incandescent.

South Italy, Sicily, Gaeta. Trial pieces, so to speak, for his published book *Un Paese*. Often strange and beautiful, but I found little to add to what is in the book.

We talked. We talked for three days!

Paul is discouraged with the state of art photography. Has nothing against journalism as such, but does not want it seen or shown as art. He feels that the only way to win respect for photography is to raise the prices. Has deep and true respect for Ansel Adams—but cannot accept the portfolio idea. When I asked what is the difference between publishing reproductions in a book and duplicate prints in portfolios, he said the photographer should not be expected to become a publisher.

I said, "But Paul, there aren't enough museums and collectors to keep an artist alive."

"There will be," Paul replied, "if we make it desirable financially to collect."

"But photographs are not unique," I answered. "The public thinks they exist in any number of prints. Let's say we compare photography with fine lithographs like that Toulouse-Lautrec there," and I pointed to a superb framed poster on the wall.

"What makes you think paintings are unique? I've seen van Gogh Sunflowers in various museums that seemed identical," Paul said. "Don't tell me old Corot didn't grind out replicas. As for engravings—often the edition is limited."

He counted Alfred Stieglitz's great contributions as four: 1) the renaissance of art photography and his encouragement of Steichen, Käsebier, and the Photo-Secessionists; 2) the introduction of modern art to America; 3) the championing of American painting; and 4) his own photography before 1920.

For the "Equivalents" Paul had nothing but contempt. "They are cloud photographs and nothing else." He felt that Stieglitz had talked people into seeing in them just exactly what isn't there. For photography, Paul said again and again, is realistic, is not abstract—and then he was off on a long diatribe against the drippers of paint—especially Jackson Pollock. And praise for the realism of the prehistoric painters and wonder of them—and of the Impressionists, above all Toulouse-Lautrec.

A full three days! I am grateful that I took the time so that we had the leisure to talk and to understand. And, before the amazing production, which is still going on as strongly as ever—perhaps even stronger—I stood in respect.

❖

Edward Weston at The Museum of Modern Art, 1946. Photograph by Beaumont Newhall. (Courtesy of Scheinbaum & Russek Ltd., Santa Fe, New Mexico)

WESTON RETROSPECTIVE

I returned to the Museum of Modern Art as curator of photography in October 1945. Nancy had been my collaborator on so many projects; she had taught me a great deal about writing, both by example and by criticism, and she was a tremendous help to me in every way. While I was overseas she had managed the Department of Photography very well under trying circumstances, and now she wanted to work side by side with me, as an equal. It had been our hope that Nancy would be retained as my associate; however, the trustees would not grant this request. This is one of the rare times the museum seemed to me nineteenth-century in its outlook, as museum policy absolutely would not allow husbands and wives to work together. (It is true, however, that Iris Barry somehow managed this successfully. The head of the film department, she was married to Dick Abbott, director of the museum. Once when Mrs. Rockefeller told her, "I think you really ought to call yourself Mrs. Abbott," Iris replied, "Well it doesn't make any difference. Iris Barry isn't my real name anyway.") Nancy was understandably upset by this decision. The trustees did, however, appoint her curator of the long-planned Edward Weston retrospective, which opened in February 1946. The largest exhibition that had ever been held of Weston's photographs, it was a handsome and highly popular presentation.

Edward and Nancy had made the selection of photographs in Carmel in 1944. Edward wanted to exhibit five hundred prints, but Nancy told him that was far too many. "Don't you think people would soon get tired of looking at five hundred pictures?" she inquired.

"If the public can't *see* five hundred photographs let them come twice" was Edward's answer. "I am a prolific, mass-production, omnivorous seeker. I *can't* be represented by one or two or even three hundred photographs to cover forty-four years of work!"

There was also considerable concern as to whether the trustees would object to Weston's frontal nudes. Weston wrote Nancy, "By all means tell your Board that P.H. [pubic hair] has been definitely a part of my development as an artist, tell them it has been the most important part, that I like it brown, black, red or golden, curly or straight, all sizes and shapes. If that does not move them let me know." Soon after, Charis sent us a note: "This is to show you what your fastidious museum has done to Edward. Lucky we had fig trees growing on the place." She enclosed a photograph of herself nude, but modestly covering herself with a giant leaf.

Nancy and Edward compromised on 251 prints, along with eleven negatives—which were then seldom shown in exhibitions. A catalog, containing a short biographical essay by Nancy and twenty-four illustrations, was published by Simon & Schuster. The first printing of a thousand copies sold out while the book was still in the bindery, and so a reprint was ordered before anyone had seen a single copy. It was a very popular show. In describing it to Paul Strand, Nancy wrote, "Edward's show a wow; every Sunday three or four thousand people cram themselves into those narrow spaces, with the guards telling them to keep moving." During his short visit Edward went to the museum almost every day, "to meet my public," he liked to say. *The New Yorker* magazine maintained that he brought his lunch and sat on a camp chair in the galleries eating it. One day we invited Edward to lunch, along with Gjon Mili, a photographer for *Life* magazine. During dessert, after a long and charming conversation, Gjon turned to Edward.

"How can you price your photographs at only fifteen dollars?" This was the price Edward had been asking over the past years.

"Well, you know, I live in a small shack near Carmel," he said, "I wear blue jeans, I don't pay an income tax, I get along very well."

"Well, we photographers here in New York don't have a small house and do pay an income tax," Gjon replied. "And we don't wear blue jeans!"

"Oh," Edward said, with some embarrassment, "I never thought of that. I'm terribly sorry. I'll tell you what I'll do. I'll raise my price for a print to twenty-five dollars, beginning right now." He was most pleased that ninety-seven prints were sold—at twenty-five dollars each.

EDWARD STEICHEN

Soon after I had returned to the museum as curator of photography, rumors Nancy had heard several months earlier began to circulate once more. What followed was one of the most painful times of my life. I write about it here because to my knowledge the circumstances are not widely known.

During the time I was overseas, Nancy had been working closely with Stieglitz, interviewing him for a biography she was writing. Nancy visited Stieglitz often during the war years, and they developed a beautiful friendship. The following is from her journal recalling the autumn of 1945.

World War II was over, at last. The horror of its terrible finale in the atom bombing of Hiroshima and Nagasaki—though the effects of radiation on the whole earth and all life upon it were as yet scarcely known—already haunted us, a spectre more fearful than any Marx dreamed of, for it was the end of our trust in mankind.

Still one had reason to be grateful, even to rejoice: so many of the men were coming back. The men we had kissed goodbye with courage so many times, but when the final parting came—and you knew, somehow, it was final, at least for years, if not forever—we broke down in uncontrollable tears. The men reported lost, the long silences, the mysteries that you lived with day and night, the jobs you tried to carry on in their spirit—all that was over. Beaumont would soon be out of uniform, though I didn't yet fully realize how disorientated he was, how small and petty the Museum seemed to him—and even the cause of photography.

Beaumont had been commanded by the Joint Chiefs of Staff to organize as efficient a photo-intelligence unit as the one he had run in

Italy; he was due to go to Okinawa in a few weeks. The aerial photo intelligence about Japan was so poor that trolley tracks were mistaken for railroads; to mount an attack would mean training of interpreters, briefing of pilots on what not to bomb—the marvelous old palaces, temples and gardens, and innocent farmers—as well as what to bomb: railroad yards, bridges, air fields, factories. The atom bomb, frightful war, had ended for him the constant trauma of thinking of what his own work resulted in—the dangling trains full of dead and dying, the sunken ships with all hands aboard. And the cities, bombed by a thousand planes a night—the dead, the dying. the living, buried in ruins.

Stieglitz, having seen what happened to men in wars before, understood Beaumont better than I could at the time. He could also see what was happening to Steichen, chief of naval photography in the Pacific War, and now a Captain—a rank higher in the Navy than the rank of Colonel, awarded [Beaumont] after World War II by the Army. [In fact, I was promoted to major in 1945, while still in Italy.]

Stieglitz had come back from Lake George looking well, and we were chatting comfortably about various things, when he suddenly said, "Look out for Steichen."

"Steichen?" I said. "Why?"

"He wants your department at the Museum."

"But why?" I asked. "What would he want with the poor, heart-breaking thing?"

Stieglitz was silent. He would not tell me what he saw: that Steichen would use the department and the Museum as a great stage from which to direct further vast exhibitions of photography as communication and exhortation, not as an art. That all Beaumont, Ansel, Dave and I had built up and fought for would be negated, just as what Stieglitz himself had built up and fought for so many years had been negated.

So he merely said, "Never underestimate Steichen. He's always doing something; he's a power. Watch out."

But I forgot the warning. There was so much going on, all kinds of plans and projects for the future. Strand's retrospective had been a spectacular success, and I was already working on the next retrospective, [that of] Edward Weston.

Thomas J. Maloney—an advertising man and publisher of *U.S. Camera* magazine and the *U.S. Camera* annual and friend of museum trustee Henry Allen Moe—sent the trustees a draft proposal that the photographer Edward Steichen be appointed the museum's director of photography. Steichen had just been relieved of duty as a captain in the Naval Reserve in charge of all naval combat photography during World War II. Maloney's three-page memorandum of December 10, 1945, stated somewhat categorically that:

> The Photographic Division of the Museum will be directed by Capt. Edward Steichen. He will be in complete charge, selecting all his own assistants....Capt. Steichen's abilities and age [sixty-six] are such that he should spend no time whatever arguing for the point of view he wishes to promote: the presentation of all the things that make America the country that it is.
>
> Naturally this presentation at the Museum presupposes that aesthetically, photography is a medium of expression that covers all of our activities, rather than the precious segment that has previously been the backbone of the Museum's presentations.

On Christmas day 1945, I wrote Ansel the news.

> The great excitement at the moment, and it is great, is the threat to the Department brought about by Steichen and Maloney. Suddenly, a week or so ago, I was told that the two had won the ear of Stephen Clark and Mr. Moe in absolute and complete charge. The plan which was submitted envisaged a greatly expanded department holding shows larger than the "Road to Victory" in a Quonset hut 80 ft. square to be built in the backyard. The plan also comprises publication of a quarterly to equal Camera Work and from six to twelve photographic books a year. All this to be started by a $100,000 subscription from ten photographic manufacturers. The plan was put to me as an opportunity to expand and carry on the department and to support it. But as you know very well such a theory would not work in practice. With Steichen in we could not carry out the work which we believe in. His program was definitely stated to be "the photographic presentation of all that makes America the country that it is," which is a long way from the broad point of view in which we are interested and which has very little to do with photography as such. Steichen would run into the ground everything that we have done during the past five years and also, from the point of view of the whole Museum, would create such turmoil and make such demands that things would be in an awful mess.

I was astonished that neither I nor the Advisory Committee on Photography had been consulted by either Maloney or Steichen before the proposal was submitted to the trustees. I was shocked when I learned that the trustees had accepted the proposal and had offered the directorship to Steichen. I found it strange that there was no mention in the proposal of my participation, especially since I was then in charge of the department and had, at the request of the museum's executive director, submitted a program of activities for the upcoming three years.

The first inkling of the possibility that Steichen was being considered as director had come in Nancy's letter to me of October 29, 1944. Nancy's assistant, Ann Armstrong, had been told of the rumor by fellow staff member Elodie Courter. I was surprised and concerned. A week later the subject again came up.

> To go back to Jim [Soby]—I asked him about Steichen. He said he's been talking about Steichen for some time and thought he'd made some headway convincing trustees and such that inside of 3 weeks Steichen would have the Museum on its beam ends in utter chaos, and that the director of painting would be lucky if he could hang a watercolor in the men's washroom—and spoke of Steichen's frustrations and megalomania in a way I didn't know he understood....I told him I felt like leaving too and he said, "Don't do that."

The following day I wrote Nancy that I found

> alarming...the news of the Steichen threat. It had never crossed my mind that he might be appointed director, and the thought of it is most discouraging, for it would mean our complete separation from the Museum....His attitude towards photography is so utterly different from ours, his personality is so self-centered and difficult, his megalomania is so aggressive, that we cannot work under him....I shall not accept Steichen....We cannot have anything to do with him, and will have to resign.

When I was selecting a committee for my history exhibition, Steichen had been my second choice, after Stieglitz. And indeed he was very helpful. For example, he made several prints of Chartres Cathedral from some 11 x 14-inch paper negatives by the nineteenth-century French photographer Henri Le Secq lent by the collector Victor Barthélemy. They were very difficult to print, and Steichen was very skilled. Nevertheless, Steichen's views on photography were utterly different from mine. Stieglitz once said if you want to understand Steichen, you must remember that he is a frustrated actor. He was very theatrical, very emotional. While my interests were increasingly in photography as a fine art, his were increasingly in the illustrative use of photography, particularly in swaying large masses of people. To him the purpose of photography was "to explain man to man and each man to himself." He was a populist in his taste, as his first wartime exhibition, "The Road to Victory" (1942), showed. A propaganda show, it was installed very dramatically on three levels at MoMA by the designer Herbert Bayer. Viewers walked through it on a ramp. Ansel, in a letter he had written to me earlier, described a second exhibition of war photographs Steichen organized for the museum in 1945, "Power in the Pacific." It points up some of the differences between us.

> The Steichen show represents almost the exact opposite of what I believe we should work towards. It is slick, mechanically excellent, superficially moving by virtue of the tremendous scale and impact of the subject. As far as I am concerned, it strikes absolutely no spiritual note, displays no reason for the war, reveals no single expression of what any of the photographers thought or felt about the tremendous scenes before them....I think the pendulum will swing to the more expressive side, but I can see quite a few years of bombastic popularization, merchandising and sheer ballyhoo which it will be our solemn duty to coun-

teract as much as we possibly can. I mentioned to Nancy the other day that for every person who is exposed to what we are trying to do there are literally thousands who are exposed to Steichen, *U.S. Camera, Popular Photography* and advertising expressions....The enormous and conscience-less ballyhoo and presentation simply hypnotize the mass of spectators.

I agree with Nancy that the Museum Department is but a step as far as we, as a group, are concerned. I think you two could found an institution—there must be a better word for it—which with very simple outlay could accomplish more than anything except Stieglitz's establishment.

I now wrote to Ansel, "If we lose and Steichen comes into the museum there is only one course for Nancy and myself to take. We resign. And immediately start making plans for a photo center of our own....We have built up a really inspiring body of supporters." Ansel replied,

I do not claim to be a telepathist but I have had a hunch that something has been going on and the news about the Maloney-Steichen business is not a surprise. In fact, I have occasionally wondered how long it would be before just such a thing took place. I should be disturbed, but I'm not. If the Museum powers accept such a program, then, ipso facto, the Museum is not the place for us and while there might be a keen disappointment at first we must always remember that what we stand for is infinitely more important than the opposition and that we can accomplish far more with the minimum of material accessories than the Museum can ever do with vast plant equipment, money and ballyhoo....

As I progress in photography I am rapidly becoming aware of the complete futility of compromise, not only with the world at large but with myself....You people have the greatest thing to offer photography of anyone and I would certainly not compromise or temporize with the Museum or any group. We will always lose out if we do that....

If the manufacturers put up the money for the Steichen melee, the direction and tone is immediately determined and you should withdraw.

One afternoon, Dick Abbott took me to the University Club, a few doors down from the museum, and over drinks explained the new policy of the photography department by comparing it to college athletics. "Steichen's plans are the equivalent of Harvard football," he explained, citing my alma mater, "while what you propose can be compared in popularity to crew on the Charles River."

I had respect for Steichen's early photography, but I felt he had by now lost his interest in art and could see photography only as documentation of the social scene, or as a journalistic medium used for propaganda. To him beauty gave way to impact.[32] Because the differences

32. In 1969, at a celebration of Steichen's ninetieth birthday held at the Plaza Hotel in New York, he told the party, "When I first became interested in photography I thought it was the whole cheese. My idea was to have it recognized as one of the fine arts. Today I don't give a hoot in hell about that." (Quoted by Thomas F. Brady, *New York Times*, March 28, 1969.)

between us were so great I did not see how I could work under him; so with great regret on March 7, 1946, I resigned from the museum. In my letter of resignation I wrote:

> If I were asked to work under a man in whom I had absolute faith and whose judgment I completely respected, I would be proud and happy to cooperate. Unfortunately my experience with Mr. Steichen has not given me that assurance. If I believed that the values of taste, scholarship and presentation which the Museum has established in all its work could be maintained under the proposed program, I would most certainly desire to continue as Curator. I had hoped that it might be possible to work out a solution satisfactory to all, whereby I would be given independent power and means to carry out a basic program. I was disappointed that this independence of action could not be granted to me.

Leaving the department I had founded with the help of Alfred Barr, David McAlpin, Ansel Adams, Jim Soby, and Nancy was very painful. The decision also caused a reaction in the photography community, which in those days was relatively small. Many of the photographers we had worked with, once they learned of the impending change in direction, wrote letters in protest to the museum administration. Harry Callahan, Helen Levitt, Brett Weston, Willard Van Dyke, Edward Weston, and, of course, Ansel were among these. Most of them were returned to me with their contents unread. Ansel, however, expressed himself with his usual eloquence, and his letter was read:

> April 29, 1946
>
> My Dear Mr. Clark,
>
> It is with deepest regret that I am constrained to write you this letter. I write as an artist as well as a spectator of the arts, and also as one who has had a genuine interest in the Museum of Modern Art. My interest in photography has extended beyond the development of my own work; I have been active in promoting the awareness and understanding of creative photography. We both know that an intelligent, critical public is the strongest support of creative expression. With the establishment of the Department of Photography at the Museum of Modern Art I felt a major step forward had been taken to secure photography among the other arts as an important medium of creative expression. I have considered my modest association with the department a privilege and a pleasure, and it was gratifying to watch the department's functions and achievements grow year by year....
>
> The recent turn of events is a profound shock and disappointment to me; to me it is an expression of a policy which can only undermine and defeat the basic principle on which the Museum was founded, and which reverses the directions of the formative years....
>
> I think it is time an evaluation of the aims and purposes of the museum be made to determine and clarify its function. Perhaps it is I who have been wrong—perhaps the Museum is not interested in *expression* as much as in *illustration*. Perhaps the museum considers the surface more important

than the substance. I do not like to believe this; your great exhibitions which have made cultural history should refute my doubts. It seems strange to me that the museum which has shown Marin, Picasso, Weston, Rouault, and many other great creative spirits would at this time turn its back upon creative photography, or, at least, dilute its values. To supplant Beaumont Newhall, who has made such a great contribution to the art through his vast knowledge and sympathy for the medium, with a *regime* which is inevitably favorable to the spectacular and "popular" is indeed a body blow to the progress of creative photography. Hundreds, if not thousands of photographers have looked to the museum's Department of Photography for knowledge, guidance, and inspiration. All types—student and professional, creative and commercial—have looked to the department for the important thing that is not found elsewhere in the world to my knowledge—a distillation of the creative and imaginative elements of the art. No other art requires such penetrating evaluations as does photography; it is the prey of superficial and glamorous showmanship, and it is an "easy" art—up to the crucial level of creative expression whereupon it becomes as intense and difficult as painting and sculpture. Were this not the case there would have been no justification for the Museum of Modern Art to have sanctioned the founding of the department in the first place....

The great exhibitions of war photography, while excellent representations of a tremendously moving and important subject, were, after all, objective and illustrative—not creative or contemplative. While they undoubtedly benefited the museum in publicity and attendance I believe they would have been far more effective in Grand Central Station—where even more persons could have benefited from them. I would believe it the function of the museum to exhibit those particular photographs which contain the creative potential, for it is this potential that should permeate and strengthen everything. Mistakes have been made, of course—as in any other department of the museum—but I can see no basic criticism on any other grounds than failure to "play to the gallery" and to compromise with the sterile world of photographic salons, magazines, and manufacturers....

As I have received no notification of termination of the Advisory Committee on Photography—to which I had the honor of appointment by you—I have presumed it still exists. If so, I would be interested in knowing why the advice of this committee was not requested in this momentous decision to reverse policy. If the committee ever had a legitimate function, this was it. Of course, I am sure you will appreciate my request that my resignation from the Committee—if it exists—be effective immediately. I tender it to you with deep regret....

Let me assure you that this letter is written with no intention of praising or condemning anyone on any personal basis. My protest is purely objective. You are trading gold for brass. Believe me, I am deeply concerned for the future potency of the Museum of Modern Art....

The following is from an entry in my journal for May 1, 1946:

Yesterday a girl from the bookkeeping office at the Museum handed me a check for salary during April and a two weeks advance for vacation. The word "final" appeared beside the total sum.

In this way I finally received official notice that my resignation has been acted upon. Not a single letter has been written to me about the whole matter. Not a single gesture has been made. The situation is extraordinary. Steichen has not procured the $100,000 that was so tempting to the Trustees. He has not found a successor to me. The Quonset hut is not built. Ann Armstrong is staying on to keep the collection open, and to bridge the gap between my leaving and the grand opening of the greatly expanded department.

My last day at the Museum as an official member of the staff was not a pleasant one. I went through all the material, trying to separate what was mine and what was the Museum's. I couldn't finish it up. Dick Abbott came in and asked me to have a cocktail with him. We went to the University Club for a couple of scotch and sodas. We didn't have much to say to one another, and the talk was mostly around the subject. I think that he has no conception of my point of view at all.

Even after my resignation, feelings continued to run high. In June Nancy wrote to Edward Weston,

The biggest news of the moment is that the Advisory Committee of the Museum, a body of younger people who were originally supposed to feed ideas to the Trustees and serve as a kind of training ground for future Trustees, has resigned *as a body* because of general discontent with the way in which the Museum is developing (or shall we say the lack of development) and they have used the whole photography mess as a specific example. A bit late, but gratifying to see that there is some opposition to the Big Business methods which the Museum is adopting.

In retrospect, I can only believe that if Alfred Barr had still been the director of the museum, the takeover of the Department of Photography by Edward Steichen would not have occurred. It was Alfred who conceived the somewhat revolutionary plan of adding photography to the museum's activities. It was Alfred who persuaded the trustees to appoint me curator of photography. It was he who accepted the plan of initiating a Department of Photography—the first in any art museum in the world. Barr wrote me:

Jim [Soby] has just told me the very sad news of your resignation. Wise or not, I suppose it was the simplest, cleanest way out—though I wish—and I told you—that you had stayed.

I think, I know, what a loss you'll be, at least to the Museum we once dreamed of in which scholarship and taste would count in photography as much as [in] big-top shows.

I think you did a very fine job pioneering under real difficulties both institutional and personal. Certainly the Museum's reputation in the field owes more to you than will be understood until a retrospective (and a reaction) of several years makes a true perspective possible.

I don't know what you'll do now; I hope you'll like it—and count on me to help in any way I can.

All my best to you and Nancy,

Alfred

When Steichen retired as director of the Department of Photography in 1962, museum director René d'Harnoncourt asked me to assist him in finding a replacement for Steichen. I traveled down to New York from Rochester for the meeting. René had a very narrow desk, and when he talked to you it was practically in your ear. "Well, what kind of curator do you want?" I asked him. He leaned over to me and spoke, his face only several inches from mine. "Someone just like you—exactly like you." There was my opportunity once again to pick up the reins, and it was an important decision. But I felt that it would not be as rewarding to move from being the director of the first photographic museum to being part of an institution, even one as great as the Museum of Modern Art. Steichen suggested a young photographer from Minnesota by the name of John Szarkowski. He had visited Nancy and me in Rochester to show us his work, and we found him most impressive. I completely agreed with Steichen on this, and Szarkowski was selected as his successor.

FREELANCING AT LARGE

Immediately upon leaving the museum, I began an intensive year of freelancing. One of the people at the museum for whom I had always had tremendous respect was the director of the publications department, Monroe Wheeler. A man of enormous intelligence and talent, in his own quiet, behind-the-scenes way he had been the virtual director of the museum. Alfred Barr depended on him. Ironically, just two weeks after I had resigned, Monroe invited me to write an essay for the Cartier-Bresson exhibition. The piece that Lincoln Kirstein had submitted did not discuss Cartier-Bresson's photographs.

I also organized an exhibition of photographs of New York City by my friend Todd Webb, began researching for a book on American daguerreotypes, and taught photography at László Moholy-Nagy's Institute of Design in Chicago and at Black Mountain College, North Carolina. In

Suffolk Street Market, New York City, 1946. Photograph by Todd Webb. (Courtesy of the photographer)

addition, I wrote ten articles, including an essay on pictorial photography for the *Encyclopaedia Britannica*. In 1947 I received a John Simon Guggenheim Memorial Foundation Fellowship, which allowed me to write the third edition of *The History of Photography*.

Todd Webb served in the Navy during World War II as a photographer. After three years of duty in the South Pacific he came to live in New York. He was fascinated by the city, and took dozens of photographs of street life. I showed a group of these to Hardinge Scholle, director of the Museum of the City of New York, in the hope that he might buy a few for his museum's collection. To my delight he suggested that I organize an exhibition of Todd's photographs. I wrote about this show in *Art News* in October 1946:

> Like all of us who were overseas, Todd Webb made utopian post-war plans. He was going to spend a year photographing New York. Unlike most of us, he carried out his dream. Although that year is not yet up, his photographic discovery of New York has been so intense and moving that 150 of his prints now hang in his first one-man exhibition, "I See a City," at the Museum of the City of New York.
>
> It is not easy to photograph a city so that its special character is revealed. It is a great temptation to concentrate on the spectacular architecture. Yet people make the city what it is.
>
> Todd found the most intense record of the people in those streets where living conditions are crowded and small shops abound. He photographed "Welcome Home G.I. Joe" decorations above the doorways of tenements as tenderly as if he saw his own name lettered on the crude and colorful

signs. He made a series of photographs of humble religious meeting places behind shop fronts and in basements, marked off from neighboring doorways by symbols as naive as those of early Christians. Third Avenue he found to be a most fruitful area: the structure of the elevated railroad casting strange patterns on the cobble-stoned street, weird architecture of stations, views from station platforms.

He has chosen to record that which is not spectacular; his approach is the opposite of the news photographer, who seeks the novel and the unusual. Todd photographs the drama of bargaining in pushcart markets; skeptical faces inspecting the wares, shrewd faces counting their change, satisfied faces weighing produce. He photographs children dancing hand in hand around the spouting hydrant on a hot day. He photographs visitors at Coney Island and a soldier having his shoes shined and people waiting for the bus and people just walking down the street.

In May 1946 Nancy and I made a trip to Massachusetts. She wanted to visit her mother in Swampscott and also to do research for *Time in New England*. She needed early accounts of the first settlers in New England and hoped to find original sources in the extensive library of the Essex Institute in Salem. While Nancy read ancient texts, I casually asked the librarian if the Institute owned any daguerreotypes. She opened the door of a closet and brought out box after box of them. I had never seen so many and I was entranced by their beauty. They were portraits on silver-plated copper sheets enclosed in velvet-lined cases of embossed leather or molded plastic. They excited me not as documents but as pictures. It was the revelation of a medium.

Nancy, New York City, 1946. Photograph by Beaumont Newhall. (Courtesy of Scheinbaum & Russek Ltd., Santa Fe, New Mexico)

As I looked at them I thought that a book of American daguerreotypes would be a fine thing to do. It could be a vivid picture of this country in the 1840s and 1850s. In addition to portraits of both known and unknown men and women, it could contain city views and such unusual subjects as gold miners at work in California. The text would be a careful account of the process, and in an index I could put a vast amount of biographical information about the men and women who made daguerreotypes. On my return to New York I had lunch with Charles Duell, of the publishing firm of Duell, Sloane and Pearce, with whom Nancy and Paul Strand had a contract for the publishing of *Time in New England*. I told him of my idea of writing a book on American daguerreotypes. He was enthusiastic, and a few days later he wrote me that they would like to publish the book in 1947.

The book proved to be far more difficult to write than I had expected. Other, more pressing, projects interfered with the research required for such an innovative subject. I traveled across the country with a copy camera and lots of film to photograph daguerreotypes in private collections and historical societies. Year after year Charles Duell would remind me of the contract. I would answer apologetically, always offering to return his $250 advance. This he never accepted. "If I do," he would say, "I'll never get the manuscript!" Charles waited patiently. Finally, fifteen years later, with his patience and encouragement, *The Daguerreotype in America* appeared, the first book on the subject.

❖

HENRI CARTIER-BRESSON

While Nancy was acting curator at the Museum of Modern Art, she had proposed an exhibition of Cartier-Bresson's work. However, she and Jim Soby could not find enough prints in New York for a show. The only material they could gather were poor or mutilated prints—retouched or silhouetted photos used by magazines. Nor could they reach Cartier-Bresson: he was in the military in France and his exact whereabouts were not known. It was rumored that he had been captured by the Germans.

One of Henri's friends was the photographer David Seymour—better known as Chim—who had been staying in France but was living in New York during the war and had a photofinishing business. Chim joined the U.S. Army, and Nancy saw him off for overseas duty. "If you see Henri," she said to him in parting, "please tell him there's a girl in New York who wants to make a show of his photographs at the Museum of Modern Art." Cartier (as he was then known) escaped from prison camp on the third attempt and joined the French Underground. He was not making his street photographs of course, because the war made this too dangerous, but he was doing indoor portraits. Surprisingly, Chim did run into Henri. "There's a girl in New York who wants to show your photographs," he sternly told Henri. "You must say yes or I'll shoot," and with that pulled out his pistol and pointed it at the photographer. Henri agreed to an exhibition to be held after the war was over.

Cartier and his Javanese wife, Eli, came to New York in the spring of 1946 to work on this exhibition and to photograph the American scene from coast to coast for *Harper's*

Bazaar, at the invitation of the editor Carmel Snow and art director Alexey Brodovitch. (These photographs were not published until 1991, however, as *America in Passing*.)[33] Shortly after their arrival, we invited Cartier and his wife for lunch. The following excerpt from my journal gives my impressions of them.

33. Henri Cartier-Bresson, *America in Passing* (Boston: Bulfinch Press/Little, Brown, 1991).

Cartier looks like a scrubbed college boy, in tweeds, with a crew haircut. His wife, in a sari, dark-skinned, with oriental eyes and a caste mark on her forehead, proved to be very easy to talk with, speaking English almost as fluently and well as Cartier. They would have nothing to drink. Where to go? We had planned either the St. Denis, a fashionable, good and expensive French restaurant up the street, or the Little Old Mansion, a Southern restaurant in a fake Italian villa made in a railroad brownstone on 52nd St. They suggested the Automat. This we vetoed only because it would be so crowded. Finally, after Mme had said something about hot sauce I thought of the Mexican place, Rudy's, and it was a perfect choice, Cartier ordering in Spanish, muttering that it was "*le véritable cuisine mexicain*," all of us with something different, special hot sauces coming in from the kitchen, and Carta Blanca beer.

We had coffee at home, and sat around talking until 4:30, all of us absorbed. Cartier has definite ideas on photography; he has a point of view which he wants to demonstrate, not alone his own, but that of a group of his friends. Photography should be plastic, it should be *aigu* [sharp]. Photography is seeing. It occupies a place midway between painting and the documentary film; each of these three forms of expression is separate, yet interrelated, like the three speeds of an automobile. He paints for himself; he paints to understand plastic relationships, and to make his seeing more *aigu*. These paintings he shows only to his friends among the painters, to Braque and to Matisse in particular. Their criticism he prizes very highly. Photography to him must not be esthetic, it must not be "art." It is like a journal, a diary, note taking. He expressed contempt for the mechanical side (yet we became involved in various technical discussions from time to time).

For the Rolleiflex he has no use at all. The square format, the waist level position, these he does not like at all. "The Rolleiflex has made photographers of too many people." For his vision, for his point of view, the Leica is the ideal instrument, except for the lenses. So he had a Contax $f/1.5$ lens fitted to his Leica. He explained that he hated flashlight, and never used it. Hence he needs the large-aperture lens. To make exposures of 1/4 second he has gone into training, like an athlete, not drinking, smoking only moderately, going to bed early. When he left he did not want to take the book on Weston which Nancy had given him because he had to have his hands free for photographing.

Cartier was very disappointed that I shall not be making the show with him at the Museum, and I cannot but share his disappointment. However I offered to help him in an unofficial way, and I am sure that both Nancy and I can be of great help to him. He has the right conception of the show, which will be a retrospective, showing the several periods of his development. At the moment his chief interest is in portraiture, of a very special kind—portraits made unawares, through a keyhole, as he put it, made in an *état grasse*, a kind of revealing of character. He said that his friends accuse him of photographing what is on the eyelid when the eye is closed, and he had much to say of the relation of the eye and the heart. Weegee's pictures he confided to us (there was much confiding, many times the words "strictly between us" were used) he found marvelous documents, but shallow, dramatic but not lasting.

To our feeling that photography is an independent art form, free of painting and other graphic art, he expressed disagreement. He does not feel that photography is in a class with painting. The weight, Nancy and I felt, of European culture in which painting has played so important a role hangs upon him as it does with other Continental photographers with whom we have talked. He has theories about sharpness, and cannot hold with the school that demands sharpness all over, although he respects those who have formed a definite esthetic. His quarrel is with those who blindly demand sharpness. He resented criticism of a *Life* researcher and writer for whom he did some work in France; she wanted his things to be sharp all over, as she wanted him to cover a story in a primitive chronological way. "A man shaving, coming down in the lift, leaving the apartment, walking down the street. Poof! That is not how to do a photo story!" By plastic relations the unsharp becomes as important as the sharp.

We felt that he had an intellectual tolerance, but that he had very definite, positive ideas about his own work. For those who know what they are doing, he had respect; for those who blindly snap away he has no use at all.

Unfortunately, we did not see a single photograph. All he brought with him were his negatives. These he is going to enlarge at the photo laboratory of his friend Chim. He will make about fifty first-class enlargements as a basis for the exhibition. He did not want to show proofs. Positively, he put forth the commendable principle that one should show only the finished product, that any apologies were to be avoided at all costs. A film, he said, should not be shown even to the actors until it has been cut and the sound track added.

It was all very stimulating. When Henri and Eli left, reluctantly, and with expressions of looking forward to a next meeting, Nancy said that she was exhausted. We had sustained for four hours a brilliant conversation which never slackened.

One month later, I bought a Leica camera.

Although I had shown the work of Cartier-Bresson in my 1937 exhibition, I had not been particularly enthusiastic about it. When Jim Soby wrote an admiring article on him, "The Art of the Poetic Accident," it made me reconsider. It was published in *Minicam*, a how-to magazine run by a curious editor with bad taste and great enthusiasm. Up until this point we thought Cartier was just a Dada photographer who went around with a prefocused camera photographing everything, then from an enormous number of images selected some that happened to be terrific. But when, during Cartier's visit, the editor of *Popular Photography* asked me to write a profile of him, I discovered during my interview that this business of the "poetic accident" was nonsense: he knew *exactly* what he was doing. His contact sheets revealed that he used the full frame for his compositions. There was absolutely nothing accidental or unforeseen in his photography.

Henri wanted to write captions for the photographs that would be reproduced. I agreed. "I've been told that you Americans want captions to answer the questions who, what, when, where, and why," he told me, and indeed he wrote them in that form. For example, for his famous picture of the man in black walking past the children, the black squares in the background repeating the form of his hat, he wrote: "Why is this man walking with the children? There is no answer."

When Cartier was asked for a portrait of himself to accompany my article, he said he had none, adding, "Ask Beaumont." One afternoon I went around to his New York apartment with my camera. He had just bought a new 85mm $f/1.5$ lens, which is common today but was extremely rare and expensive in 1946. While I was photographing him he suddenly handed me his new lens. "Try this on your Leica, Beaumont," he said. And with it I made his portrait. He then used the lens to make a photograph of me.

Very attuned in his portraiture, Cartier did not use flash in his photographs in the days before film became more sensitive. "With flashlight I can't visualize the final picture," he complained. "It's like walking into a symphony orchestra with a pistol in your hand."

Photography was everything to him in those days. He always had his camera with him, and was never without it. If someone gave him a present, he would accept it graciously, then say, "Would you mind if I sent somebody for it? I need to keep my hands free for photographing." Nancy once said, "I'm sure he takes a camera to bed, although I've never seen him do it."

Cartier could never understand the f.64 group of American photographers at all, and once commented, "They just photograph rocks." Others shared his opinion. Once, after looking through an Ansel Adams book of landscape photographs, Lincoln Kirstein turned to Ansel and asked, "Don't they have *people* in California?" He preferred Cartier-Bresson's work.

ALFRED STIEGLITZ

Throughout much of the war, Nancy had collected data for a biography of Alfred Stieglitz, perhaps most intensively in 1942. Whenever he was up to it, she would walk over to The Place and spend an afternoon visiting and interviewing. She would listen to Stieglitz for hours—without either a tape recorder or even a notebook, because she would let nothing come between her and her subject. After she left his gallery she would go to the nearest table and chair, often in a restaurant, order a coffee, and write out everything she had learned.

Alfred Stieglitz, c. 1946. Photograph by Henri Cartier-Bresson. (Courtesy of the photographer)

Dorothy Norman, c. 1950. Photograph by Nancy Newhall. (Courtesy of Scheinbaum & Russek Ltd., Santa Fe, New Mexico)

However, at one point Stieglitz's friend the writer Dorothy Norman indicated that she too was collecting material for her own Stieglitz biography. The seriousness of her intent was indicated by the fact that she found all the letters and articles he had written during his student days in Germany and had them translated by James Card at Eastman House, who had gone to school in Heidelberg. Out of respect for Dorothy, Nancy promised that she would not publish her biography until Dorothy had written hers. She put it aside. Unfortunately, Stieglitz's health became more fragile, and after his death it took Dorothy years to complete her task. By then Nancy had moved on to other projects.

Nancy and Stieglitz had become good friends. While we were living in New York, Nancy and I frequently visited him at An American Place, which was only a block from our apartment. When we dropped in on the afternoon of July 6, 1946, we found Stieglitz lying on the cot in his little office in a state of collapse. He had had another heart attack. He was under morphine; his doctor had come, and would return in an hour. There was not another soul in The Place. Stieglitz was complaining bitterly in a labored voice that was hardly more than a whisper: "What they do to me! What they ask of me! You have no idea. I tell them that if they ask me to show my photographs it will kill me. So many people. It was a wonderful day—Todd Webb and placing an O'Keeffe. Tell me what you've been doing."

And so we talked to him, sitting close to his cot, not wanting to leave him alone, not wanting to excite him, trying to find things to talk about that would interest him, take his mind away, yet not demand an answer. He lay there, dying it seemed, moving only his left arm up and down, blaming himself, depressed by everything, fearing that the fight had only begun and he was hopeless. He asked me to read aloud the article Soby had written in the *Saturday Review* about O'Keeffe. A fine, warm review, a discovery through the Museum of Modern Art exhibition of her paintings that she is "perhaps the greatest of living women painters." Then Frances Leavitt, a young woman who was living in the apartment and looking after Stieglitz, came in and we left with heavy hearts. It was painful to see such a great man physically wasting away, and to be so helpless, although we were anxious to be of assistance.

We saw Stieglitz very briefly one other time. He died a week later in Doctors' Hospital. Nancy described the circumstances in a letter to Ansel:

> A strange week. It's one thing to realize that a Stieglitz may die, at any minute, and another to come into The Place one Saturday afternoon and find him alone with a heart attack. He had called the doctor himself. No one responsible near—nobody at all, until we came. We wanted him to be quiet, but he wanted to talk, in pain, and with a racing pulse. We stayed until the girl O'Keeffe left in charge happened in. I went back later. The Place was darkened as much as the light would let it. He was worriedly dictating letters. Sunday we went over, with roses for him, but felt we had better not respond to his invitation to talk. Then, on Wednesday, as we were sitting at dinner, with the Cartier-Bressons, and Paul and Virginia [Strand], just back from the Pacific, in walked Zohler [the custodian of An American Place] and Melquist [Stieglitz's friend] with the news that Stieglitz had had a stroke and was unconscious in an oxygen tent. O'Keeffe got the telegram shopping in town [Santa Fe, near where she then lived], drove straight to the airfield, flew until grounded, then took a train. Dorothy [Norman] came down from Woods Hole. Up there in the hospital they became reconciled, those two, and took turns in that long vigil, with Henwar [Rodakiewicz, a friend of Stieglitz] helping. Stieglitz never regained consciousness; died at 1:30 Saturday morning. Dorothy, watching, said he was still very beautiful, and somehow remote, with the inevitable. We did not get the news of his death till Sunday morning, deep in Long Island, having left Saturday, early, for a vagabond trip....The cremation took place at eleven-thirty Sunday. Paul, who was there, said it was strange and sad. About twenty people. O'Keeffe, strained but under control, Dorothy utterly shattered, weeping, even on Steichen's shoulder. Not a word was said.
>
> This morning, back in town, I finally got hold of Dorothy. O'Keeffe had just called her, saying that it was all right for her to leave her things at the Place until she, O'Keeffe, should return in the fall, but then she wanted absolute control of the Place. As for the lease. Stieglitz had let Dorothy take care of it only because he and all his family liked making things difficult. In a little while, he would have let O'Keeffe take it. Dorothy's relation to Stieglitz she considered absolutely disgusting. That people should go on so many years wran-

gling! Dorothy made a few heartbroken responses, and then was quiet under the malignant whipping. Her only response can be a Twice a Year for everyone who cared for Stieglitz to make a statement in. Obviously, O'Keeffe will have no more of the Place as Stieglitz conceived it. She said he wanted her to send all his things to an institution. Dave [McAlpin] called O'Keeffe, asking if he might help; she said she didn't want to see or talk to anyone just now; later in the week, maybe. Meanwhile, she had a lot to do and Steichen was helping her. I thought this all over, my sympathies utterly with Dorothy, but realizing O'Keeffe's strain and remembering that when she came, with Dave and Sally, to our party on May first—celebrating our leaving the Museum—she looked through the door, saw Dorothy, screamed, and got back in the elevator. To make no motion toward O'Keeffe at this time would be to preclude any possibility of working together, and close the door to the greatest photographs ever made. I went over, with flowers, to offer my hands and time for any service, determined that if Steichen was there, I would work alongside him at anything they set me to, quietly. The door to O'Keeffe's room was closed. The strange little terrified woman—maybe a nurse—said she would call O'Keeffe, but that she was not well. I left the flowers and my message and came away; the outbreak to Dorothy may well have been prelude to one of the breakups that happen to O'Keeffe.

…The Place, as a Place, is dead, with Stieglitz. But what he was, what he spent his life trying to do and to say, that is greater than our little feuds. It is up to us to carry it on, each of us, with all we have to give.

When I was asked by Dorothy Norman to contribute to the *Alfred Stieglitz Memorial Portfolio* that she was editing, I wrote the following:

Those of us who came to know Alfred Stieglitz through our interest in photography will ever remember him as a great teacher. He taught by precept and parable. He opened our eyes. He helped us to discover that photography is a point of view, even a way of life.

One of his favorite aphorisms was "When I make a photograph I make love." It was a purposely extravagant remark. He wanted to tell me that a great photograph is made with the heart, at a peak of emotional intensity. It is within the photographer's power, when he is an artist, to transmute the subject and to impress his personality on the final product.

Once a handwriting analyst, a stranger to me, happened to see on my desk an envelope addressed by Stieglitz in his bold and characteristic hand. "This writer is a painter," the graphologist said.

"No," I answered, "he is a photographer. Alfred Stieglitz. Do you know him?"

"No. He must be a very unusual photographer. If he made a picture of this door it would no longer be an ordinary door, but a very special one."

It seemed as if Stieglitz could photograph anything. The subjects of his great work were often commonplace: the city from his windows, people close to him, the sky overhead.

When I brought my own photographs to show him he would look at them silently. He did not criticize them; he neither praised them nor condemned them. He seemed to accept or dismiss them as one accepts or dismisses a letter or a conversation. Sometimes he would bring forth from his vast collection a photograph in which he had solved problems similar to those I had faced, and we would discuss technique. He showed me that technique is not a thing to be taken for granted: it is a challenge. Always just a little bit more could have been gotten on the negative than seemed possible. Always just a little bit more could have been brought out in the print. Photographs made with intensity can never be recreated, prints made almost in spite of technique are not dead records. There are Stieglitz photographs that are alive. They will last as great art lasts.

Every photographer who had something to say was always welcome at An American Place. There is no record of how many came, portfolio in hand, to show their prints to Stieglitz, to talk with him and to see, if on that day he had the strength, some of his own work.

There is no way to measure what he gave, for it was intangible.

But it was very real.

❖

1946 JOURNAL

For a few weeks after leaving the Modern I began to keep a regular journal. The following are excerpts from a period from May to August 1946, and provide an idea of the life Nancy and I were leading from our small apartment on West Fifty-third Street, down the block from the museum, across the street from the home of photographer Berenice Abbott.

❖

1 May

The first day of our new adventure! I feel both sad and relieved. Giving up everything at the museum is not easy to do, yet there is no other alternative. At 8:30 our doorbell began to ring, and it rang and rang all evening as friends came to our party. After it was over we tried to remember who had come, and our list numbered 53. Nancy had invited our friends on the occasion of leaving the museum, and everybody came, bringing presents and good wishes. Betty Marshall gave us a case of champagne, which lasted throughout the first half of the party, and which was mightily enjoyed by the guests. At 3 am we shooed the last guest out and tumbled into bed.

❖

3 May

A beautiful day. Had a splendid lunch with Philippe Halsman in Vorst's Sea Grille—shad roe and bacon, beer, delicious cherry pie. I explained to him the full reasons for my resignation from the museum, and he understood the problem. His only fear is that I shall leave New York. He is editing with four others the annual of the Society of Magazine Photographers, and is doing most of the work. He would like to have me write an article for the annual on the history of photojournalism.... Halsman is a very fine fellow. I like him. He is a real success now, with a fine two-floor studio and all the work he can do. As we parted he took my hand in both his. "Let us keep in touch with one another," he said. "I shall never forget the encouragement which you gave me when I first came here."

❖

9 May

I had some errands to do at the museum and in the office I found Steichen talking with Ann. I barged right in, and was warmly greeted by Steichen....He said he wanted to have a talk with me, that he honestly and truly felt that I had con-tributed a very great deal to American photography. "I mean it," he cried, grasping my arm in both of his hands, "and I intend to prove it if it takes me fifteen years! I thought from our luncheon that you agreed with all my proposals, and I was hurt when I found out through the photographic grapevine that you were hostile." There was much of looking one another in the eye, and at one moment I thought that Steichen would break into tears. He was emotionally shaken. This was the meeting that I had anticipated long ago, this was what I feared would happen before I made the definite step; now he was turning on that powerful emotional quality of his. It is a little too late. I told him that I would want to help him how-ever I could, under the circumstances, and he said that he wanted to help me....The interview did not leave me unmoved. I was brought back to my senses by Ferd Reyher, with whom I had dinner. He said the only thing to do...was to look Steichen straight in the eye and say shit and walk out. I prefer Charles Sheeler's little motto: "Don't look back; remember what happened to Lot's wife."

❖

24 May

Stieglitz was glad to see us. O'Keeffe was in The Place. We congratulated her on her show, which we had seen at the museum the night before. Stieglitz was per-fectly swell to us, and seemed to talk more directly than ever he had before, with concrete definite pieces of advice of a kind which he usually does not offer. He advised Nancy to come to an agreement at once with Strand about the book

[*Time in New England*], for he fears that Strand does not and will not recognize the part that Nancy is playing and that it should be quite clear that the book is a true work of cooperation. As to me he saw that I did not have the talent for pushing myself forward. I told him that I realized this (and that I had tortured myself on it) and was trying to overcome this defect. He said that I couldn't, and that I shouldn't worry about it, that I had much that I could do very well indeed, and that it would be a mistake to force myself. The way he put it was most consoling to me indeed. We talked about a show at the museum. He shook his head: "Never. Never. I have made up my mind." We are both sorry and pleased at this attitude—sorry because a good big show of Stieglitz photographs would be the most important thing in photographic history—pleased because he is loyal with himself, with a decision which he made in 1940 at a time when I was trying very hard to make a show at the museum possible and had almost succeeded.

We were late for our appointment with Ferd in his spacious apartment in the Chelsea Hotel. Ferd was in fine form. He told story after story, illustrating the dramatic moments with gesticulations and shouting. Stories about Hollywood; about Mme Lachaise (picturing for us Mme Lachaise of the flesh and of the belly laugh, imagining the bedrollings, the earthquake upheavals, the love tussles throughout the house, the scenes in the kitchen, the near collapse of the kitchen table); about mediums, Houdini and psychoanalysts; about Lachaise and the Rockefeller memorial, transporting the huge block of Vermont granite through New England; digging clams in Maine, eating them raw, finding a perfect lemon washed up on shore at just the proper time and place; and I can't remember how many more stories, nor how diversified, nor how he jumped from topic to topic yet always came back and tied up each subject neatly. And he drew from us stories, about Epstean, about Cartier, about photography.

❖

25 May   Minor White came at about 5:40 for a few minutes and left at 1. Nancy says that of all our guests he is the easiest to handle. Just likes being here, and if there is talk, he is a lively part of it, and if there is not talk he finds plenty to read and do. He has grown immensely from the time we first saw him last fall, when we arranged a meeting for him with Meyer Schapiro. He is going to help Ansel.

❖

26 May   Berenice Abbott is going to teach at Moholy-Nagy's Institute of Design this summer on the same program as myself, so we got together in her studio to discuss the whole matter....Saw Berenice's macrophotographs, 16 x 20 enlargements of the works of a watch, of a shelled walnut, of a knot in a piece of wood. She has a new technique, about which she is most secretive, which gives better definition in these enlargements than by the usual methods. She seemed to me to have aged

considerably. She is having a tough time. The magazine *Science Illustrated*, which she had such hopes of being the medium for her work, and which she was instrumental in founding, has been reorganized, and Tom Maloney is taking it over, or has been called in, to make it "successful."

❖

28 May

I met Ferd at the Hotel Chelsea and we went by subway to Parkside Station, Brooklyn. It was like another world....We had made the excursion to see the photographs which a dealer named Kane had in his apartment. We found a young man in a dreary apartment cluttered up with cheap Grand Rapids furniture and sentimental color prints on the wall. He didn't have much, and didn't know what he had, but the chief item was a collection of some 200 Muybridge prints bound in book form, quite obviously a dummy for the *Animal Locomotion* book. Each was stamped "Eadweard Muybridge Copyright 1881." For this collection Kane is asking $75—a fair price. We both decided that the item was not one for either of us, but I told Kane that I would try to interest the Metropolitan in it. Ferd found a photograph of the Wall Rope building on Front Street which he thought was more remarkable than I did, and we had a little discussion over it. He bought the thing for $1 and I bought a small book on coloring photographs written by [Richard L.] Simon and dedicated to Thomas Sully.

When we got back to the house there was Herc sitting in the Sleepy Hollow chair and Barb[ara Morgan] invisible under the red puff on the bed. They had come a little early and had succeeded in getting into the apartment. We had a splendid dinner at the University Club to which they (somewhat incongruously) belong, and then we tore down to Sarah Newmeyer's for a party which we had promised to help her give. We arrived in ample time to help Sarah make the drink, which was an awful brew of May wine, papaya, lime juice, and soda water. It was a miscellaneous crowd. I kept the drinks moving. We enjoyed Ian Hugo and his wife [Anaïs] Nin very much. She is a writer and he is a wood-engraver and artist. When they came to this country his wife had no success whatsoever in selling her writing and so they got a press and began publishing her work privately. A few weeks ago Edmund Wilson praised her work in *The New Yorker*, and within a week she was offered four contracts! She has taken one option up....The example of this solution to the problem of getting one's stuff out in the world I found inspiring. We are invited to visit the Hayter workshop where Hugo does some work.

❖

5 June

Just before seven the Cartiers arrived for our party, Henri in a very neat suit and immaculate white shirt, scrubbed and looking younger than ever, Mme in a gorgeous green and gold sari. We dined rather hurriedly at Rey et Pierre, one of the less expensive French restaurants of the area. It was amusing to see how Henri got service with a few words of French. Whereas I would have gone into an elaborate story of why we needed to have quick service, all Henri did was to call, "Patron! On est pressé!" and we got things in a hurry. Mme took coca-cola with the meal, to the delight of all.

The guests arrived promptly, about thirty altogether, some of our friends and some of Cartier's. Julien [Levy] came a second time. He brought Lee Miller, who turned out to be a grand person. The atmosphere was exactly the same as in our own parties. People taking leisurely advantage of the gathering, nobody monopolizing the conversation, all very informal and delightful. Had a good talk with Dorothy Norman who wants us to visit her on Cape Cod this summer. Janice Loeb "felt" the mild punch which we served and got into a violent argument about the Museum of Modern Art, with a few staff members who were at the party....Her point was the museum was no longer worth working for; their answer was that it was better than nothing. I stayed out of the conversation. Someone brought a coil spring. A little after twelve the party broke up. Henri thanked me. He said that "This is the true America." Later we got a special delivery letter:

> Chers amis,
>
> Si nous n'avons pas téléphoné c'est qu'un coup de téléphone ne nous suffisait pas pour vous dire combien nous avons été touchés de votre gentillesse. Nous avons été si sensibles à l'atmosphère chaude et amicale que vous avez su donner à cette soirée. Nous avons été également heureux de retrouver nos vieux amis et de faire la connaissance des vôtres.
>
> Merci encore et à très bientôt je vous téléphonerai pour que l'on se voit très prochainement.
>
> Très amicalement,
> Henri Cartier-Bresson[34]

❖

6 June

Charles and Musya [Sheeler] came in this afternoon, Musya very excited over the reception which Nancy's recounting of one of her experiences had received from Bill Williams and a short story writer who lives near them. Nancy took on, in the spirit of a lark, the suggestion that Musya made that some of her experiences after having been displaced from Russia would

34. Dear Friends,
If we have not telephoned, it is because a phone call would not suffice to tell you how touched we were by your kindness. We were so appreciative of the warmth and friendly atmosphere that you provided at the party. We were as happy to rediscover our old friends as we were to meet yours.

Thanks again, and I will telephone you shortly in order to see you soon.

Very fondly,
Henri Cartier-Bresson

be good stories. She found that the writing of them was more difficult than at first appeared, but she finished up one which Musya could show to her friend Bill Williams. He had nothing to suggest, and the short story man thought that it could be sold as it stood with a few changes. Charles and I tease the girls about the stories. Musya wants to make enough money so that her sister can come to America, and she wants us to build a house next to theirs. A house with a "black room" in it for photography.

❖

15 June

Minor White came to say goodbye to us today, just before taking the train to the West. He was not well, rocky to say the least, suffering from an ailment which his doctor described as too much protein. He had to have a vegetable lunch and so we went around to Longchamps on 57th St. for a farewell blow out. We have come to like Minor very much and we look forward to seeing him in San Francisco, where he will probably be working with Ansel.

❖

7 July

Yesterday Berenice Abbott called to ask for help. She's doing a book of her macrophotographs, and wants to announce that the process is new, without divulging the technique. Did I think—and tell me honestly—that it was new? I did not know; the results were outstanding, but I couldn't say that it seemed new. The upshot was that she asked me to share the secret so that I could be quoted as an expert on the history of photography as stating that this was something new under the sun. I told her I'd think it over. I shall tell her no—I have no desire to hold a secret so jealously, and if someone else hit upon the same idea, suspicion if not accusation of betraying her might arise in Berenice's mind. I'd like to help her. But how?

❖

10 July

Paul and Virginia, Henri and Eli for dinner. Virginia, just back from the Pacific, where she has been traveling with a USO troupe playing "Blithe Spirit," looked well and was full of life. She was shocked by the morale of the troops and the official treatment of the natives. Henri, usually reticent, spoke about his 35 months in Germany as a POW, living on nothing but a small piece of bread, a piece of artificial cheese and watered cabbage soup, working on twenty different jobs. The POWs demoralized more than the DPs [displaced persons], who had a tough time, but had the satisfaction of knowing why they were prisoners.

We drank crackling wine of Anjou which Paul had given us for our tenth anniversary at dinner. While we were having coffee, Zohler and Melquist came to tell us that Stieglitz had been taken to Doctors Hospital, where he was under oxygen. We drank coffee with rum in silence, the shock was so great, and then slowly relaxed.

17 July

The death of Stieglitz has left the problem of settling the estate. O'Keeffe told Dorothy Norman off on Monday in a heartless way that upset all of us. She was to get out of The Place by November. Her relation to Stieglitz had been a disgrace. The only reason she'd been allowed to handle the rent fund was because the Stieglitz family were poor business people. Poor Dorothy was terribly hurt, and poured out the story to Nancy on the telephone. Paul Strand told about the funeral. He was horrified at the lack of ceremony, at the too open display of emotion. There was no service. Friends were driven out to the crematorium and through a window saw the coffin slid into the furnace.

❖

6 August

[Chicago]…After a hasty dinner, I gave the evening lecture [at the Institute of Design] on the tradition, the history of photography from 1839 to 1889. I talked fast for two solid hours! Divided the talk into four parts, two the lights on, two with lantern slides. I felt that I succeeded in giving or rather in imparting a sense of enthusiasm. Moholy-Nagy came to the lecture. Afterwards he and some of the faculty and older students went to the apartment of Crombie Taylor, M-N's assistant. M-N spoke of photography. The early masters he considers pictorial: they did the same in photography as had been done in painting. The expansion of vision came later. We asked him how he liked Weston. He considers him great because he has double images in his photographs! Plurality of image, the unconscious discovery of hidden forms—the witch in a concretion! My god! Ansel as a great purist. Stieglitz he finally met: great reconciliation, and great admiration. Great admiration for Strand's prints. "If I could print like Strand and make negatives like Weston, I'd be a good photographer. But I am a painter. I am not a good technician. I began with the idea that my photographs could be printed by any corner drugstore, and still have something to say and be good. I wanted to open up the field, to show the possibilities."

❖

10 August

Met Moholy and his wife Sibyl at the Institute of Design and we drove out to their summer place at Somonauk, 70 miles north of Chicago.…I found much to photograph, and made a dozen exposures before supper. The day was dull; Moholy could not understand how I could take photographs without the sun. What I had to say about the virtues of diffused light seemed almost a revelation to him. He prefers the direct sunlight, and loves harsh contrasts of light and shade.

❖

LÁSZLÓ MOHOLY-NAGY

In 1937 László Moholy-Nagy emigrated to America at the invitation of a group of Chicago industrialists who planned to open an art school they named the New Bauhaus, as it was based on the curriculum of the original Bauhaus in Germany that had been closed by the Nazis. They wanted Moholy-Nagy to be its director. The group, which called itself the Association of Arts and Industries, had been given use of the former residence of the wealthy merchant Marshall Field located on Prairie Avenue to house the school. Moholy, as his friends called him, used to delight in telling friends that he initially thought that Marshall Field was an army officer, and that he was going to see buffaloes on the prairie. He visited us on his way to Chicago, and Nancy helped him write his speech to the sponsors of the school.

Unfortunately the Association met with financial difficulties and the New Bauhaus closed within the year. Undaunted, Moholy raised enough interest and funding to open in 1939, in a loft that was formerly a bakery, the School of Design, which became in 1944 the Institute of Design. In 1945 the institute bought a large building from the Chicago Historical Society, and had an enrollment of 682 students. Photography was an important part of the curriculum, and in the summer of 1946 Moholy and his assistant, Arthur Siegel, announced an extraordinary summer course with a faculty of twelve instructors, each of whom taught for a week. The staff comprised six photographers: (Berenice Abbott, Erwin Blumenfeld, Gordon Coster, Frank Scherschel, Paul Strand, Weegee), three staff teachers (Moholy-Nagy, Arthur Siegel, Frank Levstik), two editors (Roy Stryker, Ed Rosskam), and one photographic historian (myself). There were about seventy students in the class. In the evening

László Moholy-Nagy, during the seminar "The New Vision in Photography" at the Institute of Design, Chicago, 1946. Photograph by Arthur Siegel. (Courtesy of Irene Siegel)

Arthur Siegel, photographer and teacher, 1950. Photograph by Beaumont Newhall. (Courtesy of Scheinbaum & Russek Ltd., Santa Fe, New Mexico)

of the first day I lectured for two hours on the history of photography from 1839 to the present. Moholy was at the lecture and afterward joined some of the faculty for an hour or so of discussion.

Moholy urged me to join his staff. He said that when he learned of my resignation from the Museum of Modern Art he saw at once an opportunity for both me and the school. He drew a very inviting picture of editing publications, curating exhibitions, and teaching. He wanted to have Nancy on the faculty too, and thought this could be arranged in a satisfactory financial way sometime later. For the present he could pay me the same salary I had received from the Modern. I thanked him warmly for this offer, and said that I would discuss it with Nancy. A few days later I wrote Moholy that although the prospective position was indeed attractive, neither Nancy nor I wanted to live in Chicago.

BLACK MOUNTAIN COLLEGE

Another artist and former master at the German Bauhaus was the painter Josef Albers, who emigrated to America in 1933 and joined the faculty of the pioneering educational experience called Black Mountain College, in North Carolina. I first met him in the Museum of Modern Art in the spring of 1946. He invited me to teach at the Summer Art Institute of the College in a charming way: "I offer you and your wife a free vacation! Two weeks in lovely North Carolina! All travel expenses and room and board paid! You just give four evening lectures on photography!"

We accepted the invitation, and on August 13, 1946, I joined a distinguished visiting faculty that included Walter Gropius, founder of the German Bauhaus and at the time chairman of the department of architecture at Harvard University, and painters Jacob Lawrence and Balcomb Greene, Buckminster Fuller, avant-garde artists Merce Cunningham and John Cage, along with the permanent staff. Nancy, writing to a friend, described her first impression of the environment: "The place is wonderful. The college owns around 700 acres of mountain, farmland, valley, lake, streams, rhododendrons, laurel, pine, pastures, wild mints pungent under foot. Mists rise upwards from around you in the cool morning—the nights are almost cold; the sun is really hot at noon. Walks are wonderful; the Blue Ridge and Smoky Mountains are neighbors."

A small cottage was assigned us, with a living room, a kitchenette, a bedroom, and a bath. We had lunch on that first day with Albers on the dining room porch, overlooking Lake Eden. I enjoyed the fresh salad of greens and told Albers how pleasant it was to have hors d'oeuvres.

"Hors d'oeuvres?" he replied. "That's your lunch."

I gave four evening lectures that were generously illustrated with slides on the history and aesthetics of photography. These had the titles "The Tradition," "Photography in the Twentieth Century," "Photographic Vision: An Approach to the Aesthetics of Photography," and "Photography as Expression." In addition we had screenings of films that were borrowed from the film library of the Museum of Modern Art. Included were such masterpieces as Erich von Stroheim's *Greed*,

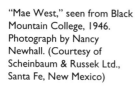
"Mae West," seen from Black Mountain College, 1946. Photograph by Nancy Newhall. (Courtesy of Scheinbaum & Russek Ltd., Santa Fe, New Mexico)

Carl Theodor Dreyer's *The Passion of Joan of Arc*, and G. W. Pabst's *The Love of Jeanne Ney*. I introduced each of the films with a statement about their significance in relation to the photographic medium.

To avoid misunderstanding and disappointment, I announced at my first lecture that I did not intend to discuss photographic technique. However, I added that I would be glad to meet any students who wanted technical advice at our cottage. Next morning a dozen or so students knocked at our door and we had an informal class on our front lawn. Unfortunately the college had no darkroom facility that year, and my teaching was more theoretical than practical. On our return to New York I was very pleased that the college rector, Theodore Dreier, invited me to join the faculty in 1947, this time to teach for the full two months of the summer session.

The college has often been referred to as "experimental." But after fourteen years of "experiments," the way of study and the way of life was far from tentative. We found the college a remarkable example of cooperative living that was fructifying to both the students and the faculty. This was quite evident at the first faculty meeting we attended, when we were told something of the philosophy of the college. The instructors are given complete leeway in conducting their classes. They name their subjects at a community meeting and describe in detail just what they want to teach, and for how many hours. On the basis of these talks the students choose their classes. During the first week they try out the classes and discuss their programs with their faculty advisor. Not more than fifteen hours a week is allowed except by special permission. The partition of the student's time is one-third academic courses, one-third creative expression, one-third work on the farm or in the basic maintenance of the grounds and buildings. The faculty owned the college, and its members were responsible to themselves only. "We suffer the consequences of our mistakes, not the mistakes of others," we were told.

The community meeting was held in the main hall. Chairs were arranged in

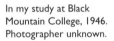
In my study at Black Mountain College, 1946. Photographer unknown.

Buckminster Fuller (*left, with notebook*), Ati Gropius, daughter of Walter Gropius (*center*), and Josef Albers (*right, with camera*) at Black Mountain College, 1946. Photographer unknown.

three concentric circles and students and faculty took places wherever they chose. The speaker opened the meeting by welcoming all present and again explaining the Black Mountain College philosophy. There was something inspiring to me in the way the meeting was held; it was informal yet dignified, and everybody was in earnest. There were thirty students that summer and sixteen faculty. The moderator of the student government spoke, the work projects were explained, and the instructors were called upon to describe their courses. It was as if they were auctioning off their wares. Fritz Hansgirg pleading for the importance of organic chemistry in the world of today, Max Dehn defending calculus as a creative expression. When my turn came I described my course in the practice of photography. Fourteen students wanted to take it. I explained that the darkroom could only accommodate eight students, so I divided the group into three teams of four, four, and six. I agreed to meet with each team twice a week.

I began instruction with my 4 x 5-inch view camera. When we had found a nearby subject that appealed to the students, I set the camera upon its tripod, threw over it the focusing cloth, and brought the image into focus. I invited the students one by one to view the image on the ground glass of the camera. To most of them this was a new experience. I slipped a film holder into the camera and made an exposure. We then went to the darkroom, where I developed and fixed the film. I did this in complete darkness, but as soon as the film was washed we turned on the lights and viewed

MY LAST DAYS AT MOMA AND AFTER

the negative. At the next meeting of the class I showed them how to make a contact print from the negative, and had each person make a print from my negative. This gave them practice in handling a sheet of paper in a trayful of liquid developer. Soon they were able to develop sheet film in a tray in total darkness. I was surprised how quickly the students mastered this basic technique. I let the students use my view camera and within a short time they were taking quite good photographs of subjects of their own choice. The next step was to help students use their own cameras and to teach them how, in that age before automated cameras, to estimate exposures.

Life at Black Mountain College was by no means all work. Always there was something going on. There was much music, both classical and contemporary. During our stay John Cage performed with his "prepared" piano. There was also dance, with a recital by Merce Cunningham. And there was Mush Day. One of the students conceived of a way of sending food packages to European students in the bleak post–World War II years: he asked the community to eat nothing but cornmeal mush on Tuesdays, and to use the savings in the food budget to buy food packages to send overseas. Joining Mush Day was optional. Of course Nancy and I joined up. Nancy conceived the idea of making the day an epicurean delight. From the college garden we obtained a lot of tomatoes, which we used to make a delicious sauce for the mush. The result, of course, was that standby of the Italian peasants: polenta. Soon others cooked with produce from the farm. After one of these meals I found the student who had organized Mush Day dejected. I asked him why. "The spirit of sacrifice is gone," he said. However, soon he was making us a Swiss apple dish.

I was invited to join the faculty as rector, but I declined, for I knew that if I did so I would no longer be able to continue my study of the history of photography.

THE HISTORY OF PHOTOGRAPHY

Early in 1947, Monroe Wheeler told me that he wanted to publish a new edition of my 1938 book *Photography: A Short Critical History*. He proposed to reprint the ninety-five-page text without revision and to add sixteen more plates. He also proposed to change the awkward title to *A Short History of Photography*. The publishing house of Simon & Schuster, Monroe said, was ready to order five thousand copies. Upon publication I would receive an initial royalty of $1,250. To this I agreed and happily signed the contract.

At first I thought that the editorial work would be simple. But when I reread my 1938 book I realized that I had learned a great deal about the subject during the past nine years that should be included. So I decided to write a wholly new text, and to revise the picture selection. I took an outline to Monroe and told him the photographs should be printed on the same pages as the text, not as a separate plate section. He agreed, but felt it would cost too much. He promised to talk to Dick Simon if I made a dummy, showing the placement of the text and the photographs. In three days Nancy and I laid out over a hundred pages. When we handed these sheets to Dick Simon, who himself was an avid amateur photographer, he looked at a dozen or so and said, "I've seen enough. Let's talk. What's your angle?"

The more I talked the more enthusiastic he became. He saw the book as a standard history. "The more complete the better," he remarked. "You should have plenty of time to work on it and nothing to limit you from making it the way it should be."

I told him I had to eat. His reply was, "We'll subsidize you," and he offered to match my Guggenheim Foundation grant. Simon told Monroe that he could sell ten thousand copies of the new book. He insisted that the title should be *THE History of Photography*. When I said I thought *THE History* was somewhat pretentious he replied, "I won't publish the book unless it is *THE History of Photography!*"

FERDINAND REYHER   I was introduced to the novelist and screenwriter Ferdinand Reyher in 1946 by his cousin, Ernest Halberstadt, an excellent painter and photographer who had been my assistant during the several months in 1935 that I worked for the art division of the Works Progress Administration. We had traveled throughout Massachusetts together on inspection trips to see what artists on the project were doing, and brought back photographs of the work. In fact it was Ernie who years before had taught me to enlarge and print photographs. He came down to Lynn and we worked in Mother's abandoned darkroom. Developing film wasn't difficult to learn; however, printing was challenging, and he helped me a great deal.

"Ferd," as Nancy and I came to call Reyher almost at once, was a jovial companion, an excellent writer, a sharp critic. A screenwriter for Hollywood films, he had sold a novel, *And I Heard Them Sing*, based on a barbershop chorus. He was a great storyteller, and dictated his novel to his secretary, just as he had the dialogue for all his scripts. Reyher disliked Hollywood, so with the pro-

Ferd Reyher and Nancy, April 14, 1946. Photograph by Beaumont Newhall. (Courtesy of Scheinbaum & Russek Ltd., Santa Fe, New Mexico)

ceeds of his fiction he moved to New York City and settled in the Chelsea Hotel to begin another novel. Entitled simply *Tin*, it was to be the story of a tintypist, a photographer who made portraits on photo-sensitized tin plates "while you wait." However, Ferd knew virtually nothing about nineteenth-century photography. His cousin suggested that I could—and would gladly—help Ferd learn about this long-obsolete photographic process. We took trips together to look at tintypes, and bought books. In the process he built up a very good personal photography library.

As we came to know each other, we made a pact: we would not read each other's book manuscripts. Discussion would wait until we felt that we were finished and ready to submit our manuscripts to the publisher. As a result I never saw his novel-in-progress, because as far as I know he never finished it. At the time I was working on revising my *History of Photography*. He didn't see it until I thought I was finally finished, and sent the manuscript down to him at the Chelsea Hotel. When I didn't hear from him for two weeks, I became concerned because I was in the process of moving from Manhattan to Rochester to begin my new job at Eastman House. I called to see how it was going. "Oh, I just finished the first chapter," he said.

"Oh, come on, Ferd, don't kid me like that."

"Well come on down and we'll kick it around." So we went over the first chapter together—and this took us a whole week, since we combed through it together practically word by word. He asked me to bring along magazine articles I had used as sources, and, still on only my first chapter, challenged me on my choice of quotes, my dry, academic narrative style, my lack of drama. He encouraged me to develop a style that had more dramatic impact, more detail, more human interest. I owe him a great debt for helping me improve my writing.

Sometime in the 1950s, after I'd departed for Rochester, we gradually lost touch. Reyher lived in Paris for a time; when he returned he remarried and moved to San Francisco. I never saw him again.

CHARLES SHEELER

I first met Charles Sheeler in 1936, when I was collecting photographs for the 1937 exhibition at the museum. Nancy and I drove to his home and studio, then in Ridgefield, Connecticut. We were delighted to make his acquaintance, and found him to be a most charming host. We looked at his work that day, and together we selected four photographs for the exhibition, two from a series he had made of Chartres Cathedral in 1929. Charles had taken the photographs during his trip back to the United States from the very important as well as influential exhibition in Stuttgart, "Film und Foto." That exhibition had included not only still photographs, but also a significant program of experimental films. Only a few Americans were represented in "Film und Foto." Another was Edward Weston, a friend of Charles's. The work of Edward's son Brett was also shown. Although only seventeen, Brett was already a master of the camera, and Edward was extremely proud that he had been recognized at this international exhibition.

Charles Sheeler, 1948. Photograph by Beaumont Newhall. (Courtesy of Scheinbaum & Russek Ltd., Santa Fe, New Mexico)

Charles and his Russian-born wife, Musya, moved to Tarrytown-on-Hudson in 1942. They had acquired a charming stone building that had formerly been the gatekeeper's house on a large estate that had just recently been purchased by a developer and made into building sites. At the time we met, I had long been interested in Sheeler's work—both his paintings and his photographs. His dual interest was very unusual for the time, and he saw no conflict whatever between the two mediums. In an introduction to the catalog of a retrospective of his work held at the Museum of Modern Art in 1939, Charles wrote: "My interest in photography, paralleling that in painting, has been based on admiration for its possibility of accounting for the visual world with an exactitude not equaled by any other medium. The difference in the manner of arrival at their destination—the painting being the result of a composite image and the photograph being the result of a single image—prevents these media from being competitive."

One of Sheeler's paintings was of a locomotive. Entitled *Rolling Power* (1929), it was a detail of the side of the train. I was rather surprised by his response when I asked him how he had made it. With his characteristic flair, he told me he had painted it from a photograph. "I called up the president of the New York Central Railroad and told him that I was an artist and that I wanted to make a painting of one of his locomotives, and would he please be kind enough to send a

Doylestown House, Stairwell, 1917. Photograph by Charles Sheeler. (The Museum of Modern Art, New York. Gift of the photographer)

locomotive to the freight yard near my place here at Tarrytown for a month or so, while I made the painting? Well he answered very politely that he was terribly sorry but that was not at all practical. And so I made a photograph instead, and from that I made my painting."

Nancy and I made frequent trips to Tarrytown to visit Charles and Musya at their house, which they called "Bird's Nest." We became close friends. Musya, herself a good photographer, was very lively, and we all thoroughly enjoyed her stories. "When I first came here I didn't speak English too good," she told us. "But I needed a sponge, so I went to the drugstore and asked the pharmacist, 'Could you please give me a sponge bath?'" But it was not all just fun. I was greatly interested in what Charles was doing, and I found he was an excellent critic and a great help to me in my early days of making photographs.

When, in 1942, during our vacation in Tarrytown as houseguests of the Sheelers, I received by telegram my commission as first lieutenant in the Army Air Force, Musya, in her lively manner, rushed out into the garden and came back with a handful of parsley. "Here, Beaumont, I give you this since I do not have a wreath of laurel."

It is interesting that Charles also reacted to the war hysteria of the period. He felt that people would not buy any paintings at that time, and so took advantage of an offer that had been made by Francis Taylor, the director of the Metropolitan Museum of Art, who asked him to make photographs for the cover of the museum's monthly *Bulletin*. The museum had been virtually emptied of its treasures after Pearl Harbor, and since Taylor knew that members either could not or would not find very much in the galleries, they should have something in return for their membership dues. He gave Charles complete freedom to photograph anything he found in the Metropolitan, in whatever way he thought would make good pictures. Some of these photographs, particularly of sculpture, were fine indeed. And in spite of Charles's fear, people did not stop buying his canvases.

Many years later, when Nancy and I moved to Rochester, we made frequent trips to New York, and always looked forward to visiting Charles and Musya. As curator of photography at Eastman House, I wrote Charles that I had checked our collection and found we did not have a representative group of his photographs; we had only two, I wrote, and I wanted to have about twenty-five more in the collection. I asked the price, and also the best time to come to look at work. He sent me a charming reply, saying that both his prints and his negatives were twenty-five dollars each, then adding: "We have had a toy white poodle for about a year and a half who has taken over the house but allows us to board with her. Given by our beloved Bart Hayes as a therapist for me. What a therapist! She is known as Vanilla, Queen of the Universe and Outer Space." When we did visit the Sheelers, I bought seven photographs and their negatives for Eastman House for a total of $350. I certainly wish I had bought more, as his work is inaccessible now. A picture he offered to me for twenty-five dollars was sold at auction in the early 1980s for sixty-three thousand—which at that time was the highest price ever paid for a photograph.

I well remember the day I came to New York in order to work with Monroe Wheeler to finalize the proofs of my revised *History*. I proudly brought back the proofs to show Charles. One of his pictures was the underside of the stairs of a house he had lived in before he was married. It was an abstract image, rather ambiguous, and I had showed it as a pair of stairs leading up. When Charles saw it he remained silent for a long time, then very quietly said, "It seems to work upside down just as well." I instantly telephoned the editor, just in time to have the plate reversed.

I always enjoyed Charles's wry sense of humor. While we were staying with the Sheelers in 1942, I photographed a Victorian house in the neighborhood. When I showed him my print, he looked at it—it seemed to me for a very long time—and then simply handed it back to me. I knew he did not like the picture, but he did not say a word. By god, I said to myself, I'll find a picture he will like. The next day, when I showed him the new photograph, he simply said with a deadpan expression, "Why didn't you do that yesterday?"

Once when I asked him if he would select a photograph and a painting for an article I was writing about the two mediums, he responded:

I always look forward to reading a letter from you. In the present one you forgot to enclose the pearls of wisdom which are usually there.

Ever since the American Revolution, I have been enmeshed in the question is Photography Art. You and I have known for a long time that it IS! I have given up sending missionaries to the Heathens. We are all born with the same equipment, eyes, and if some don't care to use them it is their loss.

Charles was a great contributor to American art, and it was more than a pleasure—it was a real opportunity—to have known him and to have profited by his criticism and knowledge. Shortly before his death in 1965 he beautifully summed up his life's quest: "The searching eye is capable of discovering in nature a combination of forms which when recorded and presented in a print have astonished those who have missed the seeing."[35]

35. Quoted in Charles W. Millard III, "Charles Sheeler," *Contemporary Photographer*, vol. 66, no. 1 (1967), unpaged, footnote 83.

A CAMERA TRIP WITH ANSEL ADAMS

In 1947 Ansel Adams invited Nancy and me to join him on a photographic trip from Yosemite National Park to the Grand Canyon. He had two objectives: to photograph the national parks, a project for which he had been awarded a Guggenheim Fellowship, and to take pictures for the Eastman Kodak Company of people in the parks taking pictures with Kodak cameras. I kept a journal of our trip.

May 29, 1947

We left Ansel's house in Yosemite and drove in his station wagon toward Tioga Pass, the eastern entrance to the park. As we climbed the air became cooler and crystal clear so that breathing was like drinking spring water. We stopped at Lake Tenaya, where both Ansel and Nancy photographed the juniper tree that we called Edward Weston's because of his beautiful picture of it. I climbed the steep granite slope to its summit and looked east to a wall of rock spotted with patches of snow and pine trees that rose sheer from the lake. Then we drove up to the Tioga Pass through deep snow. We resisted photographing one another beneath the sign "Elevation 10,000 feet" and dropped down to the ice-filled Lake Tioga. We all made negatives.

To look at the ground glass of Ansel's 8 x 10-inch view camera after he has made an exposure is a lesson in interpretive photography. His images seem to me more like mountains than the mountains themselves, for to be appreciated the mountains need, for my eyes at least, isolation. Their scale is so immense that it is difficult to judge their size or even to be impressed by a hasty, distant view. As we wound down Tioga Pass the mountains were terrifying—barren, inhospitable, challenging. It was a relief to come to plains of sagebrush and Mono Lake, the salt lake, with seagulls flying overhead and willow branches sun-bleached white along its shore.

We first hit the desert a few miles south of Lone Pine, California, where we turned east, downward into Death Valley. The hard ground strewn with pebbles, small rocks, and sparse vegetation reminded me of Egypt; I could believe myself driving on the sand-swept road north of Cairo if we hadn't been gliding so smoothly in a station wagon instead of a jeep. From a rise

Ansel photographed the distant Sierra Nevada, lost in blue haze. Then we began to climb out of the desert up into the Panamints. The earth was black—"lava deposits," Ansel said. Black rocks among the sagebrush. From the heights we looked down onto the valley floor. A tiny strip of white sand cut across it that proved to be a mile wide when we reached the valley floor after winding down a spectacular road.

Across the valley at sixty miles an hour, then up the long steady rise of Townes Pass. Three times the radiator boiled; all along the way were water barrels and on the road beside them rust stains. It took us a full hour to climb the pass up the 5,500-foot elevation summit.

The ranger at the entrance to Death Valley told us that the day was a remarkably cool one. We were in luck and did not experience the great heat of the desert. We passed through rapidly, just as the sun was about to sink. At Zabriskie Point we had a picnic supper. Ansel asked me what I thought of it. "It might be the moon," I answered. There was nothing to be seen but rock forms, and these were massive and nonhuman. There was no way to judge the scale; there was nothing whatsoever for human comparison: no sign of man nor his work. Nothing but rocks. After nightfall we climbed to the peak called Dante's View. The moon was full and we could just make out alkaline flats 5,220 feet below us. We stretched our sleeping bags on the ground. The wind tugged at me all night long. Every so often I woke up to think that it was dawn, for it was so light, only to discover the brightness came from the brilliant moon.

The now familiar reveille (Ansel braying like a jackass) got us out of our sleeping bags at first light, four o'clock in the morning. Thoughtful Ansel had coffee ready. Both his 8 x 10-inch and 5 x 7-inch cameras were already mounted on their tripods. Nancy broke out her 4 x 5-inch camera. Soon the first rays of sun hit the mountains opposite us, and then began a play of light, shadow, and color that kept all hands frantically busy. As the sun rose and as the clouds moved, the lighting of the mountains changed radically. Any instant of the spectacle would have been magnificent, and a thousand instants presented themselves in all directions. The clouds seemed to fit with the geology.

Down into the desert again and out to Death Valley Junction. Unexpectedly there was an air-conditioned restaurant open at 6:55 A.M. We sat down to a full breakfast of eggs and wheat cakes and plenty of coffee.

At Indian Springs, Nevada, at a widening in the straight monotonous road across the desert, we stopped for beer. Ansel played the quarter slot machine and won and lost all he had and a quarter more. The storekeeper was reading the latest copy of *Time* magazine. Ansel begged a look, and found in the art section a writeup of the exhibition at New York's Down Town Gallery of the *Fortune* portfolio of national parks. Paintings and photographs commissioned by *Fortune* magazine were on display there. Ansel expected some mention of his work, but he was not prepared for the article headed "Camera v. Brush," which drew the conclusion that the camera had won! "The cold glass eye of Adams," we read. We looked at Adams, could discover no glass eye, nor could the storekeeper.

Then back to the tiresome trek across the desert. Suddenly we were in the mesa country and the earth was red. Up to the mountains yet again. The atmosphere was cooler and clearer; a tremendous rich red mountain; the Santa Clara River, the Mormon town of St. George, Utah—and here we are in a neat motel, air-conditioned with private bath and comfortable beds. Nancy is scrubbing the camping dishes, we have had baths, have had steak for a third day, have changed film, and are about to turn in early for we anticipate that the donkey will bray before dawn.

❖

The donkey didn't bray at daybreak after all. About six o'clock Ansel discreetly knocked on the door, entered bearing coffee, and admitted he had overslept. A good thing too, for we all needed the sleep and it enabled us to have breakfast at the restaurant where we'd had an excellent steak last night—served with delicious homesmoked bacon thrown in as lagniappe. While we were waiting for scrambled eggs, Ansel began a catalog of the photographic equipment he had brought along.

The inventory included three view cameras (an 8 x 10-inch Agfa Commercial, a 4 x 5-inch Linhof, and a 3 1/4 x 4 1/4-inch Zeiss Jewel) and a 4 x 5-inch Graflex. For these cameras there were ten lenses and filters for each, as well as film holders and two sturdy tripods. The film supply was abundant: 108 dozen sheets, mostly of moderate sensitivity, with a few infrared and some color, plus twelve roll films and fourteen film packs. The all-important exposure meter was a Weston Master II. I had a Leica camera with one lens and six or so rolls of film.

We lunched beside the road on our way to Bryce Canyon (or as we called it, Zeiss Canyon). Ansel had a couple of Coleman stoves and a stock of food: some cheese, a cooked ham, butter, eggs, and other groceries in the station wagon. The tailgate when dropped served as kitchen and dining room. During the trip we have had excellent meals: steaks, chicken chasseur, ham with wine sauce, oysters in tomato sauce, good soups, tea, coffee, and always a little something to drink.

We arrived at Bryce Canyon at the end of the day. There was nothing particularly spectacular about the approach, but when we got out of the car and went over to the rim of the canyon and looked down we saw a most amazing spectacle. The rock had eroded in such a way that hundreds of tall spindles had been left standing "like men" as the Indians said. After a hurried look at the canyon we found a pleasant stand of pines and there Nancy cooked excellent chicken chasseur. We went on for a few miles as night fell, found a place to stretch our sleeping bags, and turned in.

❖

June 1

At four o'clock in the afternoon there was some talk of all hands taking short naps in the cabin, but instead we drive again to Bryce Point. I had been up since four and hadn't slept very well on the ground. I was tired and spontaneously burst forth, to the amazement and amusement of all, including myself: "What, nature again? I've never seen so much nature. We sleep on it, we look at it in the morning and in the afternoon and by moonlight and by sunrise and sunset. I'm looked out!" So we went back to the cabin and napped and then found a quiet spot to have dinner. Nancy made fine ham and with that inside me and nothing to look at but ordinary domestic trees I felt a great deal better.

❖

June 2

The approach to the North Rim of the Grand Canyon is a forest of aspens and firs and pines. Mile after mile of this pleasing combination of trees continued. We thought that we would never get to the canyon, despite the frequent signposts; I was impatient and kept looking for evidence, but nothing at all was to be seen until we stopped at Point Imperial and looked out and down. There is no way I can describe the Grand Canyon. Figures mean nothing: a mile deep and twelve miles across. We cooked dinner not far from the point and then went on to the Lodge, where we hired a cabin.

❖

June 3

The most spectacular moment came in the afternoon when we drove again to Point Imperial. Dark clouds in the distance approached with great speed, carrying with them furious rain. It was blowing hard and these little storms kept sweeping through the canyon. The upsweep draft at the rim edge forced the rain up onto our faces; for a few minutes we were pelted with hail. A rainbow formed in the canyon below us, staining the distant limestone cliffs. And then the sun broke through and the jagged peaks began, one at a time, to appear.

❖

June 4

In the afternoon we drove sixteen miles on a dirt road to Point Sublime, through a lush and beautiful forest. The whole canyon spread fanlike from the point. At sundown Ansel wanted to photograph the moonrise in color. First, with his view camera firmly fastened on a tripod, he photographed the landscape by the last feeble rays of daylight. Then he marked an "X" on the ground glass of the camera where the image of the moon was to be recorded when it rose. We feared that because of the overcast the sunset would be a disappointment, but at the last moment the underside of the clouds became vermillion and orange, spreading like fire. The red disk dropped; the peaks below our feet grew dim. We turned to the East; a glow on the horizon showed where the moon would rise, but not for half an hour did it finally appear sufficiently clear and brilliant for Ansel's purpose. In a state of great excitement he made a second exposure on the same sheet of film, using this time a long-focus 26-inch lens to make the image of the moon relatively large. Ansel was worried over this departure from his usual "direct approach." Was it legitimate to use two different focal length lenses on one photograph? Was it legitimate to make double exposures? Will the relatively enlarged image of the moon appear exaggerated in size?

Arizona is a country of contrasts. From the Kaibab Plateau, which bounds the Grand Canyon on the East, we descended a long, easy slope to the desert country of the Navaho Indian Reservation. Here the cattle graze on the open range. A roadside sign Watch for Buffalo set us scanning the range, but no animals were in sight.

For mile after mile we passed the red, black, and blue, and orange sand dunes of the Painted Desert. It was our private preserve; we met not a car for miles. Then, as we approached Cameron, autos came toward us by the dozen. We understood why as we crossed the Little Colorado River. A construction gang had just finished putting in a new deck section and the bridge had been closed since one o'clock. We turned west at Cameron on the third side of a rectangle. Two hundred miles of travel to reach a point seventeen miles opposite the spot where we had breakfasted! The approach to the south rim of the Canyon is through a forest of scrub pines, not nearly so impressive as the lush woods of the north rim. The mark of the tourist is more evident. There are enough buildings clustered around the original El Tovar Hotel to make the name Grand Canyon Village not an exaggeration. There we found two cabin rooms reserved for us. The roar of the diesel locomotive on a spur track of the Santa Fe railroad seemed wholly out of place.

❖

June 7

As a final climax to the trip Ansel drove us to Sunset Crater National Monument and this, to my mind, was the most spectacular sight of all we had seen, perhaps because it is completely unknown to Nancy and me. We drove off the highway onto a cinder road that climbed through low woods toward a volcanic peak, black at the base and orange red at the summit. Soon we came to a once terrifying lava flow. Great coke-like dead black chunks of lava were piled up in a mound. The slopes of the mountain were covered with cinders. Trees somehow had broken through the desolate cinder layer. On the side of the mountain the rains had washed away the earth beneath the roots and the trees had fallen and rolled down the slope. Other dead trees still stood upright, their branches intricate mazes of silver against the black cinders. I walked up a hillside. The cinders were covered here and there with pine needles and between them I could see animal tracks. This strange desolation impressed us all. I found black-and-white photography difficult. Ansel wisely got out his camera only once, waiting for a second trip before working. I could not resist snapshooting, concentrating on the dead trees as the most pictorial evidence of the desolation.

We drove through Flagstaff to Williams, Arizona, where we had a farewell dinner at the railroad hotel. Soon the train roared in. The porter took our bags and we followed him out into the darkness to the end of the station platform and climbed aboard. From the vestibule of our car we waved goodbye to Ansel.

❖

MY LAST DAYS AT MOMA AND AFTER

5

GEORGE EASTMAN HOUSE

With Arthur Rothstein at George Eastman House. Photographer unknown. (Courtesy of the International Museum of Photography at George Eastman House)

AT LAST—A MUSEUM OF PHOTOGRAPHY

In 1939 Dr. Walter Clark, head of the Applied Photography Division of the Kodak Research Laboratories and in charge of the Eastman Historical Photographic Collection, negotiated the purchase by the company of the outstanding photographic collection of Gabriel Cromer, a retired French photographer who intended to create a national museum of photography in Paris but who suddenly died before it was accomplished. Cromer spent the last years of his life in an assiduous search for everything photographic of all periods, ranging from a daguerreotype camera signed as authentic by Daguerre himself to popular caricatures of photographers at work by Honoré Daumier.

Nobby, as his friends all call Dr. Clark, had been most helpful to me when he was a member of the Photography Committee of the Museum of Modern Art. In 1940 I had been given leave of absence by the museum to spend two weeks in Rochester, at Kodak's expense, cataloging what I considered the most important photographs in its collection. I appreciated the opportunity of working with Nobby. I found him to be most congenial and knowledgeable. He realized that the value and importance of the burgeoning Eastman Historical Photographic Collection demanded its proper housing in a museum building where selections of the collection could be put on public display and the remainder stored under archival conditions. He thought at first of recommending to Kodak management the construction of a wing to the Rochester Museum of Arts and Sciences. Later he saw an opportunity to make Kodak founder George Eastman's former residence into an international museum of the science, technology, and art of photography that would be unique in the world. As he wrote me later, "I felt very strongly that Mr. Eastman would have liked the idea of his house being devoted to the collection, and I advocated this as strongly as I was able."

After Eastman's death in 1932, it was revealed that he had bequeathed his house to the University of Rochester to be used as the residence of its president, with the proviso that if it proved to be impractical for that purpose after ten years it could be disposed of by the university. Early in 1947 the governing board of the university decided to discontinue using the house as a residence and gave it to a newly formed nonprofit educational corporation, the George Eastman House, Inc. The corporation's purpose, as defined in the charter granted to it in 1947 by the Regents of the State of New York, was exactly what Dr. Walter Clark had proposed:

> (a) To establish, operate and maintain a museum of photography and allied pursuits in or about the City of Rochester, New York, as a memorial to the late George Eastman;

(b) To promote, develop, conduct and maintain public exhibitions of photography and its uses;

(c) To establish, develop and maintain a graphic and continuing history of photography;

(d) To teach photography by demonstration and exhibition and to foster public knowledge of and interest in the various methods and techniques involved therein;

(e) To promote, encourage and develop photography and its allied arts and sciences;

(f) To receive, collect and preserve relics, records, apparatus, equipment, material and other items of historic or current interest;

(g) To carry out and discharge any of the purposes hereinabove set forth either directly or by contribution to other organizations, corporations, foundations or institutions organized for any of the above purposes.

Kodak agreed to contribute funds through its Charitable Trust for the conversion of Eastman House to a museum and for the museum's maintenance. The founding trustees were seven, the majority highly successful industrialists.[36] I knew nothing about these negotiations until May 1947. While Nancy and I were the houseguests of the Adamses in San Francisco, I received a somewhat cryptic note from Oscar Solbert of the Eastman Kodak Company that was forwarded to me from New York, saying, "I am wondering if you could come to Rochester for a conference with Dr. Walter Clark and myself on some photographic business. I sincerely hope that you can come as it may be of interest to you." The following day I received a slightly more informative letter from him. "We have decided to permanently exhibit our large historical collection of photography that you are familiar with," he added. "It will be housed in the best possible place and we would like your help and advice in doing so."

36. The original trustees were: Dr. Albert K. Chapman, chairman; Thomas J. Hargrave, president; and Charles K. Hutchinson, retired vice president of the Eastman Kodak Company; Raymond N. Ball, president of the Lincoln Rochester Trust Company; James E. Gleason, chairman of the Gleason Works, manufacturers of gear-cutting machinery; Dr. Albert Kaiser, health officer of the city of Rochester; and Dr. Alan Valentine, president of the University of Rochester.

I knew Solbert only as a retired army general who was on the executive staff of Eastman Kodak in the capacity of public relations officer. It was he who had welcomed me when I first visited Kodak in 1937 and who introduced me to Dr. Clark. I replied that I would stop over in Rochester on my way back from the West Coast. On the morning of June 17, I was in the general's mahogany-and-leather executive office on the nineteenth floor of Kodak Tower, the company's office building in downtown Rochester. Solbert explained in some detail about the plans for the conversion of Eastman House to a museum of photography. All the rooms would be left, as far as possible, in their original state. The exhibition would be in three sections: historical, which Solbert called "pre-Eastman"; the Eastman period, 1879–1932; and modern. The installation of the exhibition could be started as soon as the regents of the university approved of the museum as an educational, nonprofit institution. The estimated budget was $300,000 for alterations and $100,000 annually for maintenance. Solbert asked if I would spend six months in Rochester completing the catalog of the Cromer collection that I had begun in 1940, and helping to plan the displays. I told him I would consider this offer and would write him on my return to New York.

Nancy urged me to take the job, so a week later I wrote that I would come for a thousand dollars per month. He replied no decision could be made until the fall, when the corporation would be legally set up. I heard nothing more until a year later, when Walter Clark telephoned me. "The trustees of Eastman House want to hire you as the permanent curator. Can you come here for another interview as soon as possible?"

On June 14, 1948, I sat in Solbert's office, in the same chair I had occupied a year before. After exchanging pleasantries, we drove three miles north to Kodak Park, Kodak's manufacturing center and location of the research laboratories, to meet Dr. C. E. Kenneth Mees, vice president in charge of research, who had been elected a trustee and the president of George Eastman House, Inc. On the way Solbert told me that upon his forthcoming retirement from Kodak he would be director of George Eastman House.

Dr. Mees greeted me warmly and ushered me into his office, but did not invite Solbert to join us. "Solbert has told you about the situation at Eastman House? It's been a pet project of his, but I won't let him take it unless there's someone there who knows museums and the history of photography. I understand that you're not occupied now—I mean that you have no job—that you're a Guggenheim Fellow. Well we'd like to have you join us, if you'd care to. You probably don't want to answer now, and I'm sure you have questions."

"What would be my relation to the trustees? Would I be responsible to Solbert?" I inquired.

"Yes, you would," Mees replied. "But you can always come to me. I intend to take an active interest. It's my responsibility to see that the money is well spent. I want to come around. I'll probably make a lot of suggestions that you can take or leave as you see fit. As far as the other trustees are concerned, they don't count."

"How about independent writing? I'm committed to a publisher for a book on American daguerreotypes."

"I'll tell you what I tell all my people: as long as your writing doesn't interfere with your job, write as much as you like. If it gets in the way of your job I'll warn you. I encourage all my people to write. Do a lot of it myself." He was at that time the author of nine books as well as more than a hundred scientific papers and articles.

I asked him what kind of shows he envisioned beside the permanent exhibitions.

"I'd like to see the scientific applications of photography, such as nuclear tracks. I think I can get materials from the Palomar Observatory telescope. And I want to buy photographs—the very best that's being done. The first thing I want you to do is to go abroad and buy photographs for us."

I listened with amazement to what Mees was saying. "I'd have initiative in getting up shows?"

"You certainly would," he replied. "We want you to run the museum." He asked about salary, to which I replied that I had told Solbert, after much thought and checking with colleagues, that I was asking a thousand per month.

"I wasn't prepared to go quite that high," Mees said. "But I could get authority for ten thousand a year. I don't like to beat you down, but I am afraid I can go no further."

This offer was more than twice any salary I had previously earned. The cost of living in 1948 was far below that of today. The morning newspaper was two cents, the bus fare in New York a nickel (except on the Fifth Avenue double-deckers, which cost a dime a ride), cigarettes were two packs for a quarter, lunch was sixty cents, a three-course dinner was a dollar and a quarter, and our midtown Manhattan apartment was fifty dollars a month.

I told Dr. Mees I'd like to think it over and would call him in a few days. I had already made up my mind to take the job, but I wanted to discuss everything with Nancy. She enthusiastically agreed with me, and on June 21, the day before my fortieth birthday, I telephoned Mees that I could start work on September 1, right after fulfilling my teaching commitment at Black Mountain College.

GEORGE EASTMAN'S HOUSE   When it was built in 1905, George Eastman's house, with its thirty-seven rooms, twelve bathrooms, and a household staff of twenty-eight, was the largest private residence in Rochester. The architect was J. Foster Warner, but the creator was Eastman himself. He supervised every phase and detail of the planning and construction. He insisted that the walls, floors, and roof be built of reinforced concrete, fourteen inches thick. The roof was covered with shingles split from logs brought from the Adirondacks. The concrete walls were faced with cream-colored bricks, made to order somewhat thinner and longer than standard.

The extension of George Eastman House in progress, 1919. Photographer unknown. (Courtesy of the International Museum of Photography at George Eastman House)

Work had already begun on the conversion of Eastman's home to a public museum when I arrived. To conform to the city's building code all the exterior doors had been rehung to open outward, and hideous fireproof enclosures of wire, glass, and steel had been put around several staircases.

A committee of Kodak personnel, largely from the sales force, had made plans for the photographic displays. Oscar Solbert took me on a tour of the house to explain the committee's proposals. The first room we entered was once the living room. It was beautifully paneled in teakwood, with a large fireplace. "We'll keep this room the way it was left by Mr. Eastman, so far as we can," Oscar said. "Most of the original furniture in the house was removed by the heirs, but a few original pieces remain. And here we'll hang paintings from the collection of old masters he left to the university." I never thought of George Eastman as an art connoisseur, but his collection included paintings attributed to Rembrandt, Tintoretto, Frans Hals, and Raeburn.

We passed through a rather small book-lined library and crossed the front hall into a spacious reception room, large enough to accommodate a hundred guests at recitals of chamber music. Oscar said that more paintings from Eastman's collection would be hung in this room. The photographic displays would begin here, with some of the earliest cameras from the collection in glass cases. We entered a massive room two stories high with a marble floor, a balcony on one side, and on the other tall windows overlooking a terrace and garden. "This was called the Music Room by Mr. Eastman." Always it was "Mr. Eastman," never "George," or "Eastman," and seldom "G.E."

"He loved music," Oscar continued, "and had a fine organ installed in the house. It was played from the console over there." He pointed to the end of the room. "He had a private organist who played for him every morning at breakfast—seven-thirty A.M. sharp—and at frequent recitals for his friends. We'll have the organ played frequently when we open." In this room the main exhibits would be mid-nineteenth-century photography.

The entrance to the former dining room was through a door surrounded by a beautiful ornamental wrought-iron grille. The oval table had been removed and was to be replaced by cases containing memorabilia of Eastman's life, his photographic contributions, and photographs of the many institutions with which he had shared his immense wealth. We climbed the grand staircase to the second floor. All the rooms were bedrooms, with connecting bathrooms that had been stripped of their plumbing fixtures in order to convert them to galleries. In one of these rooms a replica of an 1890 studio with a large skylight had been built. A life-size mannequin of a woman dressed in period clothes was placed on a chair with a headrest, as if posing for a portrait. A second mannequin stood near the lens of a bulky camera as if ready to make an exposure.

Another diorama featured one of the rarest items in the Eastman Historical Photographic Collection: a portable tentlike darkroom. In the 1870s, before the invention of dry plates and film, photographers had to coat their glass plates with collodion and then, while the emulsion was still wet, dip the plate in a solution of silver nitrate and expose the plate immediately. For this unwieldy process, a darkroom was indispensable. A mannequin of a photographer was placed as if focusing the tripod camera on the Falls of the Genesee River, represented by a painting. His young assistant stood ready to hand him a holder containing a prepared plate.

Oscar said the other second-story galleries would continue the display of amateur and professional still cameras, as well as motion-picture cameras and projectors. Three rooms were set aside for aerial photography, with Allied and alien cameras deposited by the U.S. Department of Defense. When I inquired about facilities for exhibiting photographs, Solbert replied "We have set aside two rooms for salon pictures on the first floor." We went down the backstairs into an empty room about thirty-five by twenty feet. It had once been the kitchen, although the stoves, sinks, and culinary equipment had been removed. This alteration we were to regret later, when it became necessary to serve formal dinners to special guests and refreshments to members on opening nights of special exhibitions. The second room, approximately the same size, was formerly the servants' sitting room.

"These galleries," he explained, "are dual purpose. They can be used as conference rooms as well as for the display of photographs." I was disappointed. I had imagined exhibitions of hundreds of photographs and meetings of hundreds of photographers.

A glazed walkway beside the garden brought us to Eastman's massive garage where at one time he kept seven automobiles. This splendid seventy- by eighty-five-foot space was ideal for exhibitions. But it was scheduled to be made into an exhibition space showing all the commercial uses of Kodak products.

A show of "Modern Uses of Photography" was being installed by members of Kodak's sales force.[37] Each of the sales divisions had been ordered to prepare exhibition material of their specialty: medical, graphic arts, astronomical, amateur. A corner of the kitchen was even set up as a darkroom. A design firm had been contracted, and there was little I could do to eliminate the chaotic, the bombastic, and the obvious. The material was often excellent; however, the presentation was that of a sales convention. At least I talked Solbert out of the "theme motif"—a column supporting a huge shutter, intermittently opening and closing, on a shaft surrounded by a spiral of greatly enlarged film, each frame a photograph. The whole was to be surrounded by a circular rail on which were dwarf-like sculptures of scientists, doctors, and other professionals, each holding a camera. I optimistically concentrated on the tremendous potential, and I planned to fill in the gaps in the collection as soon as possible.

37. The following is from their prospectus: "The exhibits in this hall show the place of photography in our life today and how it is used...to explore the universe, from the infinitely small nucleus to the atom to immense heavenly bodies...to record documents, instrument dials, and the image of the microscope...to speed up or slow down motion...to print pictures in magazines and books...to capture the fleeting image of the television screen...to send pictures across land and sea by wireless...to help diagnose our ills...to teach our young people more clearly...to preserve forever moments as meaningful as our lives, as dear to us as our families."

But to my chagrin, Oscar felt that this was not the time to collect, and that anyway, we could get all the photographs we wanted as gifts. "We must rush the installation," he said. To my protest that you can't design an exhibition until you know what you are going to put in it, he felt that we could at least order glass cases right away and fill them up with what we had. It took a year to convert the building into a museum—not a long time, but their admonition to "Hurry up, hurry up!" was constant.

The second, and more serious, problem was that they were absolutely against photography! I was greatly disappointed when it became apparent to me that Kodak had little interest in photography as an art form. I was determined to show photography as an art, and had anticipated their full support and cooperation. They owned 25,000 cameras, and it was these they wanted placed on permanent display. At one point, despondent and exasperated, I complained to Nobby Clark, "But you don't want any photographs around."

"Well we thought we could convince you to turn this into a science museum," he admitted. On several occasions during these first months, I seriously contemplated submitting my resignation. This was by now a familiar struggle, one I had waged for several years at the Museum of Modern Art. A letter Nancy wrote to Edward Weston reflects our disillusionment.

> Well, Kodak has come out from behind those whiskers. Our last vestige of a belief in Santa Claus is gone. Their beliefs, however, are rooted deep in their chromosomes or pocketbooks and are excellent examples of Superstitionia Commercialia Gigantica. (a) George Eastman is the most important man in the history of photography. (b) The whole aim and end of photography is the snapshot. (c) The technological development that has made the snapshot possible is the only interesting thing in the history of photography. (d) Nobody wants to look at photographs—a few with interesting subject matter, maybe, but not Art Photographs.
>
> They don't want a museum, they want "a shrine to George Eastman." Quote from Nobby Clark. They don't want to buy modern photographs; might get stuck with them. They don't want to fill in the gaps in their collection; it's already the best in the world.
>
> It's a little hard to make out why they bothered to lie to us, or why they hired Beau at all.
>
> Or why we fell for it.
>
> Something may still happen to save what should have been the first and greatest museum of photography. But it will have to be something like a miracle. [38]

38. Nancy Newhall to Edward Weston, January 17, 1949.

A friend of mine, a professor of art history at Smith College, visited Rochester to explore the technical side of photographing works of art for his slide lectures. He stayed with us for a time, and I expressed my discouragement that there was literally no space for photographs at Eastman: in front of every wall were glass cases, in the middle of the room were glass cases. He said, "Well you know there are three closets and a corridor on the second floor. Why don't you take the doors off and put up screens and have a show of photographs, however small?" I took his suggestion, installing a small exhibition of photographs of the Civil War. The result was that the local Rochester newspaper devoted two pages to the show, and from then on we became known as a place where photographs were being shown. By working slowly and carefully, I was eventually able to overcome their prejudice against photography as an art form.

During these first few months I made several trips back to New York, partly on Eastman House business and partly to arrange for the storage of our furniture until we found a permanent home in Rochester. One weekend I was fortunate to receive options on the purchase of two

George Eastman in his study. Photographer unknown. (Courtesy of the International Museum of Photography at George Eastman House)

important photographic collections. Philip Medicus offered us several albums of original photographs: the two-volume *Photographic Sketch Book of the War* by Alexander Gardner (1866), *Photographic Views of Sherman's Campaign* by George N. Barnard (1866), and George M. Wheeler's *Photographs Showing Landscapes of the Western Territories of the United States* (1875) taken by Timothy H. O'Sullivan and William Bell. In addition to the classics, Medicus made available to us a unique private album of Civil War photographs. Fred Lightfoot offered us five thousand stereographs—double photographs mounted on cards that could be viewed in startling three dimensions using a stereoscope.

I noted in my journal: "Went to see Dr. Mees on my return from New York and received his enthusiastic approval for the purchase of the lot for $1,750."

The first staff member we hired was Alice Coulson, who was secretary to Oscar Solbert and myself. She became indispensable. Curiously, no space had been allotted for offices of the director and the curator. For several weeks we worked in the living room until furniture, lights, and a telephone were installed in a small room near the side entrance.

The next to join the staff was James G. Card, a filmmaker in the advertising department of Eastman Kodak who came to us to produce motion pictures of historical photographic techniques that visitors could view in cabinet projectors placed alongside the camera displays. An avid collector of film classics, Jim became our curator of motion pictures. Through his efforts, enthusiasm, and knowledge, he built up over the course of years one of the largest motion picture film collections in the United States.

I learned a good deal about George Eastman from those who had worked for him and were now refurbishing his house. One of the sofas in the living room was worn out. It was leather, with ornamental brass-head upholstery tacks around the front, back, and arms. I sent it out to be reupholstered. To my surprise the upholsterer himself brought it back. He asked me, "How do you like it?"

"Why it's fine. A good job," I replied.

"You're much easier to please than Mr. Eastman. When I was a boy I used to deliver after school the furniture that my father had upholstered. When I brought this very sofa back here, Mr. Eastman looked at it carefully for what seemed a long time. Then he asked me, 'How many tacks are there in this sofa?'

"I told him I didn't know. Then he told me the exact number of tacks that had been on the sofa when it left his house. I don't remember how many, but I counted them and he was satisfied."

The hardwood floor of the spacious East Room needed refinishing. An elderly man came with an electric sanding machine and went to work. Around lunchtime I casually dropped in to see how the job was going. He instantly turned off the sander and stood up somewhat stiffly. "Oh, don't stop," I said. "I just came in to see how you're doing."

"You're not like Mr. Eastman," he said. "He came in almost as soon as I had started the sander and shouted, 'Turn that damn thing off! Do it by hand!' So I got some sandpaper, wrapped it around a block of wood, and smoothed the whole floor. It took a lot of time. When Mr. Eastman saw it he knelt down and felt the wood. 'It's too smooth,' he told me. 'Get me a spokeshave.' That's sort of a narrow plane with two handles. It's used for curved surfaces. I got one and gave it to Mr. Eastman, who went down on his knees and gently pushed it across the floor. 'Gives a hand-finished look,' he said. 'Now do the whole floor.'"

The Music Room was originally thirty by thirty feet. In 1919 Eastman felt that the square floor plan was unsatisfactory, so he had the entire house cut in two and the rear part jacked up on rollers and pushed back exactly nine feet four inches. It is said that just before the moving began Eastman exclaimed, "Don't forget the ivy on the walls!" So the roots were transplanted in dirt-filled tubs that were also put on rollers and pushed back along with the entire rear part of the house.

In order that the house could be lived in while the gaps in the walls, the floor, and the roof were being filled in, temporary partition walls were built across each of the severed parts of the house, water pipes were connected with rubber hoses, and electrical wires with extension cords. Nathaniel Myrick, chief guard and formerly Eastman's butler, told me about this most unusual operation. "I brought Mr. Eastman's breakfast to him by walking along a plank."

George Eastman, very proud of this remodeling, had photographs taken of the work in progress.

❖

It was originally planned by the Kodak committee to put in the center of each room of the house great big glass cases, six feet high, fitted with tiers of three glass shelves on which cameras would be displayed. Narrow cases of similar design were to be put against the walls. I pointed out that visitors might not like to get down on their knees to study the cameras on the bottom shelves, nor to stretch on tiptoe to see those on the upper shelves. I devised an alternate case that was simply a glass box on a waist-level wooden table. Within the boxes were fluorescent tubes to light the objects on display. Photographs could be fastened to cloth-covered, movable partitions. My design was accepted and the casemakers from Remington Rand Company came to discuss our needs. I had lined up the requirements in detail. It took us only the morning to finish up the specifications, and Oscar, elated that the estimate was $25,000 as against the $40,000 originally planned, took us all to lunch at the Genesee Valley Club. This reduction was all due to the use of smaller, single-level glass cases.

When the cases arrived, I filled them with cameras and on the background screens I placed magnificent daguerreotypes by Daguerre and his contemporaries, classic calotypes by David Octavius Hill and Robert Adamson, beautiful portraits by Julia Margaret Cameron, architectural prints by Edouard Baldus, and many other nineteenth-century photographs. Contemporary photographs I framed and hung in the two first-floor galleries that had been the kitchen and servants' sitting room.

On November 9, 1949, George Eastman House was opened to the public with a gala celebration. To a crowd of some eight hundred people, Thomas J. Hargrave, president of Eastman Kodak and a trustee of Eastman House, gave a short speech extolling Eastman, then cut a strip of motion-picture film that had been placed across the entrance, announcing the museum was officially open. That evening an audience of twenty-five hundred in the Eastman Theater heard speeches in memory of Eastman by Mary Pickford, Admiral Richard E. Byrd, Dr. Mees, and Alan Valentine, president of the University of Rochester. Among the guests was Edward Steichen, who was a trustee of Eastman House as well as director of photography at the Museum of Modern Art. He told a reporter:

> This is not just a great man's home with some of his furniture in it and a plaque on the outside. That type of institution is just as dead as the plaque....Eastman House is different....I don't know anything like this in the world. You not only have these superb collections which rescue the first hundred years of photography from possible oblivion, but you also feel the presence of a man who was the first to see with a crystal clear vision the enormous potentialities of photography.[39]

In the midst of these pressures, I finished writing the new edition of *The History of Photography* for the Museum of Modern Art.

39. "Eastman House Lauded by Noted Photographer," *Rochester Times-Union*, November 8, 1949.

Oscar, with my permission, lent the manuscript to Dr. Mees. On the following day Oscar brought it back to me. "Dr. Mees," he said, "would like to talk to you about it." I was afraid that he did not like it. But when I called on him I quickly realized that he had read the entire manuscript overnight! As Nobby Clark wrote in the *Biographical Memoirs of Fellows of the Royal Society*, "Mees had always been an avid and lightning reader, and it was fascinating to see him skim a page and hurl the essence of it at his listener who had scarcely got beyond the first line." I was relieved when Dr. Mees said his concern was only with a technicality in my explanation of the manufacture of photographic film, which he quickly corrected.

Finally the book was published. By coincidence I was in the Museum of Modern Art on the day in May 1949 when the first copy came off the press. The book was well received. I was particularly pleased with the review by Margaret Bourke-White in the *New York Times:*

With Alden Scott Boyer and General Solbert at Boyer's bank building, Chicago, 1950. Photograph © Carl Ullrich.

"'The History of Photography' is a surprising and a wonderfully exciting one, which gives the aesthetic as well as the factual side of photography's development. It's a 'must' for my bookshelf."

ALDEN SCOTT BOYER AND HIS COLLECTION   The second major photography collection to enter the George Eastman House was that of Alden Scott Boyer, a perfume manufacturer in Chicago. He was an avid collector of all kinds of antiques: coins and coin-operated devices (including slot machines and player pianos), high-wheeled bicycles, and nineteenth-century photographs, cameras, and books on photography. Nancy had met him first, when he came into the photography department of the Modern one day, took off his suit jacket, and then removed his vest. Just as Nancy began to be alarmed, he showed her the nineteenth-century detective camera he wore concealed in his vest.

I met Boyer in 1947, when Nancy and I stopped over in Chicago on our way to San Francisco. Upon our arrival I telephoned him early in the morning from the railroad station. He answered, "Come right on over," and gave me the address. So we took a cab to an apartment house on the South Side, climbed to the top floor, and knocked on the door. After a while it was cautiously opened. "Mr. Boyer," I said. The maid disappeared and presently a lady in a dressing gown greeted us, introducing herself as Mrs. Boyer. I explained that Mr. Boyer had asked us to come over as soon as we arrived in Chicago. "That's just like Alden," she chuckled. "He never tells me anything."

We had coffee at her invitation while she dressed, and then she called a taxi to take us to what she called the Factory, a warehouse-type building at 2700 Wabash Avenue, with "BOYER" painted in huge letters on the street facade. As we climbed the stairs, on a landing we were confronted by two large clocks suspended from the ceiling. Beside one was a sign, "The Time in Chicago"; beside the other, "The Time in Paris." (We later learned that Boyer had a branch parfumerie on the rue de Rivoli.) We entered a room full of desks with clerks in shirtsleeves working away, hardly noticing us. Across the room was a door with the sign "Mr. Boyer's Office" above it. We opened the door and walked down a staircase to the first floor, and then through a door marked "Private. Enter Without Knocking. *Entrez Sans Frapper*." Four little dogs rushed at us, yapping and wagging their tails. We followed them into a small office with three desks placed in a U formation: one for the telephone, one for work (with a truck rearview mirror over it), and one for junk.

In the middle of this crowded room stood a chubby, round-faced man wearing a brown shirt and a flowing, oversize red-and-blue bow tie. "Glad to meet you, young fellow!" Boyer said, shaking my hand. Then he pulled a cord dangling from the ceiling and a player piano beat out "Hail Columbia, the Gem of the Ocean."

"You want to see my collection of photographs?"

"Yes, very much indeed."

"Well, let's go over to the bank."

We went outside with the dogs to where Alden had parked his car. "Here, wear these," he said, handing us linen dusters. "The dogs have messed up the auto." When I got in I noticed the auto was a right-hand drive, and asked if he got the car in England.

"Oh no," Alden replied. "I had a tough time getting it from the Lincoln factory. 'Made for export only,' they said."

"Why did you get it?"

"Oh, I don't know. Like to be different, I guess."

It was only a couple of blocks to 2220 South Michigan Avenue, an imposing building that had once been a bank. "I bought this in ten minutes," he told us while he unlocked the great bronze door. We entered a vast room crammed with all kinds of things: wooden merry-go-round horses, a cigar store Indian, a huge and brand-new 11 x 14-inch Deardorff studio camera, Hollywood spotlights on huge booms, an ornate gilded sleigh alleged to have belonged to a Russian czarina, music boxes everywhere—I counted fifteen. At the end of the room was a velvet backdrop with glittering spangles. In the basement of the bank Alden had made a beautiful photographic darkroom, with sinks of stainless steel and several top-rate enlargers. Also in the basement was what he referred to as "the biggest collection of slot machines and every one of them crooked. This is the stuff I'll clear out. Glad to be shed of them."

We went into the main vault. Alden opened the foot-thick steel door. The walls were lined with books on photography, arranged by date. Pioneering publications of the 1830s and 1840s were in a vault within the vault. My main purpose in visiting Boyer was to see the daguerreotypes made in the 1850s by Albert Sands Southworth and Josiah Johnston Hawes of Boston. They were then the finest daguerreotypists in America. Boyer had two hundred of their portraits. They were beautiful, and I made photographs of many of them. I also found in Boyer's library several manuals of the daguerreotype process that I had never before read. I took extensive notes of what I found in them that was new to me. After three days of intensive research in Alden's collection and library, Nancy and I proceeded to San Francisco.

What was extraordinary about Boyer's collecting was that he bought almost everything by mail order. Booksellers at home and abroad found him to be a splendid customer; he ordered lavishly and paid promptly. I remember him opening a parcel from a South American "scout," as he called his dealers. In a back room of the bank he untied the string, unwrapped the parcel, folded the paper neatly (for future use), and wrapped the string around it. Then he opened the box and fished around the books until he found the invoice. He immediately wrote a check and put it in an envelope. "But Alden," I said. "Maybe you don't want all those books. Some may not be in good condition."

"So I should disappoint a scout? What's a few bucks?"

David Low, a prominent antiquarian bookseller in London, remembers Boyer in his book *With All Faults*:

> After the last war we had an order from Chicago for all the photographic items in the current catalogue. The order started "Brothers" and was signed Alden Scott Boyer. As we had not sent him a catalogue, had never heard of him before, and could find nothing about him, we wrote that while the books were reserved for him, we would appreciate the reference normal with a first order. His reply started, "Brothers, you've goofed this time," and included half a dozen references, with one from the mayor of Chicago.

On my return to Eastman House I began to receive almost daily "Boyergrams," reports from Boyer of his prodigious collecting activities. These were notes hastily scribbled on cards, the backs of envelopes, or on flamboyant letterheads. For example, when he found a duplicate of the second edition of the Daguerre manual, he scrawled on the back of an envelope, "You, only you, can have it for what I paid for it, $22.50." Notes to frequent correspondents were enclosed in envelopes on which Boyer had stamped name and address in gold letters with a hat-stamping machine. A "pluck" was a report on items just received. A "cull" was a note about something he had come across in his reading. Unlike many collectors, Alden read every book he acquired. Not only did he read them, but he marked them up freely, usually with ballpoint pens of various colored inks. His two chief references were Robert Taft's *Photography and the American Scene* and my own *Photography: A Short Critical History*. These, too, were filled with marginal notations. If I'd mentioned a portfolio of photographs by somebody, he'd write in the margin, "Must get." Then when he had bought it he'd write, "Got one" and give the date. Then "Got another" with that date. In August 1948 he wrote me on a bright yellow card: "I think if I'd read B. Newhall's 'Critical' History of Photography & *remembered* it I would do better than searching the world for Old Books and Publications on the subject—I'd save a lot of time & a whale of a lot of money—. I'm strong for 'The Critical'—I like it."

In May 1950 Boyer wrote that his wife had died quite suddenly. They had no children, and he was desolate. He wrote me:

> I have decided to quit collecting photography & now is the time to talk if you want the Collection or the Photo Library. The Crear Library will take the Photo Library

With Alden Scott Boyer in his bank building, Chicago, 1950. Photograph © Arnold Crane.

& be glad to get it, but I wondered if the GE House should not have it itself apart from Elsie's Library.[40] This decision has come from my combing thru our home which is full of collectors general items—far too many—they will have to go into the auction. There's no end of them.

40. Elsie Garvin was librarian of the Kodak Research Laboratory in Rochester.

I'd like the Photo Equipment kept together. Ditto the Photo Library. These are unreplaceable items as you know, including 750 D. O. Hills & many Talbots and several prints before the Talbot Patent.

I immediately made a tentative estimate of the value of the collection, for I thought that Boyer was suggesting that we purchase it. I estimated its worth as at least fifteen thousand dollars, and consulted Dr. Mees, president of the board of trustees. After describing the collection in a general way I asked if we could afford to pay fifteen thousand for it.

"I don't know!" he replied. "Why do you ask me? Why do you think we hired you? Go ahead. Use your judgment." So I telephoned Alden, saying I wanted to talk to him about his collection.

"You don't really need it with Elsie's library," he responded.

"We have access to it, but it's five miles away. We badly need a library right here."

I was then staggered when Alden asked, "Do you want to buy it or do you want me to give it to you?" He had had it assessed for tax purposes at fifteen thousand, but we both knew that it was worth far more than that.

"What a question, Alden. I want you to give it."

"That's the way to talk. Plain words. All right. I'll give you the whole thing—apparatus, photographs, books. What a collection! I just got five hundred paper negatives." He drew his breath. "It's a good collection, boy!"

"I can't tell you what this means to us, Alden—and to me personally. We'll give it a good home and keep it secure and well."

Around that time I received a call from my friend Daniel Catton Rich, then the director of the Art Institute of Chicago, asking if I could help him locate some ordinary commercial portraits. I told him I was coming through Chicago to pack up the Boyer collection, and he had a lot of portraits of that type, if he'd care to drop by the Boyer Museum on Michigan Avenue, just four blocks away from the Art Institute. He'd never heard of the Boyer Museum. He and an assistant came over and couldn't believe their eyes. Here was this terrific collection, and I was packing it up and taking it out of Chicago. "This is wonderful! We didn't know about you." Boyer didn't believe in the Art Institute. He didn't think it was a sound organization because they were always asking for money. "I don't know why you didn't, boys. I'm in the classified ads. Right under Art Institute. Boyer Museum of American Curiosities. Free." But he took pity on them. "Well, boys," he said, "I'll start a collection for you right now." And he did. A few months later I called him and happened to ask about the Art Institute's collection. "Oh all they do is call me up—they don't even bother to come look at what I'm getting for them. I'm going to stop collecting for them." And he did.

I spent six midsummer weeks in Chicago making an inventory of the collection and supervising the packing of it for shipment to Rochester. It was slow work, for we had agreed to take only one copy of any duplicate volumes in Boyer's library, and not to take any books already in Eastman House. That meant checking each title not only with the inventory of titles I was keeping, but also with the Eastman House library card catalog, which I had brought along with me. In the first few weeks packages were delivered to Boyer with books he had ordered, and for a while I felt I was making little headway with the inventory.

Boyer often would suggest we take a coffee break at what he called "*le bistro*"—the cafeteria next door, which was as remote from a bistro as could be imagined. He would often bring along his four dogs. They were circus dogs, he explained, and the performing life of a circus dog was very short. There was a kennel on the East Coast where retired circus dogs could be purchased. He had trained all four to go out with him on a single leash put through all their collars. He would park them outside the restaurant. One end of the leash was held by Greta Garbo, the anchor dog, who kept them all in place. When a motorcycle drove by on Michigan Avenue the lead dog would bark furiously. His act in the circus ring had been to jump onto the rear seat of a speeding motorcycle while holding an American flag in his teeth.

One day Boyer invited me to join him and a lady friend, Betsy, for a picnic supper. I helped him load his automobile with all the things he had in mind for the meal, including furniture, and then we drove along the highway to a "Victory Garden," in this case a very small triangular park formed by the intersection of three speedways. We unpacked, and there he set up a hammock between two trees and he got out a small stove, a table, and all the picnic things. We ate on gold plates. After our repast, Boyer asked me if I thought he and Betsy should get married. I thought it a fine idea. "Great!" he said, whereupon we got up and went to a nearby drugstore to order ice cream sodas in celebration of their decision.

Both Boyer and I were exhausted from packing. Finally, at the end of August 1950, in one night of feverish activity, four husky boys from Kodak packed the remainder of 3,620 items into 48 boxes. The load weighed 4 tons. I drove my Fraser to San Francisco to spend my vacation with Nancy and Ansel and Virginia Adams.

On my return to Rochester I was pleased that the collection had arrived safely at Eastman House, and that the staff had turned the former kitchen into a library. Steel shelving had been put around the walls, and Boyer's books were neatly placed in them. At the annual meeting of the trustees I announced Boyer's gift of photographs, cameras, apparatus, books, and documents pertaining to the history of photography. The books alone numbered over three thousand volumes.

We honored Alden for his most generous gift with a luncheon attended by twenty-five guests. His new wife, Betsy, accompanied him to Rochester. Alden was resplendent in a double-breasted suit; he wore a Duke of Wellington medal on a gold chain passed through his buttonhole. Around his neck was a gold chain, at the end of which was a Jacobean spoon with the hallmark of 1688, which he had had gold-plated to match the chain. He ate his lunch with the spoon, spurning restaurant, club, or caterer's silverware. He carefully wiped it off on his napkin (tucked into his collar French-style) after each course.

He was delighted with the library and the exhibition. Before we had a chance to have dessert he stood up and announced that he'd like to talk about a great American industry. He walked into the living room, leaned against the mantel, and lectured us for an hour on the history of slot machines, Pianolas, orchestrions, nickelodeons, and other coin-operated machines, including a cast-iron hen that laid a hard-boiled egg whenever it was fed a coin. He followed this with a history of Chicago "sporting houses."

Boyer died in his museum of a heart attack in June 1953. Betsy, who found him, told me that as they carried the body out she looked at all the things that he had stored away in the bank and at once thought of me. For to me alone, of all his friends and coworkers, he had entrusted the bank. I was the only one he had ever allowed to enter the bank alone.

DRYDEN THEATER AND GALLERY   It was evident that Eastman House needed an auditorium where films from the already extensive collection could be screened and meetings and conferences of photographic societies could be held. It was also obvious that a spacious, well-lighted gallery was essential for displaying prints from our own photograph collection or borrowed from other museums or private collectors. Oscar Solbert recognized this need, and suggested to Mrs. George B. Dryden, who was George Eastman's niece, that she and her husband might wish to make a contribution of $250,000 to enable a theater and gallery to be built as a wing to Eastman House. They graciously accepted the suggestion.

A gala opening of the Dryden Theater with its 550-seat auditorium and gallery took place in March 1951. In the Dryden Gallery I arranged an exhibition of nineteenth-century photography and Nancy installed a show of Brett Weston's photographs. Oscar invited his friend Lowell Thomas to give his evening radio broadcast from the stage, followed by a buffet supper and speeches in the theater. With the opening of the theater and gallery Eastman House became a lively museum of photography and motion pictures, not merely a static historic building beloved by antiquarians. On September 9, 1955, Solbert clocked in one thousand visitors.

IMAGE   We soon came to realize that to fulfill our mission of documenting the progress of the art and science of photography and cinematography we needed a publication that would reinforce our exhibitions and reach a larger audience than the thousands who visited us in Rochester. Solbert suggested that instead of mimeographing and mailing frequent press releases to newspapers and magazines we use that money to publish a monthly illustrated bulletin that would be distributed free of charge.

The father of one of our guards was a printer. He lent us a small press and type; his son set up shop in the basement of Eastman House. The first issue of *Image*, as Oscar succinctly titled the periodical, appeared on January 1, 1952. Although only four pages, it carried a surprising amount of information.

Initially I wrote the majority of the articles. Eastman House trustees feared that having a print shop in house would require a union staff. As our little magazine became increasingly popular, we abandoned the hand press and gave the work to a local print shop. In the early days of its publication, *Image* was the only magazine in the world devoted exclusively to the history of photography and film. Our articles were at first unsigned because most of them were written either by James Card or myself, but we were soon offered manuscripts by outside authors. The most successful were descriptions, with diagrams, of the evolution of camera lenses by Rudolf Kingslake, director of optical design at Eastman Kodak. In 1956 we announced that the magazine would be increased to twenty-four pages and sent to all members of the newly formed George Eastman House Associates, with annual dues of five dollars.

From 1958 to 1965 I was also a contributing editor to the elegant and highly informative periodical *Art in America*. I placed articles written by photographers Berenice Abbott, Walter Chappell, Van Deren Coke, Edward Steichen, Alfred Stieglitz, and John Szarkowski in the magazine, and wrote seven essays. These were all on photography and photographers except one account of a visit to the painter John Marin, made with Nancy and Ansel Adams.

❖

Minor White, August 1950. Photograph by Nancy Newhall. (Courtesy of Scheinbaum & Russek Ltd., Santa Fe, New Mexico)

MINOR WHITE

For seven years through the 1950s, the photographer Minor White was the editor of *Image* while at the same time he edited *Aperture*, the journal of photography. Nancy and I had met Minor earlier, in New York. "Minor White!" Nancy said on first hearing his name. "What a curiously appropriate name for a photographer!" It was August 1942, and Nancy and I, Ansel, Alfred Barr, David McAlpin, and James Thrall Soby had finished selecting one hundred photographs for the "Image of Freedom" exhibition at the Museum of Modern Art. Photographers had been asked to submit photographs anonymously, and we discovered we had chosen all four of Minor White's.

We were delighted to become friends of Minor's. He was back from active duty in the Pacific, and shocked by what he had seen. A sensitive young man, he had found combat action very searing. I gave him a part-time position as a curatorial assistant in the Museum of Modern Art, and introduced him to the brilliant art historian Meyer Schapiro, with whom Minor studied at Columbia University at night on the G.I. Bill. Together they studied the aesthetics of photography as opposed to the aesthetics of painting and drawing. They relied heavily on the stimulating writings of art historian Wilhelm Worringer, applying his principles of form to photography. We also introduced Minor to Stieglitz. Nancy later described that time:

> We took Minor with us whenever something or somebody interesting came along. He became quietly a part of our lives, this tall, pale and very strong man, with his deep voice and his background of science and poetry. At our parties,

whether large or small, he watched and listened, with humor and sympathy, to what went on around him, and you could feel him grow.

Equal perhaps to his conversations with Stieglitz was his meeting with Edward Weston, when, pushed on his first plane by his sons, he came East for his great retrospective at the Museum, which I directed. He could study Edward's work with Edward, who was on duty everyday, and then come back to our place and see Edward the man.[41]

41. Nancy Newhall, unpublished manuscript.

Years later, when Minor was asked during an interview, "How did you know the Newhalls?" his reply was simple:

I was already recognized as a photographer with my travelling shows at the WPA....I was a name for them before I arrived, and when I landed, they took me under their wing immediately and we got along really well from the start. There were no problems about getting along with the Newhalls. Beaumont was just back from the war when I arrived. That was an extremely exciting rebuilding for me. I met Stieglitz, Strand, Ansel Adams, Callahan, Smith, Barbara Morgan, Georgia O'Keeffe, and anybody who was there in New York at the time. I was also elected to the Photo League. I went up to see Stieglitz in his little gallery and I had three or four conversations with him. Within a five-minute period Stieglitz had got me back moving again. I had always had this sensation that while in the Army something had died or at least gone underground. Stieglitz came along and reactivated something.[42]

42. Quoted in Paul Hill and Thomas Cooper, *Dialogue with Photography* (New York: Farrar, Straus & Giroux, 1979), p. 345.

In 1946 Ansel founded the department of photography at the California School of Fine Arts (now called the San Francisco Art Institute). He had a teaching position there, and had raised funds for the construction of darkrooms for the students to use. He found the job a heavy burden as he was also loaded down with commercial assignments, and he needed an assistant. We suggested he invite Minor out to work with him. Minor was delighted, and moved to San Francisco. Ansel, who was training to be a concert pianist at the time, lived in a beautiful studio on the outskirts of the city, and invited Minor to live in the adjacent family residence, which was vacant. Darkrooms were installed in the basement of the residence, and students often worked there. Minor and Ansel became good friends, Ansel reporting, "He fits in like a glove fits on." After Nancy and I had stayed in this house with Minor and friends, I referred to it as "The Maelstrom."

The San Francisco years were a period of tremendous development for Minor. He often traveled down the coast to visit Edward Weston and work with him at Point Lobos. While there, Minor shared his theories with Edward. Minor had combined the philosophies of Schapiro's Freudian iconography and Stieglitz's insights of Equivalents and the sequence with his own inclination toward the mystical. He began to work out a system he called "space analysis," and to write about it.

❖

For years Nancy, Ansel, and I had dreamed together of founding a journal or a quarterly close in conception to Stieglitz's legendary *Camera Work*, but we never found the time or extra energy this would require. At the very stimulating ten-day Aspen Photographic Conference, held in the fall of 1951, the idea of the magazine *Aperture* was born. Those attending the conference included Nancy and myself, photographers Berenice Abbott, Ansel Adams, Laura Gilpin, Frederick Sommer, Dorothea Lange, Eliot Porter, Minor White, Paul Vanderbilt of the Library of Congress, John Morris of the *Ladies' Home Journal*, and other amateur and professional photographers. It was Ansel Adams who clarified our ideas, expressing the need for a professional society with a dignified publication. We discussed this informally quite a bit, feeling that what was greatly needed was a periodical in which we could talk about photography and learn from one another.

The next year, nine of us met at Ansel and Virginia's house in San Francisco and officially founded *Aperture*. Ansel suggested the title and Minor volunteered to do the actual work of editing *Aperture*. His first cover was a photograph by Dorothea Lange of a signpost pointing in all directions. In the early years we all pitched in to help out with the publication, but eventually we left it all to Minor. Whenever we protested an issue he would reply, "If you don't like it, for God's sake do it yourself."

After a few years, the California School of Fine Arts condensed its program from four years to three, eliminated photography from the curriculum, and asked Minor to take an unpaid leave of absence for a year. This of course was not possible for him, and he accepted my offer of work at George Eastman House editing *Image*, which was growing into a fine little photographic magazine. He also generally assisted me with the collection and with organizing exhibitions. He was an excellent curator as well as a photographer. For several months until he found a place of his own he stayed with us in our little house in Rochester, and seemed to like life in that city. Summers he would get into his Volkswagen bus and drive west, giving workshops along the way. His mysticism, fed by Zen philosophy and practice, increased, and his haunting personal vision became more apparent in his photographs.

Both Minor and I taught one day a week at the Rochester Institute of Technology. Minor, however, introduced students to the aesthetic side of photography and I to its history. Teaching became a very important part of his life, and it was not surprising that in 1957 he resigned from Eastman to teach full time at RIT. He was a very creative photographer, and opportunities for creating were not to be found in his job at Eastman House. In 1965 he was offered a professorship at the School of Architecture of the Massachusetts Institute of Technology in Cambridge. He received an honorary doctorate from MIT in 1975. Through his teaching, his photographs, and editing *Aperture*, Minor made a great contribution to creative photography.

EUROPE 1952

In the fall of 1952 Nancy and I flew to Europe to collect photographs for George Eastman House. In our stay of two months we visited old friends and made new ones. In London we had dinner with Denis Wratten, director of Kodak Limited and president of the Royal Photographic Society. Dennis frequently visited Rochester and was a good friend of ours. At his invitation I gave an illustrated lecture on Eastman House to members of the Royal Photographic Society. I was pleased to renew my acquaintance with J. Dudley Johnston, curator of the society's rich collection of photographs from the earliest days to the present.

Nancy had been commissioned by *Modern Photography* magazine to write a profile of Alvin Langdon Coburn, a photographer who was a contemporary of Edward Steichen and Edward Weston. Although born in America, Coburn spent most of his life in England and Wales. He invited us to visit him at his home in Rhos-on-Sea, a small town in North Wales, some thirty-five miles from Liverpool. In his letter he had enclosed a picture so we would recognize him when we arrived at Colwyn Bay, the nearest railroad station to his house. He was waiting for us on the station stairs, and

Left: Snapshot of Alvin Langdon Coburn sent to Nancy and me so we could recognize him on our arrival at the Colwyn Bay railroad station, September 1952. Photographer unknown.

Right: Alvin Langdon Coburn, Edith Coburn, and Nancy, Wales, 1952. Photograph by Beaumont Newhall. (Courtesy of Scheinbaum & Russek Ltd., Santa Fe, New Mexico)

soon we were driving in his little car to his house—named "Awen," which in Welsh means "inspiration"—where we met his wife, Edith. We liked them both at once.

We looked at portfolio after portfolio crammed with Alvin's photographs, ranging from his early, strong, sympathetic portraits of William Butler Yeats, William James, and Mark Twain, all published in a series titled *Men of Mark*, to city scenes and landscapes. We were especially impressed with his experimental abstract photographs, deliberate double exposures and distorted perspectives with the camera pointed down from high places. And there were his "Vortographs," which he had made beginning in 1917. These were photographs taken through a kaleidoscopic device he had designed of three narrow mirrors facing one another in a hollow prism through which he photographed bits of glass and crystals. These were named "Vortographs" by Ezra Pound, a member of the Vorticist group of English artists and poets.

From as much of his rich and vast collection as we could see in the brief time of our visit, Nancy made a selection of photographs to illustrate the magazine article. When we said

Alvin Langdon Coburn,
c. 1963. Photograph by
Beaumont Newhall.
(Courtesy of Scheinbaum &
Russek Ltd., Santa Fe, New
Mexico)

goodbye to Alvin and Edith we had known each other for only twenty-four hours, but as Alvin said, "There are some people you have known always."

Nancy's profile of Coburn never appeared in the magazine, although she was paid for writing it. No explanation was given. Eastman House acquired the rights and in 1962 published a handsome portfolio containing an expanded text by Nancy and sixteen tipped-in photogravures. An edition of two thousand was printed for distribution to our members.

Alvin was much concerned about finding an appropriate institution to care for his thousands of negatives and prints upon his death. I was greatly moved when he wrote me that he had decided to bequeath the entire collection to Eastman House.

The last time I saw Alvin was in 1964, when he was eighty-one years old. I was on a rush trip to London to collect photographs by Frederick H. Evans from the Royal Photographic Society for exhibition at Eastman House. I spent a memorable two days with Alvin in Rhos-on-Sea. He was writing his autobiography, and we talked more about mysticism than photography. He loved the Orient, and for many years had been drawn to mystical poets and scholars in his ardent pursuit of the spiritual. He had studied comparative religions, and explored the Kabbalah, astrology, alchemy, Druids, and early Christian mystics. In 1962, Nancy sent him galleys of her piece so he could correct any errors. She had concluded with a quote from "My Photographic Adventures," an address Alvin had just given at the University of Reading. "I will be especially happy if you will quote this at the end of your article," he wrote back to her: "'Photography teaches its devotees how to look lovingly and intelligently at the world, but religious mysticism introduces the soul to God.'"

When it came time to leave, he drove me to the railway station, and together we walked to the waiting train. I wish I had photographed him through the open window of the railway carriage as he looked up at me before the train started. Seven years earlier he had written to me in a letter, "Time has very little to do with friendship. It is the *intensity* that counts."[43] Now, as we waited, he said, "Isn't it strange that in so short a time I feel so close to you. I feel that I know you better than so many other people. I hope you feel the same."

43. Alvin Langdon Coburn to Beaumont Newhall, February 28, 1957.

"Yes. And to think we've only met three times—and spent only six days together." At the moment of parting, which he thought might be forever, he looked up with no show of emotion, asking me to give his love to Nancy. When the whistle blew for the train to start we shook hands. Gently our hands separated as the train gathered speed. I leaned out of the window to wave to Alvin. He stood there, motionless. He died two years later, November 23, 1966.

❖

It was a delight to visit Mathilda Theresa Talbot in her ancestral home of Lacock Abbey in Wiltshire. We had not seen her since 1936, when she generously lent the Museum of Modern Art ten photographs taken by her grandfather, William Henry Fox Talbot.

We drove to Lacock with Harold White and his wife, Edith. Harold was a photojournalist by profession and a photo historian by avocation; he was researching the life and work of Talbot with Miss Talbot. Nancy described our visit in a letter to her mother:

Lacock was lovely—the irregular cluster of the village, the Abbey with its two hollow squares, one the 13th-century cloisters of the old nunnery over which the living quarters now are, and the other square, formerly the shops and offices, dairy, bakery, etc., now let out as flats. We had sherry in the rooms of Miss Talbot's niece, then trotted about a quarter of a mile through corridors and galleries and had lunch in the great hall, with its stained glass rose window, and tiers of statues. Then we went walking and exploring inside and out—through the empty but still beautiful cloisters, then the attics under the roof with their still solid timbers 800 years old, then the galleries from which in the 18th century Georgian rooms were built and then Gothic revival bays and the great hall. We had tea in one of the huge bay windows, two stories high, with the sun pouring in on the shabby elegance—the fine china rivetted together, the old chairs and divans in torn and faded upholstery—and marvelous things still intact—chandeliers of glass flowers, exquisite things from everywhere. And miles of ancestral portraits, almost uniformly looking dull and dyspeptic.

Miss Talbot is 82 and looks 60; a brisk, small woman somewhat horsefaced, witty, intelligent, and very generous. Did you know she presented to the nation the finest original copy of Magna Carta, which had been in her family since it was signed? She has also given Lacock—both village and abbey— to the nation. On her 80th birthday she gave a ball—danced every dance and at two in the morning was doing a Scottish reel!

In Paris we enjoyed visiting with Henri Cartier-Bresson again, after his exhibition at the Museum of Modern Art. His book *The Decisive Moment* had just come off the press. The French edition of this beautiful collection of photographs, brilliantly reproduced in photogravure, is titled *Images à la sauvette*. Henri explained that the phrase *à la sauvette* is slang and can hardly be translated. Literally it means "to save oneself," and he gave the example of a street vendor selling his wares without a license to do so and who "beats it" when he sees a policeman, in order to "save himself" from arrest. We were invited by Teriade, his publisher, to join Henri and his wife, Eli, at a celebration lunch at an outdoor café on the boulevard Saint-Michel.

I sat beside Henri. I noticed that he was adjusting the lens opening and the shutter speed of his camera as it lay on his lap. Somewhat thoughtlessly I asked, "What are you going to photograph?" He did not answer, but put his finger across his lips, to close mine. He stood up, put his camera to his eye, pressed the shutter release, and then sat down. He told me he had made a portrait of a painter whose name I now do not recall. It was a brilliant example of his way of photographing swiftly and with perception.

I was asked to lecture about Eastman House to the members of the Societé Française de Photographie. I considered this an honor, for it was the oldest society of photography in the world. The invitation was extended to me by the president, Edouard Belin, a scientist famed for his invention of a phototelegraphic system for the transmission of photographic images by wire. After making arrangements for the meeting, as I was leaving he asked, "Of course you will speak in French?" I was taken aback. "Sir, I don't think I can manage an hour's lecture."

"Why not? We've been talking together in French for the last half hour."

"I'll try my best," I offered.

I telephoned Henri to tell him of Monsieur Belin's request. "Is my French good enough?"

"I don't know. We've never talked together in French. *Alors, parlez un peu.*" I spoke a few words.

"*Bon,*" said Henri. "You'll do."

Nancy and I had dinner before the lecture with Henri and his friends Ian Hugo and Anaïs Nin. We arrived a little late to find the auditorium packed and people sitting on the steps. Fortunately we had reserved seats. Nancy told me later she had asked Henri if I could be understood. "Perfectly comprehensible," he said, "but tell Beaumont not to lose his exotic accent."

One afternoon we visited the American Surrealist painter and photographer Man Ray in his lofty studio in Paris, near the church of Saint Sulpice. I knew him, for he was a frequent visitor to the Museum of Modern Art, where his paintings were often exhibited. I remember that whenever he gave a lecture he would use a dressmaker's arm instead of a pointer. After a warm greeting I told him that I wanted to buy some of his photographs for Eastman House. He pointed to an upper shelf of the large bookcase opposite. "Do you see that parcel? It's photographs of mine that a fellow from Chicago picked out. Said he'd like to buy them." Man Ray chuckled. "I told him to send me a check and I'd mail them to him. Well I never got any money from that boy in Chicago. If you'd like any of them you can have them."

I looked through the photographs and picked out half a dozen or so. "I'll buy these. I can't pay you for them right now, but tomorrow I can get you a check from the Kodak-Pathé office here."

"Oh, that's fine," Man Ray said, and then added, "Let's all go have dinner together."

During the meal at a nearby restaurant I asked him to tell me about Eugène Atget, who photographed extensively and exquisitely in and around Paris in the early years of the century. Man Ray knew him well. "Oh, let's wait until we get back to the studio and I'll show you my collection."

After coffee Man Ray brought out an inexpensive album, of the type amateurs keep their snapshots in, containing forty or more vintage Atget prints. They were beautiful and in perfect condition. It was a superb collection of the subjects that the Surrealists so admired: shop fronts and street fairs. As I handed the album back to him I spontaneously burst out, "If you ever think of parting with this album, please let me know."

A few minutes later I saw him talking with his wife on the other side of the room. Presently he came over to where I was sitting, bent over my shoulder, and said, almost in a whisper, "We feel like parting with it now."

I stood up and went with him into an adjoining room. "How much are you asking for the collection?"

"Well, what would you offer?"

Assuming that Man Ray was somewhat shrewd in money matters, I deliberately made a very low offer. "I thought five hundred dollars."

"Fine, fine," he said, and started to wrap up the album. Just as he was about to tie the string around the parcel, he looked up and remarked, "Oh, I forgot something. Once Gertrude Stein sold a Picasso painting. A price was agreed upon. But at the last moment she said, 'Don't forget that this Picasso is from the collection of Gertrude Stein.'"

All I could say was, "Of course. Would it be acceptable that for two hundred fifty more we say that these Atgets are from Man Ray's collection of Atget prints?"

"That's fine," he said, as he finished tying the parcel, his wife placing her finger on the string for him to secure the final knot. Then we all went out and had a drink to celebrate.

LIVE TELEVISION

In the winter of 1952 , I was asked by station WHAM-TV in Rochester to do a fifteen-minute television show about photography and George Eastman House every Thursday night for thirteen weeks. I accepted with anticipation. Although the show was billed as "Focus on Photography," it would have been more accurately titled "The Curator Opens the Glass Cases," for I brought to the studio some of the rarest objects in Eastman House, which I demonstrated and explained to my partner, Larry Mann, who played the part of a visitor to the museum.

I first showed him a large wooden box camera designed by Louis-Jacques-Mandé Daguerre, the inventor of the daguerreotype process, for making photographs on silver plates. This was almost a unique camera, for it had a label on one side signed by Daguerre himself in 1839 as a guarantee of authenticity. I showed a few daguerreotypes and all the apparatus used to develop the plates.

In the early days of television, all shows were "live." What the camera saw was transmitted instantly to hundreds, if not thousands, of television viewers. Unlike with film or videotape, there was no lasting visual record of what the cameras saw. Post-production editing was impossible, and mistakes could not be corrected. Nancy and I were entranced by the medium, and we wrote a detailed description of an early program.

NN: Beaumont and I arrived at the WHAM-TV studio with assorted historical photographic apparatus for his TV show. It is 7:40. The floodlights, the banks of fluorescent tubes, and the spotlights are all on, the two huge TV cameras are being jockeyed around, Beau is unloading a daguerreotype camera and developing boxes and arranging them on a long table in front of curtains. Pictures are being set up on music racks for the cameras to copy.

BN: I huddle with my partner, Larry Mann; with Ross Weller, the chief announcer; with George Geiger, the director, who will give me time signals throughout the show; and with Bud Senke, the producer, who puts the show on the air.

NN: It's time for the first rehearsal. Beaumont and Larry are working out their sequences; cameramen with headphones on follow them. Overhead, on a long boom, hangs a microphone that can be placed above the head of anyone speaking. The control rooms, way off where the balcony would be if the studio was a theater, glimmer darkly, mirroring the lighted stage. Very dimly one can see the producer and other men working at the controls. They look like fish in an aquarium at night. The TV term for this room is "heaven." Thank the Lord that Beau is a spieler. This is all ad lib! Nobody works from a script—just an outline of what to do and say. What a turret of lenses on the TV cameras! How quickly they move, with the cameramen kicking aside the cables on the floor. Red lights on the front of the camera mean it is "on the air." After the first run-through, the producer asks the director over the loudspeaker, "How's the time, George?" Back comes the answer, "One fifteen over."

BN: He means the rehearsal ran one minute and fifteen seconds beyond the allotted time of fifteen minutes. Thirty seconds is a long time

on the air; a show is spoiled if there are even five seconds of "dead air."

NN: 8:55. Now I'm up in the main control room with the producer, Bud Senke, looking at three TV receivers. Over two of these we can see what each camera is focused on. The third screen shows what Bud will put on the air by switching from camera to camera. The three screens are fun, but distracting.

BN: Everything about TV is distracting. While I spiel and demonstrate, cameras are moving silently around, people are moving around, red lights are blinking on the cameras, a microphone almost touches my head as it hovers over me, the monitor is showing me almost mockingly as I stand here. George, the director, is right beside the camera. He twirls his finger to tell me to talk faster; he pulls the palms of his hands apart very very slowly; that means to speak slowly. If he points his finger to the red light on the camera it means that I should talk right straight into the lens of the camera—he wants me to speak to one person—to you—and no one else, at your TV set.

              At long last he holds up a big card with three huge letters on it: OFF. But I cannot relax, for I and whoever else is on camera must stand absolutely still while the next show is preparing to go on. When George draws his forefinger across his throat the show is over. Then Bud, the producer, shouts over the loudspeaker, "That was a darn good show, everybody!"

NN: I tear out of the control room in great excitement— they can have their cameras and lights and microphone booms down there, and Beau or anybody can do all the acting—me for the controls in "heaven"! With four eyes—one for each screen and an encyclopedic one for the stage, and living always in the next ten seconds and making fast decisions. I had no idea how much was actually done by the "producer." Me, I am a convert to TV from the control room. Beau is a convert from the sheer excitement of solving the manifold problems of being thrown into star performer's status—with only two appearances as a professional before.

BN: It is one of the most exciting experiences I know—all these people that Nancy has described—all this miraculous equipment—all focused on me, to bring my story, my interests, my enthusiasm, to more people than I have ever been able to reach directly. To reach them immediately, now, at once. To see myself talking and moving—not as in a mirror, not wrong-way around, but as others see me. And to have people on the streets, in stores, in Eastman House, speak to me, and to know by their questions that they looked and listened. Two little boys saw me in Eastman House. They looked at me as if they thought I was glass and would shatter if they spoke.

"You're the television man!"

"Yes."

"We're going to look next week!"

"Mister, what's the littlest camera you have?"

I told them where to look for the camera no bigger than a watch, with a picture made with it. It did me good to think that kids come to see the House and to ask questions. Then there is the thrill of learning a new medium, learning by doing, without books, directly. I think TV is the first thing I've done without reading about it first.

A year later, in 1953, WHAM-TV asked me to do another TV show, with a theme that was quite different. On the air I taught a friend, Patricia Caulfield, how to take photographs, how to develop the film, and how to make prints. Pat, a senior at the University of Rochester, knew nothing at all about photography when she volunteered to join the show. On the last show of "Focus on Photography" she took a portrait of me, developed the film, and made an 11 x 14-inch enlargement—all on camera in fifteen minutes. I was very pleased that very soon after our television venture Pat became the editor of *Modern Photography* magazine.

TEACHING

In 1952 both Dr. Mees, president of George Eastman House, and Dr. Cornelis de Kiewiet, the president of the University of Rochester, felt that their institutions should cooperate in offering a course of lectures on the history of photography. On December 8, 1952, a vice president of university development wrote me:

With the magnificent development of Eastman House as a world center for the photographic arts and the history of photography, it is becoming increasingly apparent there is some common area of cooperative interest between Eastman House and the University of Rochester which should be identified and explored and, if possible, implemented.

For our own part, the idea of developing here a center of study and teaching in the field of the photographic arts and particularly in the use of photography as a basic medium of communication appeals to us very much.

I wrote the following memorandum for presentation to the university administration.

Photography is second only to the spoken or written word as a medium of communication. It has become an important part of our daily life. Yet our universities have not considered the teaching of photography with other academic courses. Such instruction that is offered has come under the physics or journalism departments, and is largely technical. Photography as a means of communication, and as an art, has not been considered as an academic discipline.

A department of photographic arts, offered jointly by the University of Rochester and the George Eastman House, would be innovative. It could offer the general student an introduction to photography. It could also train students who wish to make photography their vocation. Such a program might well attract students to the university. Almost everyone today is interested in photography, but few are able to pursue this interest in college. It is obvious that, as in any professional field, the broad understanding that is the very purpose of a university education is essential to a success in photography. To put photography aside for four years is discouraging for the student who wishes to make photography his life work. The program suggested for the University of Rochester and Eastman House would enable such students to work in the field of photography while also pursuing more classical courses of study. The emphasis in the course would be on the use of photographs, and on the establishment of critical standards by which to judge finished work. A Department of Photographic Arts might well have as its first goal training in understanding the potentials of photography: what can be done with a camera and light-sensitive material. The history of photography would show students how photography came into being, and how it has become an essential part of our lives. The masterpieces of photography in the Eastman House collection could be studied as evidence that the camera can go beyond the field of communication into the realm of expression. The use of photography in books, magazines, and on exhibition walls would be an important part of the course. It is possible that experts in various fields of photography, from

Rochester and other cities, might be available to give lectures and lead informal seminars in their special fields.

I proposed a one-semester evening course at Eastman House of fifteen two-hour lectures. I would give nine of these, the other six would be handled by guest lecturers. We were very pleased when the course was approved by the administration in 1954. In 1955, I was appointed senior lecturer in photographic arts by the School of Liberal and Applied Studies.

The course was given again in 1955, in a slightly altered form. Two meetings a week were scheduled at Eastman House, and the number of guest lecturers reduced to three. In addition several staff members addressed the students. I was dismayed that only five students came to the first meeting, as a minimum of ten students was required by the university. At the second meeting I was encouraged. Ten students also joined the class, all of them eager. Also, we now met around a table in the library. This change of location was welcome, for I could bring to class photographs from the collection. The students could see and handle daguerreotypes, ambrotypes, tintypes, as well as platinotypes, calotypes, and other prints that tend to look alike in reproduction. The informality of our meetings led to lively discussions. At examination time I gave each student a box of miscellaneous photographs to describe for the catalog of the collection. The course as given in the university night school was so successful that a Professor Hersey proposed that it be given by the Department of Art of the college, and that I be invited to join the faculty as a professor. The plan was rejected by the Committee on Academic Policy. "This is not a trade school!" I was told.

I then accepted, in 1956, the invitation of the Rochester Institute of Technology to teach in its Department of Photography. The institute *was* a trade school and had applied to the Regents of the State of New York for accreditation. The addition of a course in the history of photography was most welcome. The course, which met once a week, was a required one for photography students.

MARGARET BOURKE-WHITE

Margaret Bourke-White, who was one of four staff photographers for *Life* magazine when it first began publication in 1936, enthusiastically accepted my invitation to show her photographs at Eastman House in a large one-person exhibition. I visited her for five days in December 1954 at her home in Darien, Connecticut, to select the work for the show.

I arrived by train at Darien about 9 A.M. Peggy—as she told me she liked to be called—was standing beside a brand-new Studebaker—low, rakish, robin's-egg blue. She wore plaid slacks, a short coat of fluffy wool, and a Canadian trapper's fur hat that looked like an overseas cap. We at once went shopping. The butcher understood veal, and cut wonderfully thin scallopinis, while Peggy picked up two little squabs. In the wine shop we chose a Saint Emilion, a rosé, and an assortment of domestic vintages.

Arriving at Peggy's house in ten acres of suburban country about two miles from town, we had coffee brewed in Italian espresso pots from freshly ground beans that Peggy had brought back from Guatemala. We breakfasted in the sun room, on plates made for her by a Korean potter, with toast in individual baskets from Italy and butter in pots from Japan. On the living room walls were hung memorabilia of various tributes Peggy had received: diplomas of two honorary doctorates (Cornell and Rutgers), a thank-you letter from the U.S. War Department for her work as a field correspondent in World War II, and a certificate of honorary membership in the Grasshoppers Club, named for the pilots of the tiny observation planes in which she flew over the Italian front with her cameras.

We began selecting photographs, some old, some new, without any thought of chronological order. Soon we were going through magazines in which her stories had appeared, especially old copies of *Fortune*, for which Peggy was the sole staff photographer from 1929 to 1936. In the attic we found stack after stack of these magazines, as well as envelopes of tear sheets. Soon Peggy's tidy living room had become a shambles. Harriet, the maid, had prepared a lunch of lamb chops, and we ate in the dining room, sitting on camp chairs at a table made of one great slab of heavy plate glass laid across two upended tree trunks.

After lunch, somewhat to my surprise, we got out the bikes. These were very special French bicycles made of aluminum, with three gear speeds. I wondered if, after all these years, I could ride, but it all came back to me in a few minutes. We chose a route that would give us the best long and gentle hills down which to coast. After biking two or three miles we stopped to have some tea, then began once again selecting photographs.

While I was looking and familiarizing myself with her work, Peggy was telling me of her experiences: how she got into photography, her favorite things to do, what she considered her best work. Time and again, pictures she particularly remembered seemed to both of us less important now, and we came to realize that many of her selections were reminiscent of experiences she went through while making the photographs. If I felt a picture was not up to some of the other work, out it went, without question. One group of pictures would call to mind another; there would be a frantic search: somewhere in the house were prints or tear sheets, or some news clipping that would complete the essay. So we went on until it was long after dinner and we could hardly walk around the room, it was so full of photographs.

Then Peggy announced that the time had come to break with the past. We were to have a ceremonial dinner. I was to choose one of three Japanese kimonos she had brought back from Japan, specially made outsize for western men. I chose a quiet striped brown and white one and got into it, along with sandals. Presently she joined me wearing a gorgeous white kimono with great red and green designs on it. With our cocktails we had Japanese tidbits—roasted pimentos, fish, ripe olives—all served and eaten with delicate chopsticks. Peggy had planned to cook the squabs, but found she had forgotten the chicken livers she needed, so I made scallopini and she prepared a most unusual salad. She described it in her autobiography:

It would seem that those who lean toward photography should also lean toward good food. Beaumont Newhall, the curator of George Eastman House in Rochester and a prolific author of books and articles on the history of photography, brings to his cooking a kind of mystery. His secret is stock. The process is a little like putting negatives in the developer. Almost anything can come out. We spent many days at my home going through some two thousand of my pictures, retrieving some from old magazines and scraps in the attic, to make a major exhibition of four hundred photographs. During the entire monumental task, a kettle of soup stock simmered on the back of the stove. At intervals, Beaumont would add various liquids to make up just the precise amount that had boiled away. And when it was at its pungent best and combined with beef or chicken or fish and set on the table, who could tell where the subtle flavors and aromas came from?

At one of our suppers, I carried highest honors for a salad I had made, using twenty-seven different salad greens—everything from long, canoe-shaped Chinese cabbage, through various shapes and crinkled forms, down to tiny clover-like leaves of delicate fresh chervil. It was a photographer's salad, composed of large and small objects for contrast and depth and the long green scale for gradation of tone. This mainly was a triumph of marketing. To get the range, I had canvassed the greengrocers for miles around.[44]

On the second day of my visit we made a list of everything we had put aside as candidates for the exhibition. When we had finished, there were some forty major photo essays to be shown, from the earliest industrial subjects to her current work in color—low-altitude aerial photographs of the American harvest. The more I studied the photographs the more I became impressed with the journalistic character of everything Peggy had done on assignment. To consider her a "one-picture artist" would be a mistake; there were many great single images in what we had looked at, but they were rare. The photo essay, with several pictures, formed the gist of her work. Nor could one separate the work from the personality.

Peggy was an extrovert among photographers. Hers is not the velvet hand and hawk's eye of a Cartier-Bresson; she is not an invisible presence on the sidelines. She was a warm, generous, gracious, attractive woman who immediately established a rapport with the people she photographed. She made being a woman an asset, and created an image of being a daredevil, adventure-loving, world-roaming foreign correspondent.

Late Sunday afternoon, taking a break from work, we drove down the freeway to visit Barbara and Herc Morgan. On the way a great moment occurred: the odometer turned to 19999. Peggy pulled the car over to the shoulder of the road, and turned the engine off to admire it.

We worked two more days, interrupting our work for delicious meals and spins on the bicycles. We decided to present the first photo essay that Peggy did for *Life*, a 1936 story of the Montana boomtown called "New Deal," where ten thousand construction workers on the huge Fort Peck Dam lived. We also settled on the photographs of the boomtown she made ten years later—when

44. Margaret Bourke-White, *Portrait of Myself* (New York: Simon & Schuster, 1963), p. 304.

only a single building remained standing. The boomtown, so lively in 1936, had come to exist only through her photographs.

Once we completed our selection, Peggy and I drove to New York, and I went up to the offices of *Life* magazine with her. Managing editor Ed Thompson, and his right-hand man, Joe Kastner, who recalled with fondness a piece he did on my book back in 1937, art director Charlie Tudor, and his assistant, Bernie Quint, were all in shirtsleeves, rushing about with layouts to be approved and copy to be edited, and yet there seemed to be time somehow to speak to me and make me feel at home. We met with Bob Elson, assistant editor, about the Eastman House plans, then went to the fifth floor to speak with the head of the lab about making prints for the show. I was invited to their staff party that evening, but declined. When I went back after lunch to say goodbye to everybody I felt a glow of pleasure that I seemed to be so welcome all around.

Steichen was at the Museum of Modern Art when I called the next day to ask could I come over right away? Our conversation, which I had intended to limit to obtaining his answer to two questions—would the museum like Minor White's show? Would they like Eisenstaedt's?—took up the better part of the morning. With more emotion than usual, Steichen described the problems he was having with his upcoming mammoth show, "The Family of Man." He seemed to be putting everything he had into it—at unbelievable cost, working long hours, finding sleep possible only with the assistance of drugs. He declined both exhibitions, saying, "I've never had a one-man show here, and if I did I wouldn't start with Eisie." Steichen went on about his big project, then became very emotional about me and what a fine job I was doing at George Eastman House. As we said goodbye he put his arms on my shoulders, looked me in the eye, and shed a tear.

And I was very thankful that I had gotten out and wasn't obligated to him in any way. In my mind I compared the Modern with *Life*. An outsider, I was given the run of *Life*'s top offices; all the big wheels, although on deadline, found time to talk to me. Yet I was a stranger in my own museum. I saw Monroe Wheeler, who confessed that Steichen had gone so overboard that the show was costing sixty thousand dollars, and they were in the hole twenty thousand—and couldn't Kodak do something? This was very ironical, considering the promise of bringing in a hundred thousand dollars that Steichen had originally made to the Museum of Modern Art trustees. I explained to Monroe I simply could not ask Kodak for anything for somebody else. "Would you ask the Rockefeller Foundation for money for Eastman House?" I asked.

The Bourke-White exhibition opened at Eastman House in March 1956. It was a great success. *Life* chartered a plane to fly Peggy's editors and other staff members up to Rochester. At her insistence, the *Life* photographic laboratory made a duplicate set of all the photographs in the show for simultaneous exhibition at her alma mater, Cornell University. Peggy was greatly pleased, and boasted, "I am the only woman photographer to have two one-man shows at the same time!" Those of us who knew her as a friend and brilliant photojournalist were saddened that she suffered from Parkinson's disease. She faced her last years courageously, and died in 1971.

❖

"Epicure Corner"

One evening in 1956 our friend Andrew Wolfe burst into our house in Rochester with the startling news that he had bought a weekly suburban newspaper, the *Brighton-Pittsford Post*. He explained that he planned to report local news and to publish columns on a variety of subjects, such as reviews of the theater, concerts, motion pictures, and cooking. "You'll be the food editor," he told me.

"What?" I exclaimed. "I can't do that."

"Why not?" he replied. "I know you can write well because I like to read it. You can cook well, because I like to eat it."

I agreed, but made one reservation: the column would not be signed. That way either Andy or I could drop it without embarrassment if it was not well received. Andy agreed, and suggested the name of the column: "Epicure Corner."

We decided the column would contain not only recipes and cooking know-how, but also anecdotes, a touch of history, visits to famous restaurants, and interviews with chefs. I had one rule: I would never write a recipe unless I had cooked it myself and somebody else had enjoyed eating it. Here are two of the 234 columns I wrote between 1956 and 1969.

French Omelette

Of all the ways to prepare eggs, the French omelette is classic. The varieties are limited only by your imagination. In her New York restaurant, Madame Romaine de Lyons serves nothing but omelettes—and the menu lists over a hundred different kinds!

We used to be superstitious about the iron pan we used. It was never put in water, and was cleaned with a paper towel. If any egg particles were left sticking to the sides, we rubbed them off with salt. But recently we have been using an aluminum electric fry pan that is washed out thoroughly with detergent and water after every use. The omelettes made in these pans are identical.

The critical thing about cooking an omelette is not the pan or the mixture put into it, but the temperature of the butter. When butter is heated it goes through a series of changes. First it melts to a golden brown liquid, then it becomes frothy, and gradually clears. For an instant or so it still remains golden, then it rapidly becomes brown, starts to smoke, and finally turns black and thin. To make a good omelette you should put the eggs in at just the point where the butter is turning from gold to brown.

For each person, break two eggs into a bowl, add a tablespoon of milk, a pinch of salt, and a grind of pepper, then beat it vigorously with a chef's wire whisk until the mixture is frothy. While still frothy pour it quickly into the pan. As the edge solidifies, push it back gently with a fork, and let the uncooked part run in the sides of the pan by rocking it gently. When the bottom is brown, fold over half the omelette with a spatula. Have a warm plate ready. Tip the pan until the omelette falls onto the plate.

A simple, delicious variant to the plain omelette is to add to the eggs, before beating them, a generous bunch of parsley chopped fine. A mushroom omelette is always a delight. Cook a plain omelette, and just before you fold it over, add mushrooms that you have sautéed in butter. Peas, string beans—almost any leftover vegetable can be added in this way.

If your taste runs to real fantasy, the "Symphony of Eggs" described by Ali-Bab[45] in his great *Treatise on Gastronomy* might appeal to you: "When a lain omelette is almost ready to fold, drop a half a dozen eggs into it. They will poach. Fold the omelette and garnish with chopped hard-boiled eggs." We must confess that we have yet to try this extravagant recipe.

45. Pseudonym of Henri Babinsky, 1855–1931.

Chicken Sauté Sec

We first enjoyed chicken sauté sec—chicken delicately sautéed in butter and white wine with mushrooms and artichoke hearts—at Jacks, a small, old and famed restaurant in San Francisco. The chef invited us into his kitchen. It was hardly larger than you would find in any house, and each order was made individually.

Cut up a small chicken. The pieces should be fairly small—cut the leg at each joint, and cut the breast in two pieces. Dust the pieces with flour seasoned with salt and pepper. Now brown the chicken in butter over a medium fire. If the pan smokes, reduce the heat. Turn the pieces frequently using tongs or two spoons; do not puncture them with a fork for then the juices inside will run out and the meat will become dry. Slice six mushroom caps very thinly, parallel to the stem, so that each piece retains the semicircular profile. Chop up the stems very finely. Add to the chicken.

Now slowly pour into the pan one cup of white wine. Be careful to choose a wine that is dry, not sweet. Stir gently, so that the mushrooms are well moistened. With a metal spoon scrape the bottom of the pan to detach browned places where the meat has "caught on." If the sauce tastes too much of wine, dilute it with chicken stock or even water. Salt to taste. Cover the pan and let it simmer over a low flame for at least thirty minutes. Longer cooking will improve the flavor, providing the sauce remains liquid. Should it get too low, you can add a little warm water. Just before serving add six artichoke hearts, well drained. Allow them to garnish each serving.

Rice or noodles go well with chicken sauté. Perhaps you would like to add a halved avocado for each guest, set on a bed of watercress and filled with a sharp dressing of olive oil, tarragon vinegar, salt, ground black pepper, oregano, and parsley.

LUNCHEON FOR MR. BEARD   Occasionally I would cook some of my "Epicure Corner" recipes before a paying audience to raise money for charitable purposes. The first, in 1961, was for the scholarship fund of the Columbia Preparatory School in Rochester. The local gas and electric company generously set up a brand-new electric stove on the stage of the gymnasium. Over three hundred people looked on as I cooked chicken sauté sec, filet mignon, and zabaglione, an Italian dessert of egg yolks, sugar, and Marsala wine beaten in a double boiler into a delicious froth. I was delighted to learn later that the proceeds brought a girl from South America to the school.

Eight years later I gave a more spectacular demonstration. My friend, Chef James Foley, Rochester's premier restaurateur, offered to close his dining room in the Holiday Inn to the public while a hundred or so paying guests not only saw me prepare suprême of chicken, but ate that dish, which Jim Foley had prepared from my recipe. The proceeds of this demonstration went to the Rochester Philharmonic Orchestra.

James Beard, hailed as "the Dean of U.S. Cookery," came to Rochester to spend several days demonstrating cooking for the benefit of the Museum of Arts and Sciences. The museum director, Stephen Thomas, invited me to have luncheon with him and Mr. Beard at the faculty club of the University of Rochester. I thanked him, saying, "I don't think we should take Mr. Beard to the faculty club!" Then almost as an afterthought I added, "I'll cook luncheon at my house!" I chose to prepare a rather uncommon dish: choucroute garni, an Alsatian sauerkraut. Here is my recipe as printed in my column for November 25, 1965.

Finely shred a head of cabbage, wash it well in several changes of water, then put it in a deep pot with one cup of tarragon red wine vinegar. Let it steep overnight. In the morning wash it again, and add one cup of beef stock and 12 peppercorns. Cover the mound of cabbage with, for each guest, two pieces each of cooked Canadian bacon, cooked ham, and Italian prosciutto. Simmer over a gentle heat for two hours.

Four of us sat down at the table: Mr. Beard, Stephen Thomas, William Gambel, president of the Rochester Museum Association, and myself. Naturally the prospect of cooking for so illustrious a guest as James Beard was somewhat worrisome. I brought the choucroute to the table in a casserole of large diameter, with the slices of meat in the center, and a border of parsley potatoes around the edges.

When Mr. Beard asked for a second helping, I was pleased. When he had a third helping, I was overjoyed.

In 1958, I was saddened by the death of Oscar Solbert, who over ten years had become a friend as well as a colleague. He had served Eastman House well, raising funds for new

At George Eastman House, c. 1971. Photograph © Don Eddy. (Courtesy of the International Museum of Photography at George Eastman House)

construction and excelling in public relations and social gatherings. He was rightfully proud of Eastman House. A brigadier general who served with distinction in two world wars, Solbert was given the traditional, highly ceremonious last rites of a military funeral at Arlington National Cemetery.

In September 1958, I was appointed director of George Eastman House by the trustees. I looked back on our first ten years with satisfaction. We had put on display 159 exhibitions, many of which were circulated to other museums. We had founded the magazine *Image*. We had built a fireproof vault for the storage of the some two thousand films we had already acquired. The Dryden Theater Film Society grew from one thousand to three thousand enthusiastic members who viewed rare motion pictures from the collection. James Card and I initiated courses on the histories of motion pictures and photography at the Rochester Institute of Technology and the University of Rochester. To my knowledge these were the first courses on these subjects offered for academic credit by any university anywhere.

When I left Eastman House in 1971, after twenty-three years, I felt proud of my achievements, for during the course of another long struggle to have photography accepted as a fine art, I had helped create the world's first museum of photography, with an outstanding collection of photographs. Today there is hardly an art museum in this country that doesn't present photography exhibitions, and many support departments dedicated to the medium.

❖

6

WORDS AND IMAGES

With Nancy and some of our publications, George Eastman House, 1968. Photograph © T. Gordon Massecar. (Courtesy of the International Museum of Photography at George Eastman House)

MAKING A PHOTOGRAPHIC BOOK

In 1967 Ansel, Nancy, and I thought the University of California might be interested in forming a department of photography at its new Santa Cruz campus, which was then under construction. I wrote a proposal for this, envisioning a photographic center with a gallery for the display of photographs, a lecture and demonstration room, and darkrooms for the students. Ansel sent the proposal to the chancellor, who sent it to university president Clark Kerr. Although enthusiastic about the place of photography in the curriculum, Kerr concluded it was not the time to add facilities. It was suggested that we begin with a summer course, but the regents were not at all interested in a historical approach. We then proposed a practical workshop in an area in which we all had a great deal of experience: making a book of photographs.

The workshop was intended for photographers, writers, editors, historians, and curators who wanted a basic knowledge of the principles and techniques involved in making and procuring photographs for publication, editing them, preparing captions, and combining them with a text. The idea was that using a short text as a basis, the workshop group would produce, within two weeks, a presentation dummy of a photo essay ready for production by a printer.

We suggested students bring a 4 x 5 camera. Ansel requested support from Polaroid, which lent us a number of their cameras and provided a supply of instant film for students who did not have their own cameras. Those using traditional materials used a laboratory in town for processing. Twenty-eight students signed up for this unique course—students of all undergraduate levels, from incoming freshmen to seniors. All expressed great enthusiasm for the project.

There were two all-day field trips with Ansel, who taught what he called the Zone System (a very refined system for exposure control). Mornings we worked on the dummy of the book. Ansel talked about technical materials, and I worked with the students on page design and scaling photographs. We had a grid for placing the images. Nancy taught the principles of picture editing and led the group in editing the photo essay. Afternoons we divided into teams and photographed in the town of Santa Cruz. In the evening we screened films.

We orchestrated our summer workshop for five years, through 1971, with very enthusiastic response from the students. The first year we made a forty-page dummy, complete with text, in twelve days, and Polaroid printed it. We did this for four years. The second year we divided the forty-six participants into groups and sent them out into the community with a local welfare worker to meet the senior and disabled citizens in conjunction with a community outreach program. They interviewed them and took many moving photographs. A very strong, eighty-four-page book was

With Nancy and Ansel at the Images and Words Workshop, University of California at Santa Cruz, July 1967. Photograph by Libby Wilcox.

produced, *Twelve Days at Santa Cruz*, which Polaroid again printed. To our amazement the federal government's Office of Economic Opportunity ordered twenty-five thousand copies.

On the last day of class each year, the students were invited to tea at the Adamses', and they had the opportunity of watching Ansel make a print in his darkroom. He concluded the workshop by playing jazz on the piano.

Ansel Adams

Ansel was an extremely important person in my life. Through the years he was a splendid colleague and an inspiring and supportive friend. He shared my passion for photography, and working with him meant a great deal to me. Our friendship really began after I had read and reviewed his extraordinary book *Making a Photograph* in 1935. I was so moved by it that I wrote him a letter. He sent a cordial reply, and this began a lifelong correspondence between us. Ansel turned out to be a prodigious letter-writer—so much so, our letters fill three entire file drawers.[46]

Although Ansel was a wonderful friend, we did not always see eye to eye on photographic technology. One issue we always disagreed about was his emphasis on the technical aspect of picture-making. When I began to photograph there wasn't such a thing as a photo meter. It was done by guess and by golly. And by experience, which was the best teacher. Walker Evans and I used to photograph together on weekends in New York, and we had a little gadget called a Welcome Exposure Guide. It was a memorandum book given away by an English company that had in the back detailed charts of f-stops and shutter speeds for various times of the day and months of the year. Still, I was one of the first to get GE's electric exposure meter

46. These letters are in the archive of the Center for Creative Photography in Tucson, Arizona.

when they were novelties in the 1930s. It greatly improved the chances of taking a successfully exposed image.

Edward Weston used a meter, but he didn't need to. In the 1940s, when he made color photographs for Kodak ads, they would ask his exposure for the pictures, but then dismissed them as not within the acceptable range, so they made up what they thought a typical exposure should have been. Weston didn't need a meter: he'd been photographing for decades. He just *felt* the exposure.

For Ansel an exposure meter became an indispensable instrument. He felt that the precise calculation of film exposure was crucial in photography, and that it hadn't been given enough study. In 1941 Nancy and I had a small two-room apartment in Manhattan. When Ansel came to New York to work with me in the Museum of Modern Art's photography department, he stayed with us as a houseguest. At that time he was full of the work he'd done in California on his Zone System, and in those days he was continually experimenting with it. He chose the bookcase in our bedroom as a test subject on which to perfect his system. Using an exposure meter, he calculated the precise exposure using two measurements, the size of the diaphragm of the lens and the length of exposure. Of course these both are critical for accurate exposures. With his meter in hand he would measure the shadows of his subject, then he would measure the highlights, then he would measure the middle tones, then calculate these in relation to the others before deciding on his exposure. For Ansel, this system worked beautifully. He did magnificent work using it, and so have many other photographers. But to many of us, including me, it was too mathematically demanding, and too time consuming. He was very patient, and tried very hard to teach me the Zone System, but I couldn't take the time to work it out. Things were happening in front of the camera. I didn't want to interrupt the flow of life to do math. That was the influence on me of Cartier-Bresson. Like him I preferred to use a 35mm camera, if necessary shoot a lot of film, shoot fast, build toward a climax.

Ansel Adams, Ranchos de Taos, New Mexico, 1980. Photograph by Beaumont Newhall. (Courtesy of Scheinbaum & Russek Ltd., Santa Fe, New Mexico)

I remember helping Ansel at one of his summer workshops at Yosemite. He had worked out his teaching technique in an unusual way. He sprayed a whole sheet of wallboard middle gray, then lined up the students and asked them to walk by and take a reading with their cameras or separate exposure meters to check if their meters were out of kilter. Then he gave them a little talk about music. If a musician tries to play with an instrument that's not in tune, it's absolute chaos. It's the same in photography, he said: a photographer must keep the exposure meter in tune. Exposure's really a very simple thing, he confided to them. All you need to do is to set the diaphragm at the square root of the ASA, and the time at the reciprocal of candles per square foot. The students would come around to me and whisper, holding their hands over their mouths, What are candles per square foot? What is the square root of the ASA? What is a reciprocal?

During the war, Ansel was very eager to help me and my photoreconnaissance team improve the technical side of taking aerial photos. To help us get better results, he volunteered to help me learn his Zone System, and sent me a lot of instructions. I wrote back to thank him for the material but said I couldn't use his techniques because we weren't using an exposure meter. This shocked Ansel. He couldn't understand it. *No exposure meters?* Here was his friend, and a whole group of people, making literally millions of photographs without an exposure meter. I explained that when you're photographing from five miles up above the earth, you don't need the Zone System. We didn't have the time; the Zone System requires the photographer to take time out to make precise calculations. Moreover, I explained to Ansel, we were photographing a *war*: we were using three cameras per plane, each one loaded with 250 feet of film, and our planes traveled at speeds of over 400 miles an hour. We went back to the Welcome Exposure Guide, and set the shutter to the time of day, and set the timer to overlap according to the speed of the plane. Furthermore, if we couldn't find the details in the shadows, we just ordered the boys in the darkroom to make us fresh prints that did reveal what was not visible—to print for the shadows and give longer exposures for the highlights.

In terms of technique and subject matter, I was far more influenced by Henri Cartier-Bresson than by Ansel, but I always admired Ansel's superb craftsmanship and his passion for the medium. In August 1950, after packing up the Boyer collection in Chicago, I drove out to California to meet Nancy and vacation with the Westons and Adamses. I concluded a letter to Ferd Reyher about my cross-country trip with a description of Ansel.

> Long arguments with Ansel about photography and modern art. Ansel defending his position that he is the interpreter of the natural scene, I asking what is unnatural about man and both of us coming to the conclusion that what moves him to photograph is the primeval scene on which the hand of man has not left a trace. I contend that it is not the subject which makes his pictures great but his photographing them—that Mount McKinley probably looks more exciting in Ansel's photographs than it would to my own eyes. What a craftsman! We stood by while he printed a hundred and twenty-five prints from a single negative in part of a morning. And when he got through there was not one print that could be distinguished from the other hundred and twenty-four.

With Ansel at Ranchos de Taos, New Mexico, 1980. Photograph by David Scheinbaum. (Courtesy of Scheinbaum & Russek Ltd., Santa Fe, New Mexico)

Ansel was a great party man and loved to entertain. He had a very dominating personality, and would always be the center of attention. The painter John Marin once described the first time he met Ansel, when they were both guests at Mabel Dodge Luhan's artists' colony in Taos, New Mexico. Marin told me he saw a tall young man talking very loudly in the middle of the room, with everyone gathered around him. I don't like that man, Marin said to himself. "Then he sat down at the piano. He sounded one note—*one note!*—and I'd never heard the piano played so well!"

By the time I went overseas Ansel was staying in a hotel in Manhattan, but because he spent so much time with us, he had moved a concert grand into our small apartment and came over to play it every day. He was studying to be a concert pianist at the time and needed to practice. I'll always remember Ansel at the piano. He seemed to belong there. Relaxed by drink and sympathetic friends, a whole other world seemed to open up, and he played and played until everybody, exhausted, quietly left the house, then he played on alone. I have heard him play pieces that were buried within his unconscious for twenty years without once referring to a note of music. His was the smashing, bold technique. Later, in California, he made the rafters of his studio—a big simple room with a window looking out on the Golden Gate Bridge—ring, and then played with great delicacy the soft passages. He had in his studio a six-foot Chinese bass drum that he would pound now and then. One evening in San Francisco, we stopped in after dinner to say goodbye to our friends the McKays. In their playroom was a miniature pump organ, a child's plaything. Ansel couldn't resist it. Somehow he settled his six foot frame onto the tiny bench (first removing the teddy bear) and felt out the instrument amid shouts of glee from the rest of us. Then he began to make that little box sing a Bach fugue. Ansel played on and on. That little organ had probably never felt a musician's fingers before.

In New York Ansel's company was often sought. If there happened to be a piano at a party he was attending, he needed to play it—but only if the piano was in tune. Of course he couldn't directly ask his host if the piano was tuned, so he devised a way of discovering this on his own. I know nothing about music at all, but Ansel showed me how to play just one bar of Bach, making it resound throughout the room. So at some point in the evening, Ansel would signal me, and I would sit down and play this one bar, very dramatically. Everyone would stop their conversation and turn to look at me. If the piano was off, Ansel would say, Look at that clown. Newhall thinks he can play the piano. But if he liked the way it sounded, he'd sit down next to me on the bench, we'd repeat the same bar together, then I'd quietly slip away and he would entertain the group by playing for an hour or two.

❖

Teaching full-time

In 1970 I began to think about retirement. I had been happy at George Eastman House; it was wonderful to see it respond to my suggestions, and it was very moving to receive such excellent reports of our activities. But after twenty years, I needed a change. When I moved, in 1958, from being curator to being director of Eastman House, I became very involved with administrative duties—working with trustees, managing the physical plant and even the parking lot, and was not able to do what I was best at and loved most, collecting and researching photography. I promised the trustees to stay on until a new director was found.

The news about my decision to leave spread, and Van Deren Coke, at the time a professor of photography at the University of New Mexico, indicated interest in applying for the position. I gave him a detailed account of the responsibilities of the job, and he was very much interested. He made a formal application and was granted the job. He began in 1970, a bit earlier than my retirement date, to work with me as an understudy.

Neither Nancy nor I had any idea of where we would go or what we would do in our retirement. Our first decision was to spend a couple of weeks at the Wild Horse Ranch north of Tucson, Arizona. Van Deren Coke suggested I give a telephone call to Dean Clinton Adams of the Department of Art at the University of New Mexico. I was not one bit interested in doing so, for I was leaving one institution and had no desire to even contemplate joining another one. But during the last week at the ranch I did phone him. He warmly invited me to stop off on my way back to Rochester and have a look at the university. I agreed, but very reluctantly. I was puzzled when he added, "We'll be delighted to see you, but you will have to give a lecture."

"I'll *have* to give a lecture? But I don't have any material, I have nothing prepared, and I have no slides with me."

"Well, we have an exhibition of Farm Security Administration photographs on display. Surely you are familiar with them. Perhaps you would consider giving a gallery talk to the students."

To be polite I obliged, then was surprised to be invited to a luncheon given by the dean, and attended by the chairman of the art department and several faculty members in the department. We had a lively conversation throughout lunch. When dessert arrived the dean pushed back his chair and addressed me directly. "Would you be interested in joining our faculty?"

I was taken aback by this sudden, informal invitation for a position for which I had not applied, and I hedged. I called Nancy at the ranch to suggest she stop off on her way home to look over the town of Albuquerque, the university, the museum, and to meet some faculty members.

"Take it! Right now!" she shouted. I replied that I couldn't do that until she decided whether she wanted to live there or not. "Take it now!" she pleaded. "Right away!"

So I accepted the job, and Nancy and I returned to Rochester to sell the house and pack up all of our goods. We settled in La Luz, a beautiful development of modern row houses in Albuquerque, and I began to teach at the university in the fall of 1971. No plan or schedule was provided for my classes. I did not give instruction in the technical art of making photographs because there were competent instructors already on board. However, for a great many years I had given a course in the general history of photography one day a week at the Rochester Institute of Technology. I was offered twice as much time at the University of New Mexico, so I decided again to teach a history of the medium, covering the nineteenth century during the first semester, and the twentieth century the second. There were over a hundred students in the lecture room each semester. A second course, offered for graduate students preparing for their master's degree, was a seminar in which we combed over the history of photography in far more detailed fashion than in the survey course. I particularly enjoyed these small, intensive sessions. Later, when I moved to Santa Fe, I held seminars in my own library. Once a week five or six students would come up to do research in my personal photography library and extensive archive of correspondence, manuscripts, reviews, and photographs.

A third course, Museum Practices, introduced students to the art of arranging exhibitions. In addition to selecting small weekly exhibitions, we worked as a group on larger ones. One class organized a show of the color photographs of Eliot Porter. Once a week we drove to Eliot's house near Santa Fe and pored through his collection, which at that time numbered about five thousand prints. He assisted us with many welcome suggestions. Unlike many photographers, he did not insist that certain photographs be displayed. After the exhibition closed Eliot generously donated the final selection of over two hundred prints to the university.

In Rochester students had access to the extensive Eastman House collection of photographs and library, but the University of New Mexico did not have those resources available. There was very little literature available, and I was particularly concerned that instead of adopting *my* retrospective view as a historian, students read the early historical documents—contemporary nineteenth-century accounts that, as early as 1839, chronicled what the pioneers of the medium were doing and thinking. I reproduced a book for them, using photocopies of rare material from my own library. A typical example was "An Account of a Method of Copying Paintings Upon Glass, and of Making Profiles, by the Agency of Light upon Nitrate of Silver," written by Thomas Wedgwood and Sir Humphry Davy in 1802. Another was Henry Fox Talbot's account of the calotype process, written in 1841, and Oliver Wendell Holmes's 1859 description of the stereoscope and stereograph. It was a history of photography as it was written by many of the photographers themselves, and provided an entirely different perspective on the historical record. The students responded so enthusiastically I wondered if we couldn't make these historical documents accessible by publishing a book they could buy. I approached the Museum of Modern Art, who published *Photography: Essays and Images* as a companion volume to my *History of Photography*, which over the years I had continued to revise. In American towns and cities that don't have major research libraries, it is often the students' only access to these early writings.

I often invited whomever was in town to come and talk to my students. One guest is my German friend Karl Steinort, who is bilingual. A lawyer and public relations director for Kodak in Germany, he has a wide knowledge of the history of photography. Over the years we have sent each other our published reviews and books. Ansel stayed with us whenever he was in New Mexico, and he would frequently drop in to my classes. One day I asked him to sit down while I introduced him, so he could then stand up and receive their welcome. Ansel didn't bother about that at all. As I was fussing around looking for a chair he just walked to the front of the stage and said one word: "Hi." The students clapped and laughed. When I finally did start my lecture, he suddenly interrupted me. "Oh, professor, I didn't bring a notebook!" The students rushed to give him pages torn from their notebooks.

Together my colleagues and I created a major program in photography at the University of New Mexico. I felt very rewarded during my thirteen years there, and I am very proud of the record of my students over the years, for many I have trained are teaching, writing, directing exhibitions, and building photography collections in this country, Canada, and Europe. Many hold major positions as curators of museums and of both private and public photography collections.

Books have always played a central part in my life, both as a reader and an author. Several years ago I was asked by a photography magazine to list the five photography books that had most influenced the development of my interest in photography as a creative art. I enjoyed a few days of careful thought on the subject, selecting and then rejecting various titles that had been important, but not influential. Here is my list.

Josef Maria Eder, The *History of Photography*, 1932

> Originally published in Germany in 1932, this book was the most complete history of photography in print at the time I was organizing "Photography 1839–1937" and when I was writing the first edition of my book *The History of Photography*.

Ansel Adams, *Making a Photograph*, 1935

> The extraordinary reproductions of Ansel Adams's photographs greatly impressed me, for I had never seen such fine prints anywhere. His meticulous explication of his technique was my introduction to fine printing.

Walker Evans, with an essay by Lincoln Kirstein, *American Photographs*, 1938

> I was greatly influenced in my personal photography by Walker Evans's straightforward documentation, particularly in his architectural work.

Henri Cartier-Bresson, *The Decisive Moment*, 1952

> Henri Cartier-Bresson is one of the great photographers because he has trained himself to see in a fraction of a second the inner structure of a

fleeting subject. For him photographs are discovered, not made: the subject is never altered or contrived.

Edward Weston, *The Daybooks*, 2 volumes, 1973

Seldom has an artist in any medium written about his life and work with the detail and perception of Edward Weston in his *Daybooks*. Every time I read these volumes I discover new dimensions of his extraordinary camera vision, and I am inspired to look more sharply at the world through my camera.

I consider myself most fortunate to have been able to share a close personal relationship with the photographers listed, all of them masters in photography who made profound contributions to the medium in this century. It was always so fascinating to hear Alfred Barr speak about when he last saw Picasso, or visited Matisse, but there were not many other people in that rare position. I consider myself privileged that I had a similar opportunity in photography.

LECTURES   Lecturing to large audiences on various aspects of the history of photography has been an important part of my career. Although I find it enjoyable now, and even relish the prospect of entertaining an audience while informing them, it was not always so.

I began to lecture, in a very elementary way, before attending Harvard. The subject was usually Gothic architecture, and the minister of our church helped me with public-speaking techniques. I had also taught the history of prints at a private girls' school in Boston, to acquaint the students with art. But students are a captive audience. There is a great difference between lecturing to an audience that knows little, and to a group of students who have done required reading and are ready for further illumination on the subject.

After losing my docent job in Philadelphia, and then at the Metropolitan Museum of Art, and returning to Harvard to begin doctoral study, I was once again looking for employment. I landed a job giving sit-down lectures about the magnificent collection at the Museum of Fine Arts in Boston, one of the finest museums in this country. It was the custom for Nancy and me to go together to the museum on Sunday afternoon and give this spiel, then walk to the Ritz-Carlton Hotel and spend the entire fifteen dollars that I'd earned on a fine dinner. This helped me develop my lecturing style. Eventually I realized that every job I had held required me to lecture. Rossiter Howard, my mentor in Philadelphia, had been right, I found. The most important thing to remember is that a lecture is a performance—it is not bringing to a lecture a typewritten script and reading it out loud, looking at the book rather than making contact with the audience. That's absolutely useless. They can read the book themselves. Instead I talked directly to my audience, and got in the habit of picking out individuals to concentrate on. As a result, when I began to appear on live television in Rochester in the 1950s, the early days of the medium, I found it very difficult to lecture just to the television camera. The cameramen eventually learned to push their fingers down right beside the lens, using a method of hand-talking to focus me. At intermission they would say, "Think of looking at one person in his living room who is looking back through his television. Look at him, not at this wall, the way you do." I never quite mastered that technique. I am better able to connect with the audience if I don't need to rely on notes, so I memorize my outline beforehand. Since my lectures involve slides, I will use my projector and tabletop viewing screen and look at the pictures several times beforehand. Every picture evokes several thoughts.

One of my earliest experiments with the theatrical was in my talk on Henri Cartier-Bresson at the Museum of Modern Art in 1976. For Henri the Leica was the ideal instrument for making photographs, and since at that time most people in the audience did not know what a Leica was, for a hundred dollars I purchased one in beautiful condition for the occasion. Holding it up to my eye, I quickly focused, then pressed the shutter, as photojournalists do. Then I opened the camera, removed the film cartridge, and zzziippp! pulled the film out of it to show what will occur in the darkroom of the film laboratory. At that point the projectionist knocked out the spotlight, and projected on the screen one of Henri's contact sheets. I took the audience over all thirty-six pictures, showing how Henri builds up to a climax to get the one picture he will print. It is interesting to note that when Henri taught photography he asked his students to bring not their finished prints, but their contact sheets. Like any good photo editor, he would look at them to determine if they got their photograph by chance or through skill. As I've noted previously, Henri's photographs were the result not of lucky accident, as some believe, but of a quite deliberate concentration on his subject. With each frame he came closer to achieving the picture he wanted.

Perhaps my most radical attempt to humanize a lecture was in my talk for the Edward Weston exhibition for the San Francisco Museum of Modern Art in 1983. I found a young photographer who knew Weston and who owned an 8 x 10-inch camera just like Edward's. So, lights out, spot: in walks a photographer lugging all his heavy view-camera apparatus; over his shoulder he carries a large tripod, and in his hands are two suitcases, one holding the camera, folded up, and the other containing film in holders. He puts all the equipment down, opens the boxes, sets up the tripod, takes out the camera and unfolds it, puts it on the tripod, takes out the plate holder, inserts it in the camera, gets under the focusing cloth, makes the exposure. It made a dramatic point about Weston in later life, clambering around the rocks of Point Lobos carrying this load of paraphernalia.

I admit to a fascination with doing a bit of detective work on the technical aspects of certain photographs. Three particular examples come to mind. The first is the subject of my lecture "The Unreality of Photography," which concentrates on the various illusions created by the medium. I address, for example, a photograph by the French photographer Jacques-Henri Lartigue of a racing automobile, which he took when he was just a boy (and incidentally, his father was at the wheel). In order to keep up with the racing car, Lartigue swung his camera and followed it. The result is rather strange: instead of being circular, the wheels were ellipses. I like to discuss the tools the photographer uses. In Lartigue's case it was a camera with a focal-plane shutter. The shutter was like a curtain across a window, with a slit in it. The slit could be changed in size. As he released the shutter the slit moved down the piece of film, exposing it; while the position of the wheels was changing all the time, this slit was capturing the different attitudes of the wheels. The result was a wheel that looked like an ellipse. This gave it a sense of speed. There was also a spectator standing nearby who looked as if he were falling over backward. That was because in portions that were seen by the film only through the slit, he had moved. It resulted in the curious image of an amazed spectator, someone who seemed knocked over by the rush of the racing car. It became an idiom, and people began to choose to make photographs with the focal-plane shutter.

A second bit of sleuthing involved Ansel Adams's famous photograph *Moonrise, Hernandez, New Mexico, 1941*. Ansel was not certain when that picture was taken. I asked an astronomer's assistance in calculating it. By studying the position of the moon and the stars and the landmarks, he was able to narrow it down to the year and the day. Recently he found that through further study with the computer he has ascertained the hour, which he believes is accurate to within seconds.

A third piece of investigation involved a photograph by Alfred Stieglitz and came about as a result of a bet. My friend Van Deren Coke is a very good photographer and teacher of photography, and very much interested in the development of modern art. One day he challenged me: he bet me I couldn't talk for one hour about one photograph. I chose one of Stieglitz's most celebrated pictures, *The Steerage*. In 1907 Stieglitz traveled to France with his wife on the SS *Kaiser Wilhelm II*, the largest of the transatlantic ocean liners of its day. It had at least two luxury items: an electric hair dryer for the ladies, and an electric cigarette lighter for the gentlemen. Like all steamers, it was divided into classes for passengers: first-class, or cabin quarters, which were almost like a hotel, several decks high; and steerage, crowded and miserable places in either the stern or bow of the ship. In this particular steamship, steerage was between the bow and the forecastle. Stieglitz's photograph has always been thought to be of European immigrants about to land at Ellis Island. The passengers were presumed to be looking at the Statue of Liberty after their long voyage. An immigration museum in Washington has even used the photograph as a lead image for an immigration exhibition. However, I had long suspected that this photograph was not taken on a steamship sailing to America, but that instead Stieglitz had photographed the scene on his 1907 voyage to Europe. Although U.S. immigration was at its peak in 1907, a great many people were not admitted, and others could not find work. It was reported in the *New York Times* that year that in one week between sixty thousand and seventy-five thousand emigrants left the United States to return to Europe.[47]

Again I worked with an astronomer. We began with the position of the sun, and studied the shadows made by the stanchions on the gangplank in the photograph, which all pointed to the right side of the picture. Since northern-hemisphere shadows always point in a northerly direction, the bow of the ship must have been pointed west when Stieglitz took the picture. The logbook told me that the first port of call was Plymouth, England. With its draft of almost thirty feet, the ship was far too large to dock at Plymouth; instead it anchored two and a half miles out in the harbor, and passengers were ferried ashore. The ship, at anchor, was free to swing in a circle according to the tide and undercurrents. Although pointing toward America, it was bound for France.

Stieglitz recollected taking the picture while the ship was under way in a heavy sea, but we could not feel secure that this was an accurate statement. The captain pointed out how relaxed the subjects were, for example the little girl standing on the edge of the ladder: one wave

47. G. W. Schwab, of the American office of the North German Lloyd steamship line, which owned the SS *Kaiser Wilhelm II*, reported this to the *New York Times*, November 29, 1907.

and she would have been thrown off. Of course this investigation occurred long after the photographer died. It would have been very interesting to have worked this out with Stieglitz himself. The detective work here was very challenging. In any case, I very easily spent one hour lecturing on a single photograph and won the bet.

STRAIGHT PHOTOGRAPHY

Of all the lectures I have given on the history of photography, one of my favorites is "Straight Talk on Straight Photography." To me it's still something of a contradiction that so many of the people admired as "straight" photographers manipulated their prints—and even their negatives—and that so many photographers cropped their images in the darkroom. Edward Weston, as I described, taught me some darkroom techniques to improve my print quality. For him cropping an image was not acceptable; he said about cropping, "Father used to do that to the tail of the horse." And when a magazine shaved a quarter of an inch off an 8 x 10 photograph, Paul Strand not only wrote a sizzling letter to the editor responsible, furious that he had utterly ruined it, but he drew up a letter of agreement that he wanted signed in advance by anyone wanting to reproduce his photographs, and he sent copies to Edward and Ansel encouraging them to do likewise.

Although Stieglitz was a champion of straight photography, he shared many tips with me on how to manipulate the photographic image. He would help me with photo techniques, teaching me how he developed his negatives, showing me how to crop the image, and giving me his for-

By David Scheinbaum, 1982. (Courtesy of Scheinbaum & Russek Ltd., Santa Fe, New Mexico)

From Our Apartment in New York, c. 1938. This cropping was suggested by Alfred Stieglitz. Photograph by Beaumont Newhall. (Courtesy of Scheinbaum & Russek Ltd., Santa Fe, New Mexico)

mula for intensifying negatives, which he also taught to Paul Strand. Stieglitz told me that he favored a full exposure of the negative and a weak development in Rodinal. After fixing and washing, he advised locally intensifying areas that seemed to lack density with mercuric iodide. He gave me the formula: 20 ounces of water, 4 ounces of sulfite, and 90 grams of mercuric iodide. Both Stieglitz and Paul Strand actually built up shadow details that way. Now this is not straight photography—it's absolutely manipulated; however, the result looks like a straight photograph, and that's the point.

One day, Stieglitz gave me a print of *The Steerage*, which was one of his favorite photographs, and I spent an entire afternoon watching him retouch the print with a brush. As he painted away on the ship's mast, increasing the shadows with a watercolor set he'd asked me to purchase, he remarked, "I always thought this mast should look *rounder*." I was using an inexpensive 4 x 5-inch camera at that time, and he urged me to buy a more expensive one, one with tilts so I could take architectural photographs without distorting the buildings. However, I was still under the influence of the German architect Erich Mendelsohn, and particularly loved to photograph architecture by pointing my camera straight up, so I neglected to take his advice.

Years later, many of Stieglitz's negatives melted into a pool of nitroglycerine, from a combination of the intensifying chemistry and the nitrate film stock. Strand also lost many of his negatives that way, and he was extremely upset about it when he returned from France one time and took his negatives out of storage. He phoned me in Rochester, begging me to help him make copy prints of the work we had in the George Eastman Collection. Many of his "original" prints are actually copy prints: that is to say, because he lost his negatives he was compelled to photograph his prints, making copy negatives from which he made subsequent prints.

A profile of Paul Strand once appeared in *The New Yorker* magazine. Now Strand was of course a legend in his total dedication to straight photography, and was one of the earliest practitioners of it in this century. His work was enormously influential. However, he was not as pure and uncompromising in his use of straight photography as is commonly thought. *The New Yorker* cites the time when the photographers around Stieglitz thought one should never enlarge negatives, but make contact prints only, yet Strand was shooting his early photos (for example, *Blind Woman*) with a small Ensign reflex camera. He enlarged the negatives onto 11 x 14-inch glass plates, and then made contact prints from those.

I wind up my lecture quoting the profile writer saying, "'Well, Mr. Strand, they tell me that you're a straight photographer: you don't retouch your negatives.'"

Paul replied, amazingly enough, "Well, you know, I'm not that way at all. For example in a picture taken from the courtroom looking down on Wall Street, I didn't like the three people together so I took one out right in my darkroom. I've done all sorts of retouching when there's been a reason for doing it. And I crop negatives in the enlarger all the time. I've always felt that you can do anything you want in photography if you can get away with it."

When the audience is serious students of photography, that brings the house down.

NANCY

When I met Nancy she was a painter, and a very good one. She had no knowledge of or interest in photography when we met; but I talked about it constantly during our courtship and she became an earnest student. She soon gave up painting and became involved with photography, eventually collaborating with photographers on books. Nancy often said, "When I married Beaumont I married photography," and that is true. She also made very fine photographs herself.

Nancy's first important book project was *Time in New England* with Strand, and it became a model for later books they both would do. She curated the terrific retrospective exhibitions of Strand and Weston at the Museum of Modern Art, and edited Weston's *Daybooks*, which were published by Aperture in two volumes. Although she intended to do a biography of Weston, she didn't receive the Guggenheim Fellowship she had applied for, which would have made this possible.

Instead she began a long-term working relationship with Ansel Adams, and over the years they collaborated on many projects. In 1951 *Arizona Highways* magazine commissioned Ansel to make photos for an article, and he suggested Nancy write a text for it. The following year the magazine asked them to do an article on Death Valley, which they published, but in 1954 Nancy and Ansel also brought it out as a book, by the Adams family publishing enterprise. It was so popular, five editions were printed. This led to a long and very creative working relationship. Nancy, who was herself an extremely independent person, found it far easier to work with Ansel than with Strand. Ansel didn't attempt to interfere with the text, while Paul did, and that wasn't his strong point.

At George Eastman House Nancy was unable to work alongside me as we had hoped because the trustees did not allow spouses to work together on the staff. Dissatisfied with the long, snowy winters of Rochester, she began spending more and more time in the West and Southwest, which she loved. Between 1944 and 1967 she made fourteen extended working trips to the West to work with Ansel, and in the 1950s she was in California at least a third of the time. Many of the pieces she and Ansel did initially for *Arizona Highways* were published in book form, and she also wrote a biography of Ansel, *The Eloquent Light* (1963). Their great triumph was *This Is the American Earth*, which was published by the Sierra Club in 1960.

Nancy was a terrific writer, yet for all of her talent, she found writing difficult. She would spend a very long time revising, revising, revising. She would hand me something to read, and I'd say, "That's fine," or, "This is great." She'd go back to her typewriter. I'd say, "I told you, it's really fine. Don't change it." She'd say, "I can tell by the tone of your voice."

In the summer of 1974, Nancy and I vacationed in the Grand Teton National Park in Wyoming. She had written a book with Ansel about the spectacular Rocky Mountain landscape and the early explorers of the area. I had not seen this lush country, and she was eager to share it with me. On our last day we took a trip down the Snake River in a raft. Our guide and oarsman, while pointing out the natural features of the riverbank, told us the water was unusually high and was eroding the bank around the roots of a huge, overhanging tree. He said that someday that tree would fall. Suddenly, without warning, it fell across the raft on us. Nancy was struck down with such violence that she died a week later. Her death was very tragic and extremely painful. Ansel gave the following tribute at the funeral ceremony.

> Nancy Newhall was one of the few personalities of our time who recognized beauty as the major component of art. In this she occupies a rare position beyond the modes, manners and doctrines imposed by the social and political currents of our period.
>
> In her approach humanity always retained superior values; the relation of man to the world he lives in is a dominant rationale for art and aesthetic expression. She was intolerant of despoliation of natural resources and beauty; she did not subscribe to the pessimistic opinion that we have done too little and are too late to save a habitable environment. The highly intellectual, albeit subjective attitudes of contemporary arts and literature may be moving away from the realities of life and nature and may be dominated by cults and concepts in which the fragile meaning of beauty and spirit are minimized or discarded.

Highly cultured in various domains, Nancy could pull together disparate images and statements in various mediums, penetrate their inner structure and meaning, clarify and render luminous their final expression. Nancy's abilities in the realms of free poetic expression were extraordinary. Some find the term "beauty" actually embarrassing; one wonders what the purpose of human life may be as the beautiful, the frankly emotional and the magical elements are discarded for fact and function alone.

Nancy's services to creative photography and its applications are historic; its true measure has yet to be evaluated. *Time in New England* (with Paul Strand) and *This Is the American Earth* (the first of the series of the Sierra Club books, and the most effective) are typical of her inspiration and conviction. Warm and impulsive in spirit, she was nevertheless ruthless in rejection of the phoney, the pretentious and the empty intellectual forms of art. Her standards of creative perfection were matched by her standards of scholarly perception. We all remain indebted to her for elevating our craft, our awareness and our confidence in creativity. The world has benefitted greatly and will benefit in the years to come because of her presence among us.

CHRISTI

My partner, Christi, has been a wonderful companion and helpmate. We first met in 1969 while Nancy and I were in Carmel, visiting our old friend Brett Weston. He introduced us to his friend Christi Yates, who was also visiting. After looking at photographs for several hours, Brett and Christi went into the kitchen to fix cocktails, and he proposed to her there. She accepted his offer of marriage and Nancy and I were the first people they told. What a happy day that was! We danced and celebrated. They married six weeks later and spent a year traveling and photographing the United States, Canada, Baja Mexico, and Japan. Unfortunately, their marriage ended shortly afterwards.

I met Christi again in 1974, when I was visiting her mother and stepfather, Ginny and Wally Goodwin, at their beautiful ranch in Pojoaque, New Mexico, just north of Santa Fe. I had known Wally as a publisher in New York and also as a photographer and student of Ansel's in California.

Christi had spent several years earlier studying in Tucson with Hazel Archer, who as a student at Black Mountain College had studied photography with me, design with Josef Albers, and synergetics and comprehensivity with Bucky Fuller, among others. Later, as a teacher there, Hazel taught photography and the design class after Albers left. In early 1975 Christi came to Albuquerque to talk to me about her passion for education and about Black Mountain College. We found we both greatly enjoyed many of the same things—art, music, and photography. I had been very lonely and very upset about the sudden loss of Nancy, and I greatly appreciated Christi's affectionate and

With Christi on our wedding day, May 22, 1975. Photograph by Sarah Greenough.

very thoughtful companionship. We were married later that year. Simultaneously, I received a second Guggenheim Foundation grant and took a sabbatical year from the university to write the fifth revision of my *History of Photography*.

When I married Christi, I had agreed to live in Santa Fe. We rented a small adobe house on the west side of town and Christi began looking for land and found a beautiful parcel in the foothills of the Sangre de Cristo Mountains. I drove down to the university twice a week to teach my classes and always loved the hour-long drive.

Christi envisioned and designed the house set around a central patio planted with cottonwood trees and surrounded by extensive flower and vegetable gardens. She has an extraordinary feeling for nature, in fact for all living beings, and every summer creates the beautiful gardens, which I have photographed so much in the past seventeen years.

The house itself has a very open feeling, with many windows, clerestories in the roof, passive solar panels for heat, two large studios facing each other across the patio, and sliding-glass doors that open onto the gardens and patio. Our herd of five dogs wander in and out freely.

Ever since my ship-model days, woodworking has remained my hobby. I built floor-to-ceiling bookcases to house our libraries, along with furniture and tables for the darkroom I added on later. I keep a hand in the culinary arts by baking various whole-grain breads every week and preparing for guests one of my favorite suppers: omelettes with fresh herbs and vegetables from the garden.

Christi is, as she says, "a student of spirituality, consciousness, and transformation." I understand her deep love and concern for mankind, education, and the planet. She is an

Our home, 1992. Photograph by David Scheinbaum. (Courtesy of Scheinbaum & Russek Ltd., Santa Fe, New Mexico)

artist/designer, writer, videographer, musician, and singer, among other talents, and all this revolves around this extraordinary house, this extraordinary environment she has created.

Christi and I were officially divorced in 1985 but continue in close partnership and share this beautiful house. Most recently, our family has grown. For Christi has adopted an amazing little baby boy, Theo Christopher.

Serendipity, those unexpected and surprising connections, have been so much a part of my life. It so happens that Christi's stepfather, Wally Goodwin, was the nephew of the very same Philip Goodwin, the architect and Museum of Modern Art trustee who, with his brother, had lent the brownstone next to the museum for Nancy's Photography Center during the war. Wally was also first cousin to Sally McAlpin, wife of David McAlpin, who funded the first "History of Photography" show and the Photography Department at MoMA, and who, until his death, continued to be a beloved patron of photography.

Making photographs

My interest in the history of photography grew out of my love for taking pictures, which I began to do as a teenager. I was particularly drawn to architectural subjects. As I've stated, I went to Harvard somewhat as an obedient son, for what I really wanted was to make photography and film my profession. Since in those days there was no possibility of study in either of those fields, I moved into art history. But I continued to love making photographs. During the war I yearned to taste again the creative side of photography, to take pictures again. Continuing to investigate the history of photography, although fascinating in the past, from the vantage point of a world war seemed a dry and uninspiring academic pursuit. I hoped that making photographs again would renew my spirits. I wrote a letter to Nancy in which I elaborated on this aspiration.

I have been thinking about how to master photography. I am resolved to discipline myself, and sweat out—to use the inelegant but expressive G.I. slang—a technique. The legendary self-discipline that Steichen imposed upon himself after the last war is something that I can now readily understand. He found that the interruption of his career by the war gave him time to reflect upon his past, which the busy and successful artist does not have otherwise. And when the time came when he could be his own master again, he decided to go into the question thoroughly, from the egg to the human model. I do not propose to photograph eggs—do not be alarmed! But I do mean to start learning photographic technique anew by doing still life, because I can leave my camera set up and continue to make exposures until I get just the quality which I had visualized.

From still life—which will be lighted naturally, of course—I mean to go on to close-up views of whatever may strike my fancy. Not ultra close-ups, which border on the abstract: I mean precisely the sort of thing I did in my last photograph as a civilian, that detail of the Victorian door handle, with the scratches around the keyhole and the marks of Friend Dog's claws beside it. This is where I differ from Edward and Ansel—I want to work out a kind of photograph which will capture those evanescent or unnoticed traces of the human hand. I want to do more of the kind of picture which Oliver Wendell Holmes envisaged when he said, "What is the picture of a drum without the marks upon its head caused by the beating of the sticks?" Such things as the favorite tool of a craftsman, the handle burnished by constant use. The fortuitous beauty of a butcher's chopping block, worn into a gentle concavity by incessant cleaver blows. Not just the lines of a ship, but the scores on the gunwale where the lines have chafed. To make evocative photographs, that present a clue to the observant spectator, appreciated perhaps only unconsciously, but so strongly that he will say, "A fellow traveler was present, he did thus and so." As Atget did, but I will not do it by the same means. And for this type of photograph closeness is essential—not too close, for few have looked enough through the magnifying glass to be able to appreciate more than the form. I do not want people to be stumped. Let their question, "What is it?" be at once answered by a careful scrutiny of the print.

Having mastered the technique of the close, so that I can bring forth significant detail as vividly as the Dutch Little Masters, I want to work on the more difficult photography of the extremely distant. Perhaps I shall begin with the sea, and try to make a picture of the place where the water and the sky meet. Can it be done photographically? Nothing but the sea and the air—no object to give scale—just the subtlety of tones to push that horizon far out and to cause the heavens to curve overhead like a vault. Perhaps I'm seeking the impossible: I want to find out. Then architecture afar, without the Newhall trick of a horizontal object in the foreground. Now comes a hard test: to make mountains rise and hills roll.

Then the real test, the most difficult part of my work, without which I shall not have succeeded: people. I'm after informal pictures of people in their natural surroundings, at ease and so characteristic that recognition of the individual (if the sitter is a personal acquaintance) or type will be instantaneous. I do not seek the "candid" portrait, which can perhaps be compared with the chance glimpses that one has of people when they are not aware that they are under observation. These may be magnificent and they may be disgusting. I'm after a feeling of hospitality in these pictures, a perfectly natural welcoming of a friend, within the home of the subject. The way people look who say, "Do come in and have a drink." The way Diego Rivera looked when I sat down beside him on the scaffolding when he was painting the fresco in Rockefeller Center—knowing that I was present, eager to show me what he was doing. The way the Italian family looked who invited me to share on New Year's day their charcoal fire, their wine, their oranges and their candy. The way a dear friend looks with whom you are talking. And the way one's beloved mirrors in her face all her love and admiration, her hopes and fears. I want to have in my pictures of people a vivid sense of participation: I want the spectator to realize that the subject was indeed aware of the camera, but that he neither feared it nor gloated over it, but allowed the photographer to observe him as he stands—unashamed, unpretentious, natural. This kind of picture is not easy to produce, and yet I feel that it is worth attempting to produce. It is, of course, the kind of photograph which Stieglitz has made by the score. It is not a new concept, and I describe it only to tell you how I have been thinking of photography, and how it seems to have acquired in my mind an importance which—for all my enthusiasm—I did not earlier realize. I want to do all kinds of people, and to combine with these pictures the kind of still life I described above. The ship builder and his tools, for example. Above all I want to produce pictures which will not be startling or obtrusive, but which will compel attention through their depth of feeling and their "rightness."[48]

48. Beaumont Newhall to Nancy Newhall, February 2, 1944.

My desire to return to making pictures was underscored when, during my leave, Nancy and I returned to California to visit the Westons. I wrote the following to Charis shortly after our 1945 visit: "If anyone were to write my history (which god forbid) they would find that the two trips to Carmel were landmarks. In 1940 when I first began to photograph in a meaningful way, and in 1945, when after the isolation of foreign service I rediscovered photography and began to create again."[49]

49. Beaumont Newhall to Charis Weston, date unknown.

The photographers whom I count as decisive influences on my vision are Stieglitz, Ansel and Edward, Cartier-Bresson, and Moholy-Nagy. Ansel, the person with whom I've had the greatest friendship, had the least influence. I never could keep in step with his insistence on technical perfection; for me it got in the way. In terms of my own photography, I was most influenced by Cartier-Bresson: his philosophy, his concept of photography, as well as his way of making his camera an integral part of his vision. He did not stand aside and watch events happen, but he was really in there, moving with them, making his camera an extension of his own body. When we met in 1946 he pointed out the flaws of using my Rolleiflex and teased me about viewing the world from waist level. Inspired by his photographs, I became a great fan of the miniature camera.

And yet my work was different from his too. I wrote the following in my book of photographs, *In Plain Sight*:

> Photography has been to me what a journal has been to a writer, a record of things seen and experienced, moments in the flow of time, documents of significance to me, experiments in "seeing." But it's the journal *written*, not just jotted down diary-fashion, that interests me: writing as a piece of literature. Over the years I have sporadically kept a journal. When I say that to me my own photographs are the equivalent of journal entries it does not mean I use them as a memory book. I don't use photography in the sense that George Eastman said the Kodak is a notebook in which the owner can put down what he saw or thought and later enjoy it by the light of the fire.[50]

50. Beaumont Newhall, *In Plain Sight* (Salt Lake City: Peregrine Smith Books, Gibbs M. Smith, 1983), p. xiii

Throughout my adult life I have been making photographs. I seldom exhibited them publicly, however. In fact, I felt very strongly about that. I never showed my photographs when I was in the position of curator or director of an institution. This was simply because when I was at Harvard, my mentor Paul Sachs, in his course "Museum Practices," taught us ethics. He made it quite clear that there was a problem if the curator collected for himself as well as for the museum, so I never bought a picture that my museum or collection did not already own. Nor would I exhibit my own work or promote myself as a photographer when I was a curator. In either case it would have been a conflict between my personal interests and those of my institution.

When I retired from the museum profession the situation was different; however, it didn't occur to me that I could show my work if I was only teaching. Although I had taken photographs throughout my life, I did not think of myself as a photographer, and with the exception of a brief period during and immediately after the war, had no aspirations in that direction. Christi often quotes me as asserting, "Well Ansel's a photographer, Edward's a photographer, but I'm a historian."

I have particularly liked to photograph architecture, and to a lesser extent landscapes and portraits. I began showing Christi some of my photographs, and from there we began looking at the contact sheets and negatives I'd made during the course of five decades. She encouraged me to gather together fifty photographs and have new prints made, with the idea of putting together a small exhibition. Yet when Christi's aunt, Kay Bonfoey, invited me to show my work in her small and very lively art gallery in Tucson, I automatically demurred. Her reassurance eventually changed my

Exhibition of my photographs, curated by my students in the Museum Practices class, University of New Mexico, Santa Fe, 1972. Photograph by Beaumont Newhall. (Courtesy of Scheinbaum & Russek Ltd., Santa Fe, New Mexico)

mind. So in 1978, fifty years after I began making pictures, I had my first one-person exhibition. I kept my prices low, as I considered myself a young photographer since I was new to exhibiting my work, and I was very surprised when the Center for Creative Photography at the University of Arizona bought twelve pictures for their permanent collection. Bit by bit my pictures were shown and published. Then in 1983 the Smithsonian Institution's Traveling Exhibitions Service circulated an exhibition of fifty of my photographs and funded a video on my photography. Over the years my photographs have been shown in thirty-eight museums in the United States and South America, Europe, and Japan. These photographs were published by Peregrine Smith as *In Plain Sight*. My work was also becoming known in Europe; while I had previously given history lectures abroad, now I began showing my own slides as well as images of historical masterpieces.

In recent years my prints have been made by a master printer, David Scheinbaum. In 1978 David came to visit me and asked to work as my assistant as part of a doctoral internship, in return for credit toward an advanced degree. He began by reorganizing my library. At the time I was having a lab in New York print my negatives. One day, as David was helping me ship a package off to the lab, he asked, "Would you let me print your negatives if I can do as well as New York?" I agreed to try him out and was so impressed with the quality of his work that I asked him to print all of my negatives after that. In addition to his masterful printing, he is an excellent photographer and teacher. David and his wife, Janet Russek, own a photography gallery in Santa Fe—Scheinbaum & Russek Ltd.—which I am pleased represents me.

❖

In retrospect

People often ask me what it is I feel I have achieved. It is always a difficult question for me, since although I am a historian I do not think in those broad retrospective terms about my own life. However, looking back, there was enormous enthusiasm about the 1937 exhibition. This was in part because the Museum of Modern Art was a highly influential organization, and the press and public paid careful attention to whatever it did. Alfred Barr was a real showman, with an amazing flair for garnering publicity, and in the 1930s crowds flocked to this Rockefeller townhouse to see the exhibitions. The message of my historical survey exhibition, and of my catalog, and of all the work I did for the museum, was simply this: photography is a fine art, one on a par with all the other arts—painting, sculpture, prints, architecture, film. My 1937 exhibition and catalog, and the founding of the Department of Photography, changed the way people viewed the medium. It started people looking and collecting, and it started galleries exhibiting photographs. Eventually photography began to be taught at the university level, and that has made an equally important contribution to its development. Perhaps one of the highest honors I was paid carried with it a bit of irony: receiving an honorary doctorate in 1978 from Harvard, the school that did not offer an academic course in photography when I was a student there.

It should be remembered that at the time photography began to have a wider audience, Stieglitz himself was at the point of destroying his own personal collection of other people's photographs that he'd gathered over the years from those whom he had published in *Camera Work*. He said he was tired of paying the storage on them. Fortunately somebody from the Metropolitan heard about this and came to the gallery. Stieglitz loaded all the work into a taxi and it was taken uptown to the museum. This is a major collection.

Like the rest of the world at large, the photography world has changed radically since 1937. Many of my former students are now curators or professors at major institutions—the National Gallery of Art in Washington, D.C., the Victoria and Albert in London, Houston's Museum of Fine Arts, the National Gallery of Canada, Princeton University, the University of California, and the University of New Mexico, among many, many others. The books on photography that are published constitute a minor industry. Over twenty-five books on photography have been written by my students alone. There has been a wonderful expansion of the field. I and others of my generation who always wanted photography to be appreciated today witness an extraordinary respect for the medium.

Many contemporary technical advances have improved photography. The technology of electronic camera design, for example, has advanced amazingly—cameras today set the ASA, focus the lens, measure the light, then choose the aperture and shutter speed, advance the film, then rewind it. And we no longer are confined to black-and-white film. The quality of color photography is evidence of a remarkable advancement in the last thirty years. Just a few years ago it was exceedingly difficult to do good color work. I applaud this new technology. These innovations are discovered by us, not forced on us. Why drive a horse and buggy when you can drive a sportscar?

Regarding straight photography, it's a good thing that photographers are now free to experiment in all kinds of ways. The f.64 school was very narrow—and the school of straight

In my study, 1984.
Photograph by David
Scheinbaum. (Courtesy of
Scheinbaum & Russek Ltd.,
Santa Fe, New Mexico)

photography was a very small group, after all, to have set up the rules of the game, so to speak. Today a new aesthetic and technical freedom is happening all around. Certainly this is an age in which the images are of great importance, whether they are electronic images on television or in video or pictures in books. I don't feel photomontage is at all an inferior type of photograph—the seeing and quality of the work are what is important.

However, in spite of the technological advances, it is amazing to realize that photography today uses exactly the same technique as a hundred years ago. If a photographer could travel back to a daguerreotype studio of 1850, he wouldn't know what in the world to do. But if he traveled back to an 1888 photographic portrait gallery, he'd know exactly what to do—precisely what he's doing today. Film processing and printing are done the same way; and although the chemicals and papers have somewhat different formulas, the basic process has not changed.

It pleases me enormously to see how many people are now professionally involved in photography. The medium really has come of age in the most marvelous way. In the early 1950s my old friend Helmut Gernsheim and I had a pleasant luncheon together in Essen, Germany. Helmut jokingly rapped on the table and said, "The Society for the History of Photography will now come to order!" We two comprised the entire membership! There just wasn't anybody else in the world at that particular time—and for a long time afterward, I might add—as qualified as we were. And that was not so very long ago.

❖

BOOKS AND CATALOGS

BY BEAUMONT NEWHALL

Photography 1839–1937 (exhibition catalog).

New York: Museum of Modern Art, 1937.

Photography: A Short Critical History (revised edition of *Photography 1839–1937*).

New York: Museum of Modern Art, 1938.

The Photographs of Henri Cartier-Bresson (with Lincoln Kirstein).

New York: Museum of Modern Art, 1947.

The History of Photography from 1839 to the Present Day.

New York: Museum of Modern Art, 1949.

(Revised and enlarged in 1964, 1971, 1978, and 1982.)

- Japanese edition (same title).

Tokyo: Hakuyosha, 1956.

- French edition: *L'Histoire de la photographie depuis 1839 et jusqu'à nos jours*
(French ed. by André Jammes).

Paris: Bélier-Prisma, 1967.

- British edition (same title).

London: Secker & Warburg, 1982.

- German edition: *Geschichte der Photographie.*

Munich: Schirmer-Mosel, 1984.

Illustrative Guide to the George Eastman House of Photography.

Rochester: George Eastman House, 1952.

Arthur Rothstein: 200 Photographs (exhibition catalog).

Rochester: George Eastman House, 1956.

On Photography: A Source Book of Photo History in Facsimile.

Watkins Glen, NY: Century House, 1956.

Masters of Photography (with Nancy Newhall).

New York: George Braziller, 1958.

The Daguerreotype in America.

New York: Duell, Sloan and Pearce, 1961.

(Revised edition Greenwich, CT: New York Graphic Society, 1968;
reprint edition New York: Dover, 1976.)

Beaumont Newhall's Vademecum to French Wines.

Geneseo, NY: Gaudeamus Press, 1964.

Frederick H. Evans.

Rochester: George Eastman House, 1964.

T. H. O'Sullivan (with Nancy Newhall).

Rochester: George Eastman House; in collaboration with
the Amon Carter Museum of Western Art, Fort Worth, TX, 1966.

Latent Image: The Discovery of Photography.
>> New York: Doubleday, 1967.
>> • Italian edition: *L'Immagine latente.*
>>> Bologna: Zanichelli, 1969.

Project Find (with Ansel Adams and Nancy Newhall).
>> Santa Cruz, CA: University of California at Santa Cruz, 1968.

Airborne Camera: The World from the Air and Outer Space.
>> New York: Hastings House, 1969.

Of an Exhibition of Platinum Prints (exhibition brochure).
>> Carmel, CA: Friends of Photography, 1969.

Faraday's Presentation of Photography.
>> London: Royal Photographic Society, Historical Group, 1970.

Photo Eye of the Twenties (exhibition catalog).
>> Rochester: George Eastman House, 1970.

William H. Jackson (with Diana E. Edkins).
>> Fort Worth, TX: Morgan & Morgan, 1974.

Frederick H. Evans: Photographer of the Majesty, Light, and Space of the Medieval Cathedrals of England and France.
>> Millerton, NY: Aperture, 1975.

Photographic Views of Sherman's Campaign (with George N. Barnard).
>> New York: Dover, 1976.

Die Vater der Photographie: Anatomie einer Erfindung.
>> Seebruck am Chiemsee: Heering, 1978.

Beaumont Newhall: A Retrospective Exhibition of Photographs, 1928 – 1978.
>> Andover, MA: Addison Gallery of American Art, Phillips Academy, 1980.

Photography: Essays and Images. Illustrated Readings in the History of Photography.
>> New York: Museum of Modern Art, 1980.

In Plain Sight: The Photographs of Beaumont Newhall.
>> Salt Lake City: G. M. Smith, 1983.

Photography and the Book: Delivered on the Occasion of the Eighth Bromsen Lecture (May 3, 1980).
>> Boston: Trustees of the Public Library of the City of Boston, 1983.

Edward Weston Omnibus: A Critical Anthology (edited with Amy Conger).
>> Salt Lake City: G. M. Smith; Peregrine Smith Books, 1984

Supreme Instants: The Photography of Edward Weston.
>> Boston: New York Graphic Society (now Bulfinch Press), 1986.

❖

Christmas card, c. 1939.
Photomontage by Beaumont
Newhall. (Courtesy of
Scheinbaum & Russek Ltd.,
Santa Fe, New Mexico)

INDEX